Structures of Language

Studies in Critical Social Sciences Book Series

Haymarket Books is proud to be working with Brill Academic Publishers (www.brill.nl) to republish the *Studies in Critical Social Sciences* book series in paperback editions. This peer-reviewed book series offers insights into our current reality by exploring the content and consequences of power relationships under capitalism, and by considering the spaces of opposition and resistance to these changes that have been defining our new age. Our full catalog of *SCSS* volumes can be viewed at https://www.haymarketbooks .org/series_collections/4-studies-in-critical-social-sciences.

STRUCTURES OF LANGUAGE

Notes Towards a Systematic Investigation

JOAN CASSER

Haymarket Books
Chicago, IL

First published in 2022 by Brill Academic Publishers, The Netherlands
© 2022 Koninklijke Brill NV, Leiden, The Netherlands

Published in paperback in 2023 by
Haymarket Books
P.O. Box 180165
Chicago, IL 60618
773-583-7884
www.haymarketbooks.org

ISBN: 979-8-88890-014-7

Distributed to the trade in the US through Consortium Book Sales and
Distribution (www.cbsd.com) and internationally through Ingram Publisher
Services International (www.ingramcontent.com).

This book was published with the generous support of Lannan Foundation,
Wallace Action Fund, and the Marguerite Casey Foundation.

Special discounts are available for bulk purchases by organizations and
institutions. Please call 773-583-7884 or email info@haymarketbooks.org for more
information.

Cover design by Jamie Kerry and Ragina Johnson.

Printed in the United States.

Library of Congress Cataloging-in-Publication data is available.

The nature of the following work will be best understood by a brief
account of *how* it came to be written

CHARLES DARWIN

∴

Contents

Preface

Language may be – but in many cases is not – treated as a branch of physics. The humanities and social sciences use language, however, this usage is typically achieved *without* the real application of scientific principles. Hence, it is possible to differentiate certain impressions of language produced by these 'disciplines' from the real science of such experience. These experiences will not become scientific until it can be shown how language conforms to the laws of nature. In view of the fact that physical sciences have established general laws for the behavior of natural phenomena such methods will, indeed, provide the most accurate means to advance the science of language. Language is fundamentally physical and involves interactions of energy, matter, space, and time that can be unified by applying the principles of physics. Yet, strict physical analysis of how language functions does not typically occur in the research practice of the humanities and social sciences. One explanation for this conceptual oversight is evinced by ideologies: the pre-scientific beliefs sustained by real incomprehension.

In the terminology of physics ideology does not appear to exhibit an empirical *frame of reference*. In consequence, ideology 'represents' a metaphysical view of empirical reality circumscribed by historical forms of pre-science. The science of language – as inaugurated by the work of Ferdinand de Saussure – attempts to separate the science of language from its ideological prehistory and Saussure, in some respects, follows physical principles in his studies of linguistic phenomena. His research programme, however, is compromised by the ideology of meaning. Saussure is unable to reconcile the objective – physical – properties of language with the subjective reception of individual speech acts. The research in *Structures of Language: Notes Towards a Systematic Investigation* does no more than raise for consideration a number of problems that issue from this ideology of meaning. The leading theoretical protagonist presented here is Michel Pêcheux who registers both the scientific importance of Saussure's epistemological break and the ideological basis of social science.

In diverse ways the principal thesis considered – the ideology of meaning – is addressed by all of the researchers included in the notes that follow. Michel Pêcheux, Ferdinand de Saussure, Noam Chomsky, John Searle, B. F. Skinner, J. L. Austin, Jacques Lacan, Ludwig Wittgenstein, Zellig Harris, Roman Jakobson, Jacques Derrida, Mikhail Bakhtin, Jürgen Habermas, Émile Benveniste, and Michel Foucault, each evince particular theories concerning the meaning of discourse. In general, these theories of meaning are speculative accounts of semantic phenomena. Nonetheless, in certain cases their findings offer important insights concerning the possible future of linguistic science. For example, Pêcheux, Skinner, Wittgenstein, and Harris, endeavour to establish that meaning is an obstacle to the real science of language. I emphasize that *Structures of Language* is only a *preliminary* set of notes on the topic of semantic scientificity. This modest commentary simply marks the recommencement of Saussure's epistemological break via Pêcheux's materialist theory of discourse.

Acknowledgements

Allow me to thank series editor of *Studies in Critical Social Sciences* (scss) David Fasenfest and the staff at Brill. For without their efficacy, you would not be reading *this* text and I could not have published it.

Introduction

The following quotation from the *Oxford Guide to English Grammar* provides a remarkably clear statement to introduce the main topic of this book *viz.* the ideology of 'meaning':

> The *Oxford Guide to English Grammar* is a systematic account of grammatical forms and the way they are used in Standard British English today. The emphasis is on meanings and how they govern the choice of grammatical pattern.
>
> EASTWOOD, 2002: VII

'Meaning' is thus assumed to be a *self-evident* 'part' of grammar in so far as it 'governs' certain forms of language use. The *Oxford Guide to English Grammar* (2002) does not, however, appear to pay any heed to the research of Ferdinand de Saussure published in 1916 as *Cours de linguistique générale* and translated into English by Wade Baskin in 1959 as *Course in General Linguistics*. Saussure describes how 'grammar' and with it 'meaning' persist as *normative* beliefs that are incompatible with linguistic science. Saussure establishes there is no *necessary* connection between grammar and meaning, instead, any supposed relationship is conditionally based on psycho-linguistic associations manifested in forms of discourse that are regulated by patterns of social experience. Michel Pêcheux refers to this discovery as the 'Saussurian break' of linguistic scientificity. A science begins by detaching itself from existing ideologies and the prehistory of a given field evinces those early myths that pervaded the epistemological space now occupied by the established science. The present-day physical sciences began with initial – speculative – accounts of phenomena that are now without *practical* relevance to real knowledge. Aristotle's 'unmoved mover' of physical causation, the 'magic' of alchemy, and the geocentric (i.e., earth-centred) universe, have not survived theoretically vis-à-vis the objectivity of scientific practice specific to physics, chemistry, and astronomy. In Pêcheux's view much of 'social science' is pre-scientific with its theoretical basis representing socially prescribed ideologies that function as state-authorized structures of language. Pêcheux thus historicizes the production of scientific knowledge following the work of Gaston Bachelard,[1] Georges

---

1 According to Bachelard: "In the formation of a scientific mind, the first obstacle is primary experience ... because no explicit criticism has been brought to bear on it, primary experience cannot in any circumstances be regarded as *utterly* reliable" (Bachelard, 2002: 33;

Canguilhem,[2] and Louis Althusser[3] to conclude that the social sciences must undergo a critical transformation to become real sciences and 'discourse analysis' is the instrument that Pêcheux advances to initiate this process (Helsloot and Hak, 1995). Pêcheux suggests that 'meaning effects' are generated via particular psycho-social situations which are unconsciously associated with given discursive formations. Following from this research there stems three important conclusions:

1)   The meaning of everyday discourse (i.e., a 'natural language'), is, in certain respects, an ideology supported by state apparatuses;

2)   Saussure inaugurated the scientific break of linguistics as a double structure between the signifier and the signified (e.g., syntactic/semantic; individual/social; phonic/graphic &c.);

3)   Social science is pre-scientific because it has not objectively resolved the Saussurian break.

Pêcheux suggests that meaning effects are the result of imaginary associations that are 'connected' by practices of speech and writing. Meaning, therefore, can never be revealed as a physical object *per se* it is always the result of performative conditions which are socially mis/recognized via normative *training* of the imagination. Scientific practice has superseded the imaginary presumptions of grammar yet *explanans* of individual and social phenomena continue to invoke the subject as an origin or cause of the *explanandum*. Pêcheux identifies this process as the 'Munchausen effect' whereby the subject is attributed the cause of itself.[4] Grammar is but one mechanism by which the Munchausen

---

emphasis added). Pêcheux attempts to discover how 'meaning' functions as primary experience in certain forms of social practice administered by ideological state apparatuses. Such semantic primacy (self-evident meaning) is thus an obstacle to the science of language (Pêcheux, 1982).

2   Canguilhem notes: "Nature is not given to us as a set of discrete scientific objects. Science constitutes its objects by inventing a method of formulating, through propositions capable of being combined integrally, a theory controlled by a concern with proving itself wrong" (Canguilhem, 1994: 26). For Pêcheux meaning is typically taken for granted (self-evident) and, as such, untested, i.e., not subject to falsification.

3   Pêcheux's references to the 'Saussurian break' align with Althusser's Bachelardian postulates regarding scientific practice. "The ideology/science opposition is thus always based on *retrospection* or *recurrence*. It is the existence of science itself which establishes the 'break' in the history of theories which can then serve as grounds for declaring the prehistory of science ideological" (Althusser, 2003: 268).

4   The subject of meaning appears as an invocation which elicits certain forms of agentic behavior, however, the real basis of such semantic inscription is defined by socio-historical institutions such as the family, the school/university, the workplace, and other ideological state apparatuses.

effect is realized. In addition to the grammatical subject and its 'meaningful' or 'meaningless' discourse there must also exist certain institutional structures to support the 'self-evidence' of subjective meaning in the form of interpretive disciplinary systems: media, law, psychology, philosophy, criminology, sociology, psychiatry &c.

Pêcheux's research represents an epistemological rupture with the subject-form of discourse by following Saussure's discoveries regarding the *associative* relation of signifier to signified. I am, therefore, suggesting that in the future grammar may be to linguistics what alchemy is to chemistry today. Ludwig Wittgenstein arrived at much the same conclusion in the *Tractatus Logico-Philosophicus* when he declared that the best way to solve a philosophical problem is to stop practicing philosophy because it can't produce what is required *viz.* certainty.

CHAPTER 1

Michel Pêcheux (1938–1983)

I begin with a presentation of Michel Pêcheux's research because he fore-grounds the broad scope of this book: the *possibility* of semantic scientificity. *Language, Semantics, and Ideology* (1982) and *Automatic Discourse Analysis* (1995) – by Pêcheux – are the main sources of the general theoretical frame-work I subsequently apply to the other researchers in the field of linguistics who are included for discussion here. In his writings Pêcheux refers (in greater or lesser detail) to most of the researchers who are presented in the text that follows, including: Noam Chomsky, Roland Barthes, Roman Jakobson, Michel Foucault, Zellig Harris, Jacques Lacan, Ferdinand de Saussure, Burrhus Frederic (B. F.) Skinner, John Langshaw (J. L.) Austin, Émile Benveniste, and John Rogers Searle. By studying these linguists and philosophers of language in relation to Pêcheux's problematic I expect, at the least, to define some points of reference for the explication of a *semantic* science.[1] Pêcheux's theoretical 'Marxism' is notable but this observation should not deter anyone who is willing to discern the *linguistic* basis of ideology.

Linguistic phenomena may be categorized according to specific functional criteria, e.g., syntax representing linguistic rules between signs, semantics rep-resenting the connection of syntax to meaning, and pragmatics representing how syntactic and semantic conditions are determined by a given social context. Pêcheux questions the very *notion* of semantics in as much as he finds it replete with ambiguity and 'non-sense'. Is the field of semantics a speculative ideology? This question defines Pêcheux's research agenda (i.e., problematic). He finds that the term 'semantics' – in some cases – also incorporates what is called rhet-oric, the theory of knowledge, and logic. "How can this all be held together as semantics, a branch of linguistics?" (Pêcheux, 1982: 3). Linguistics, according to Pêcheux, is yet to reach the threshold of scientific objectivity because it remains a form of philosophy, i.e., linguistics is a speculative and ideological 'discipline'.[2]

---

1 According to Bachelard: "Scientific research demands, instead of the parade of universal doubt, the constitution of a *problematic*. It really starts with a *problem*, however ill-posed the problem" (Bachelard, 2012: 27).

2 Not all disciplines are sciences. There are a number of disciplines that do not conform to the expectations of exact sciences. For example, art history, philosophy, the 'humanities' and other literary disciplines do not achieve the objective precision of chemistry, optics, and physics. Indeed, Althusser suggests that the human sciences rely on certain philosophical

Furthermore, linguistic phenomena are manifestly historical and social – as demonstrated by the development of natural languages throughout human history – thus the domain of linguistics appears at once historical, social, and *philosophical* (in so far as it is pre-scientific). Given this theoretical issue Pêcheux attempts to explain how the discipline of linguistics is determined by *philosophies* of language which are un/consciously adopted within certain conditions of social interaction. Thus he articulates a theoretical relationship between historical materialism and philosophy – as an ideological system – which supports certain forms of social subjection.

Before proceeding to describe Pêcheux's semantic theory more specifically the object of linguistics requires further elucidation. Ronald W. Langacker in *Language and its Structure: Some Fundamental Concepts* (1972) suggests that knowledge and culture are stored and transmitted in linguistic structures, yet, this process is only vaguely understood.[3] Without such linguistic transmission, however, society would be *inconceivable*. Linguists, therefore, attempt to represent how languages 'work'.[4] Society is language-dependent and relies upon certain communicative structures for organizational functioning and linguistic units are found practically everywhere within it and are usually self-evident to those who use them. A linguist, then, deconstructs a particular language to identify how it can be described and what rules or - potentially - laws it obeys. The domain of linguistics exhibits distinct sub-disciplines, such as: historical linguistics, anthropological linguistics, sociolinguistics, psycholinguistics, &c. Historical differences, anthropological differences, social differences, and psychological differences, are exemplified across divergent linguistic forms (e.g., differences across history, culture, society, and 'personality' are represented by specific linguistic characteristics). By studying these differences, a linguist describes the various features of verbal structures (spoken and/or written).

---

ideologies to elevate the perceived status of prescientific 'disciplines'. "The philosophies or philosophical categories thus 'exploited' by the human sciences are used practically by them as an *ideological substitute* for the theoretical base they lack" (Althusser, 1990: 91).

3 Following the research of Althusser this lack of knowledge confirms the use of *philosophies* of language as a 'stand-in' for linguistic science. "Whereas in the exact sciences everything proceeds without any *visible* intervention on the part of philosophy and its apparatus, in the human sciences the structure of relations between the sciences and the human sciences seems to require, for ill-explained and therefore confused reasons, the intrusive intervention of this third character that is philosophy: in person" (Althusser, 1990: 90–91).

4 While languages may appear to 'work by themselves' the performative basis of speech acts is subject to certain institutional norms. What appears as 'spontaneous' articulation is the result of particular forms of training, i.e., various practices of socialisation and pedagogy. Thus a supposedly 'natural' language is *actually* the result of relatively strict forms of social control.

The formal description of a given language is a 'grammar' of that language and the attributes of such a structure typically include the rules declaring how the language functions vis-à-vis particular norms of use. These rules include assorted criteria - semantic, syntactic, and pragmatic - for combining words to form sentences.

Sentence formation – by definition – follows the rules of grammar and this performative process provides a symbolic representation of how a given society is linguistically structured via specific statements, questions, imperatives, and sometimes, exclamations! (i.e., sentential forms). Some definitions of 'sentence' include:[5]

> Way of thinking, opinion; An authoritative decision; A judgement pronounced by a tribunal; The judicial determination of the punishment to be inflicted on a convicted criminal; An indefinite portion of a discourse or writing ... a short passage of Scripture in liturgical use; A series of words in connected speech or writing, forming the grammatically complete expression of a single thought.
>
> OED Online, 2020

A given society is comprised of sentences as enacted opinions, decisions, convictions, punishments, statutes, regulations, speeches, tv scripts, &c. (i.e., anything that can be thought using grammar). Because human culture and knowledge are stored and transmitted 'in' language it is not surprising that the study of linguistics can be applied to the full breadth of human experience. Historically the Western grammatical tradition finds its origins in Ancient Greece. Indeed Aristotle (384–322 BC) is an early representative of the problem addressed by Pêcheux given that Aristotle questions *how* a word has a meaning. Aristotle's work introduces a distinction between necessary and arbitrary signs. Furthermore, he also attempts to define how sentences 'signify' in relation to parts of speech, e.g., nouns, verbs, and conjunctions (Larkin, 1971). As language is capable of systematization it can be studied in ways that permit *structural* analyses. Thus, a given language exhibits structural elements that comprise the relations between the parts of which it is composed. "To understand the changes that occur in such a system, the linguist must first have some knowledge of the *structure* of the system at one or more points in time" (Langacker, 1972 9; emphasis added). The form of a *natural* language contains

---

5   I note that sentence and sentience only differ morphologically by the inclusion of i(I) in the latter case. Hence the close etymological link between the two words derived from Latin *sententia* (a thought expressed).

various sub-systems that, in aggregate, structure the elements of communication. Such discourse, then, functions as an 'amalgam' of semantic, phonological, and syntactic structures. Semantic structures represent the meaning of words, phonological structures pair sound and meaning, and syntactic structures define how words are arranged and combined to form sentences.

Pêcheux maintains that a science always begins by 'breaking' with certain ideological presuppositions that were epistemological obstacles to the emergent field in question.

> This leads me to posit that, for a given 'scientific continent', every epistemological event (the break inaugurating a science, the 'discovery' and production of knowledges, 'recastings', etc) is inscribed in a conjuncture ... up to the cumulative point which constitutes the conditions of possibility of the epistemological break in which the *founding concepts* of science are produced and which thus marks the historical initiation of the latter.
>
> PÊCHEUX, 1982: 135–136

For the study of language Pêcheux suggests that the work of Ferdinand de Saussure marks the inauguration of linguistics as a scientific field, however, Saussure's break with ideological pre-science is incomplete. Along with Claudine Haroche and Paul Henry in "La Semantique et la Coupure Saussurienne" [Semantics and the Saussurian Break] Pêcheux notes that without the *critical* continuation of Saussure's research the theoretical principles found in the *Course in General Linguistics* remain impeded by semantic empiricism.[6] This problem issues from the *idea* that meaning is self-evident, yet, words change meaning according to the positions held by those who articulate them (Haroche *et al.*, 1971).[7] Writing under the name Thomas Herbert in "Pour

---

6   Thus, self-evident 'meaning', i.e., the obviousness of what is 'meant' by a given enunciation must yield to a real science of language that establishes the 'mechanisms of meaning' for a given linguistic structure. According to Althusser: "The important point is that a science, far from reflecting the immediate givens of everyday experience and practice, is constituted only on the condition of calling them into question, and breaking with them, to the extent that its results, once achieved, appear indeed as the *contrary* of the obvious facts of practical everyday experience, rather than as their reflection" (Althusser, 1990: 15).

7   Semantic authority ('meaningfulness') apparently corresponds to particular pragmatic conditions of speech (i.e., speech situations), for example, the statement "I am the boss" may be uttered by a child 'playing' with friends, a husband 'joking' with his wife, a employer 'addressing' her employees, yet, in each case *the same words* "I am the boss" are assumed to convey *different* meanings via their 'context'.

une théorie générale des ideologies" [For a General Theory of Ideologies] Pêcheux remarks how "all science – regardless of its current level of development and its place in the theoretical structure ... is principally a science of ideology from which it is detached" (Herbert, 1968). Following this reasoning his research suggests that the science of language (i.e., linguistics) must detach itself from everyday language (i.e., 'natural' language) by means of scientific practice. Furthermore, in so far as everyday language is pre-scientific it is, therefore, in a certain sense ideological (i.e., pre-Saussurian). According to Pêcheux, the given – self-evident – structure of society is a result of particular ideo-technical practices embedded 'in' the practice of language. Therefore, ideology is represented as a linguistic structure where the 'realization of the real' is determined by intersections of semantic, syntactic and pragmatic co-reference.[8]

Pêcheux/Herbert divides ideological phenomena into two kinds, Ideology A: Technical-Empiricist, and, Ideology B: Political-Speculative. Empirical ideology (A) defines semantic 'reality' (i.e., self-evident meaning) and speculative ideology (B) defines syntactic reality (i.e., grammar/law). Using concepts obtained from linguistics Pêcheux/Herbert suggests that empirical ideology designates 'the coincidence of the signifier with the signified' – as self-evident meaning – and speculative ideology connects such signifiers by forms of tacitly accepted syntax (Herbert, 1968). Ideology A refers to the assumed semantic 'facts' of social reality and it functions via the mutual integration of meaning and 'sociality'. Certain forms of self-evident linguistic interaction designate accepted 'meaning' – Pêcheux defines this as the 'empiricist' form of ideology. Ideology B refers to the coherence of social relations in terms of the discourse articulated between subjects who are the bearers of such self-evident grammar. The empirical/speculative conditions of ideology bear specifically upon signifying structures vis-à-vis mis/recognized realities. "Empirical: function of reality/signifier-signified relation; Speculative: function of recognition/signifier-signifier relation" (ibid.). Pêcheux is thus working towards a *linguistic* science of social relations: his project, then, generally corresponds to Langacker's proposition that 'human knowledge and culture is stored and transmitted in language'. According to Pêcheux the research of Saussure demonstrates that a rupture was made in the field of linguistics via the concepts of phonology, morphology, and syntax, however, the material implications of Saussure's break are unfulfilled due to existing ideologies of linguistic phenomena. Saussure's

---

8 Paradoxically the 'realization of the real' may be the result of certain ideological practices. The always-already-there of a historical epoch will 'realize the reality' of a given social system, yet – as is the case in the history of modes of production – this can take effect via pre-scientific practices (e.g., the role of the Church in feudal times).

conceptual displacement in the field of linguistics induces a new research domain where language no longer has the function of expressing 'meaning' and becomes an object that can be determined scientifically. The problem of intersubjective discourse vis-à-vis ideology can thus be represented as a particular linguistic operation – under specific conditions of production – rather than the assumed result of self-evident – ubiquitous – 'meaning' (Pêcheux, 1982). For ideology type A, according to Pêcheux/Herbert, a process of metaphoric substitution from signifier to signifier produces an effect of semantic domination as empirical 'proof' of reality. For ideology type B the metonymic connection between signifiers produces syntactic dominance resulting in the recognition of inter-discursive guarantees of 'real' experience (e.g., the 'always-already-there' of existing social reality).[9] Furthermore, this metonymic process determines how subjects are positioned in the syntactic structure and typically occludes how such subjection occurs by an identificatory mechanism which permits the reproduction of this experience throughout the whole structure of 'accepted' meaning.[10]

For Pêcheux/Herbert empirical and speculative ideologies induce particular forms of 'guaranteed' illusion-misunderstanding via ideological discourse.[11] Empirical guarantees (type A) 'reflect' social reality by producing the knowledge which 'guarantees that we see what we see'. Speculative guarantees (type B) support the mutual mis/recognition of empirical ideology (type A) in terms of intersubjective illocution. Both the empirical guarantee and the speculative guarantee are found to function in terms of existing institutional structures.

9　The 'always-already-there' designates the existing norms and social conditions that are associated with a given mode of production. For example, the slave mode of production, the feudal mode of production, and the capitalist mode of production each exhibit an always-already-there which presents the assumed structure of such social formations, however, these norms and conditions change when a transition occurs from one mode of production to another historically. "The theory of history – a theory of different modes of production – is, by all rights, the science of the organic totality that every social formation arising from a determinate mode of production constitutes" (Althusser, 1990: 6).

10　Althusser proposes that when one is 'in ideology' a break may be set in motion by establishing a scientific discourse (a discourse without a subject) *ipso facto* ideology. This idea appears to have greatly influenced Pêcheux whose research programme in *Language, Semantics and Ideology* also attempts to define how such a break could proceed.

11　Pêcheux/Herbert applies Althusser's theory of ideology to the study of discursive formations where the always-already-there is guaranteed by the existence of the state apparatus. "Ideology makes individuals who are always-already subjects (that is, you and me) 'go'... each subject (you and I) is subjected to several ideologies that are relatively independent, albeit unified under the unity of the State Ideology ... Their subjection-effects are 'combined' in each subject's own acts, which are inscribed in practices, regulated by rituals, and so on" (Althusser, 2014: 199).

In *Automatic Discourse Analysis* Pêcheux writes: "Discursive processes are at the origin of the production of meaning-effects, the language constitutes the material site in which meaning-effects are realized" (Pêcheux, 1995: 133). Form A and Form B ideologies guarantee empirical and speculative effects with reference to particular conditions of discursive production.[12] Empirical and speculative ideologies are seemingly embedded *in* language and Pêcheux addresses how these ideological structures can be understood in Saussurian terms. Pêcheux, therefore, seeks to explain how such semantic and syntactic systems are associated with particular forms of communication (e.g., the institutional materiality of linguistic norms defined by ideological state apparatuses). He questions the 'stability' of these discourses in relation to objective conditions and divides 'logically stabilized discursive universes' from 'non-logically stabilized discursive universes' specific to socio-historical space.[13] Thus, the enunciative coherence of a given discursive formation exhibits material support from certain social institutions (e.g., political, educational, commercial &c.). This is what he calls 'institutionally guaranteed discourse'. Social science, as it is presented in "For a General Theory of Ideologies", constitutes an application of A and B ideologies to social relations. Structures of language permit the 'realization of the real' via these Technical-Empirical (type A) and Political-Speculative (type B) ideologies as they are manifested in 'accepted' forms of discourse, including the institutional discourse of social science (Herbert, 1968). Syntactic and and semantic dominance is, according

---

12   The suggestion that ideology functions as a 'guarantee' for social order occurs often in the work of both Pêcheux and Althusser. Etymologically the word 'guarantee' is derived from Old French *garant*: a person who gives security (e.g., defender, protector, pledge, justifying evidence) and a 'guarantor' is one who vows that the obligation of another shall be performed. For Pêcheux certain discursive formations guarantee existing social relations by monitoring the 'meaning' of a given mode of production and typically such security is provided by the habitual use individuals exhibit in everyday speech acts. The guarantor of the guarantee is the subject who speaks and provides its own system of surveillance as a form of ideological self-subjection. This 'subjective' process is a consequence of the ideological state apparatus which enables each individual to recognize itself 'automatically'.

13   Scientific laws (e.g., the laws of classical mechanics and thermodynamics) are considered 'stable' by virtue of the repeated confirmation of experiments, however, the 'knowledge' associated with literary disciplines does not evince the same 'stability' as the exact sciences because it is not subject to experimental verification. Althusser also addresses this line of enquiry in *Philosophy and the Spontaneous Philosophy of the Scientists* where he discusses the differences between scientific and literary disciplines vis-à-vis the exact sciences and philosophy.

to Pêcheux, directly associated with 'social science' as a system of intersecting ideologies and pre-scientific practices.[14]

The 'realization of the real' is the combined result of type A and type B ideologies assumed by the 'always-already-there', however, such ideological effects typically go unnoticed in daily life. This is due to the structure of mis/recognition functioning in its effects where the subject is never presented with an ideology 'pure and simple' (i.e., immediately recognized as such), instead, it is determined by contradictory ideological beliefs that vary from site to site according to the conditions that are required to institute the accepted structure of social domination. How, then, do ideologies manifest different forms (e.g., from empirical to speculative forms and vice versa)? "What we can say now is that the *mutation* always results in a shift, a 'shift' in the system of guarantees" (Herbert, 1968). Discursive guarantees – empirical or speculative – no longer imply-secure the same ideological effects and this necessitates the syntactic and/or semantic reconfiguration of a given discourse. Saussure's break demonstrates that form B ideologies are associated with form A conditions, i.e., speculative ideologies are generated from 'empirical' conditions (e.g., new semantics 'facts').[15] For Pêcheux all discourse is constituted under specific relations of production. Speech and writing are thus produced vis-à-vis specific socio-historical conditions which determine what is linguistically 'acceptable'. Discourse of a given type will be connected to particular circumstances which constitute the background/context of the speech situation in so far as the intelligibility of speech act is prescribed by certain social norms (Pêcheux, 1995). For example, an empirical ideology (type A) may be contextualized in terms of a speculative ideology (type B) via an accepted social situation (context). Pêcheux posits that a sociological study of discourse could potentially exhibit variations in dominance between relations of 'meaning' and syntax manifested in power relations. In this sense, certain discursive behaviors are associated with specific socio-economic conditions to reveal how *meaning is a tacit power structure* that is not always obvious to those

---

14　For example, empirical ideologies may function under the guise of the educational apparatus and speculative ideologies may be 'legitimated' by the juridico-political apparatus – whereas the family apparatus instills the proclivity towards *acceptance* of existing ideologies by way of primary socialization. "For the family is the site of the biological reproduction of the reproduction of representatives of the 'human race', of their rearing and training, and so on (let us say that it reproduces *the existence* of labour-power)" (Althusser, 2014: 77).

15　Pêcheux attempts to discern the genesis of meaning as an ideological process of discursive realization. Language appears as a fact, yet, upon closer inspection linguistic facticity is, in a number of ways, open to doubt.

subjects who are ostensibly using the language. The obviousness of the 'always-already-there' is, therefore, not understood as a social construct in which particular ideologies generate meaning effects associated with certain forms of social subjection. Networks of self-evident meaning are then a normative effect of power structures which are determined socio-economically (Pêcheux, 1995). (Gadet *et al.* 1995: 49) note how Pêcheux had read Saussure 'very carefully' and identified that modern linguistics owes its foundation to Saussure's fundamental postulate of linguistic systematicity, i.e., language forms a system. Furthermore, I find that not only does Pêcheux broadly follow Saussurian linguistics, he also supplements Saussure's research to explain how the associations made between syntax and semantics are related to un/conscious socio-economic structures.[16]

In "Reflections on the Theoretical Situation of the Social Sciences and Especially, of Social Psychology" Pêcheux/Herbert maintains that the social sciences fulfill an ideological function within the division of labour in so far as empirical practice (what he calls 'the existing life of men') is doubly determined by technical practice (transformation of raw materials from nature) *and* political practice (transformations of social relations) (Herbert, 1966). Certain discursive structures, according to Pêcheux, convey how empirical practice is 'understood' by generating speculative meaning effects within social relations for the purpose of technical transformations of nature under ideological conditions (e.g., philosophy, literature, media, and law).[17] Moreover, Saussure discovers that meaning effects are the result of conventional linguistic 'associations' between phonation and audition, and, for Pêcheux/Herbert, the primary meaning effect produced by the social sciences is the 'always-already-there' of existing ideology (cf. Saussure, 1959; Herbert, 1966).[18] The 'the-always-already-there' represents the self-evident structure of social reality: "political practice meets the raw material to be transformed in the form of social relations 'always-already-there' ..." (Herbert, 1966). Pêcheux also uses the example of law as an 'always-already-there'. "Law as legal practice can only exist on the basis of 'established law', customs, rules which have the status of the

---

16   As a composite: Marx + Saussure + Lacan = Pêcheux's materialist theory of discourse.

17   The social sciences produce a system of 'facts' which is quite different from those of the natural sciences. In Pêcheux's view such scientific ideologies cannot establish objective knowledge because they are used primarily as agencies of repression by the state apparatus (cf. Pêcheux, 1982; Herbert, 1966).

18   The always-already-there is the 'obvious' and 'indubitable' system of norms, behaviors, and practices that allows a given mode of production to assume legitimacy over those individuals who are always-already subjects.

'always-already-there' at a given historical moment" (ibid.). The university and its faculties reproduce the always-already-there of society epistemically (i.e., as structures of 'knowledge') and the social sciences have a specific role to play in such ideo-technical reproduction. According to Pêcheux social science combines certain technical practices with various ideologies of agency (e.g., the subject as cause of itself). Thus the 'social sciences' are an ideological adjunct to political practice. "Ultimately, we will say that the 'social sciences' exist, in their present form, in the application of a technique to an ideology of social relations" (ibid.).

The primary technical means of 'social science' is *writing* and, more generally, written and spoken 'communication'.[19] Saussure's theoretical break presents a way to transform the ideology of language into a linguistic science. "A science ... is always born by the transformation of an initial ideological generality, by means of an intermediary, which disappears in the result ..." (ibid.). The object of linguistics is studied by Pêcheux to reclaim, and further, Saussure's findings regarding the *systematicity* of linguistic structures. In *Language, Semantics, and Ideology* Pêcheux returns to the division between empirical and speculative ideologies in terms of metonymic and metaphoric linguistic structures. Metonymy and metaphor deliver the mechanisms of embedding and articulation that subjects encounter in the relations of production. Because such linguistic devices exhibit apparent 'meaning' for a given subject Pêcheux explains that his theory of discursive processes necessitates a *non-subjectivist theory of subjectivity*. 'Meaning' does not *originate* from the speaking subject, rather, institutional structures define various 'subjective' types of discourse that are socially accepted (e.g., the grammatical person and other forms of personification). The discovery of such ideological effects leads Pêcheux to outline a non-subjective theory of subjectivity to further his materialist theory of discourse for the reason that 'meaning' is an ideology.

Empirical guarantees ('I see what I see') and speculative guarantees ('everyone knows that ...', 'it is clear that ...' &c.) are enunciative mechanisms of embedding and articulation that find realization vis-à-vis institutional guarantees in so far as *situated* speech and writing are related to ideological orders of discourse (Pêcheux, 1982). In this sense, words, statements, propositions, and other speech acts obtain their meaning from those discursive

---

19 Pêcheux suggests routine forms of communication prevalent in the capitalist mode of production typically represent the extant forms of social domination that are generally accepted-endorsed-justified by the social order (Pêcheux, 1982). He proposes – following Althusser – that state apparatuses are the *inconspicuous* cause of such pre-constructed linguistic subjection (Pêcheux, 2014).

formations which define and represent the linguistic structures of ideological systems. Pêcheux suggests that ideology conveys a given linguistic 'always-already-there' via certain discursive processes which constitute such 'reality'. Moreover, meaning is constituted in specific discursive formations and such semantic self-evidence is only obvious once a particular ideology has been 'accepted'. Pêcheux uses concepts from linguistics to demonstrate the ideological functioning of discursive practice (both empirically and speculatively) via lexical mis/recognition. 'I see what I see' and 'everyone knows that', i.e., type A and B ideologies, are institutional guarantees of preconstructed discourse. According to Pêcheux lexical substitution, paraphrase, and synonymy operate within the 'discursive process' upon the signifiers that convey 'meaning' within given linguistic acts.

Gadet (1989) notes that Saussure's research leads to a fundamental question regarding the relationship between representation and meaning given that both phonic and graphic structures appear to transmit meaning, yet, such semantic structures must somehow be 'attached' to sound or text. This leads Gadet to suggest that signifier and signified are associatively connected by psychological 'imprints'. Such psycho-signification unites signifier and signified in particular systems of re/presentation. For Pêcheux, the transmission of meaning is 'accepted' in forms of discourse which represent contextual norms. Meaning is transmitted by the syntactic recognition of signifiers, however, systems of signification must be 'stabilized' for effective semantic specification, i.e., the signifier must *represent* the signified psycho-linguistically. Consequently, the associative relation of signifier to signified may be mis-recognized under ideological conditions of interaction due to the 'obviousness' of an accepted meaning.[20] In an interview regarding the book *La Langue Introuvable* Pêcheux discusses 'the lecture (interpretation) of ideological discourses' (Pêcheux, 1983: 24). He ascribes a certain religiosity to the notion of 'lecture' (i.e., a reading) whereby the *meaning* of a given discourse is defined by protocols that have an ecclesiastical character.[21]

---

20   In Pêcheux's research such associative relations are typically unconscious given that the subject's discourse may appear as the automatic result of ideological experience. Althusser's theory of the unconscious appears to support Pêcheux's investigations regarding the symbolic basis of subjection. "The unconscious is a structure whose elements are signifiers. Inasmuch as its elements are signifiers, the laws of combination of the unconscious and the mechanisms of its functioning depend on a general theory of the signifier" (Althusser, 2003: 48).

21   Pêcheux and Althusser challenge the supposed 'divinity' of textual authority. The meaning of a text may manifest itself as gospel to the reader/listener, however, such

In each case, there was actually a theological representation of a relation between an origin (God, the Author) and an end (the subject-
consciousness) through the Text, which was in turn considered to be a
more or less transparent medium of this relation.

PÊCHEUX, 1982: 25

Pêcheux also includes formal 'content analysis' and philosophical hermeneutics as 'secularized forms of this theological *lecture*'. 'Lecture' has been historically defined in the following terms:

the action of reading, perusal; the way in which a text reads; the 'letter' of
a text; the action of reading aloud. Also, that which is so read, a lection or
lesson; a discourse given before an audience upon a given subject, usually
for the purpose of instruction (the regular name for discourses or instruction given to a class by a professor or teacher at a college or University);
applied to discourses of the nature of sermons, either less formal in style
than the ordinary sermon, or delivered on occasions other than those of
the regular order of church serves; an admonitory speech; esp. one delivered by way of reproof or correction.

OED Online, 2020

Etymologically 'lecture' is derived from Medieval Latin *lectura* 'a reading': "to
gather, collect, pick out, choose ... Thus to read is perhaps ... to pick out words"
(Online Etymology Dictionary, 2021). Pêcheux's research suggests that social
science is a kind of reading or 'lecture' in which speculative and empirical
ideologies are disseminated and instituted for the purpose of social cohesion/
reproduction vis-à-vis certain discursive formations (e.g., ideological state
apparatuses).[22] Resistance to – and subjection by – ideological structures is
symptomatic of the 'fluidity' of a given social context in so far as syntax and
semantics are 'mobile' forms of mis/recognition (Pêcheux, 1983). Moreover,
Pêcheux reflexively explains that his over-reliance on historical materialism
was a theoretical error for the development of discourse theory due to the

---

'direct' comprehension of a given text is only possible as an instance of discursive preconstruction (e.g., certain historical associations of sound and meaning).

22   According to Althusser: "Ours is the age of the 'Human Sciences', which include besides
history and political economy, sociology, ethnology, demography, psycho-sociology,
linguistics, and so on ... The extensive methodological and technical apparatus that
these disciplines put to work is by no means proof of their scientific nature" (Althusser,
2003: 202).

speculative structure of social 'classes'. He questions the metaphysical presuppositions of class structures as autocentric and preconstructed forms of
discourse. Evidently the *meaning* of a class structure is dependent on the institutional guarantees provided by certain *lectures* (instruction by oral or written
discourse), i.e., particular 'readings' of social reality. These ideological interpretations are not, however, *naturally* embedded in social structures they are
derived from phonic and graphic materialities that are assumed to be obvious.

In a concise article with Etienne Balibar called "Definitions" Pêcheux
describes the formation of scientific physics as the non-linear arrival of experimental objectivity emerging from an ideological prehistory (Pêcheux and
Balibar, 1971). "The discontinuist position rejects the notion that 'knowledge'
('savoir') is a continuous development, from 'common sense' to 'scientific
knowledge', from the dawn of science to modern science" (ibid.: 11). Scientific
practice, methodologically, supersedes ideological practice and defines reality
objectively via historical ruptures in the evolution of knowledge. When a discovery reconfigures a particular domain of investigation earlier philosophies
and theoretical ideologies are displaced by the new paradigm.

Pêcheux and Balibar suggest an epistemological break is comprised of three
moments:

1. the break has the effect of rendering impossible certain philosophical or ideological discourses which precede it;
2. the break has the effect of making validations, invalidations or seg-
   regations within the philosophies implicated in the conjuncture in
   which it takes place;
3. the break has the effect of determining a relative autonomy of the
   new science which corresponds to it ... the possibility of instituting
   an experimental procedure adequate to it.

   PÊCHEUX and BALIBAR, 1971: 11–12

According to Paul Resch the historical conditions that inaugurate an epistemological break are accompanied by a challenge to the subject-form and the
'self-evident' meaning attached to its pre-scientific ideology (Resch, 1992).
In "Definitions" Pêcheux and Balibar apply the epistemological break to the
domain of physics, however, this concept may be applicable to other fields of
research by theoretical adaptation (e.g., linguistics). Pêcheux maintains that
Saussure's research represented a rupture in the history of ideologies by the
scientific principles outlined in his *Course in General Linguistics*. Saussure's
research thus constitutes a theoretical point of no return for linguistics as a
science. "Everything is at stake here, including the very future of the scientific

path opened up by Saussure" (Pêcheux, 1982: 174). Pêcheux, however, also suggests that Saussure's theory remains problematic due to the disjunction of individual speech acts in contradistinction to language as a *social* system.

> Hence the opposition between the creative subjectivity of *parole* and the systematic objectivity of language, an opposition which has the circular properties of an ideological couple ... In short, in the couple *langue/parole*, the term *parole* reacts on that of *langue*, overloading the systematicity characteristic of the latter (phonological, morphological and syntactic) with the supposedly extra-linguistic systematicity of thought as a reflection or vision of 'reality'.
>
> ibid.: 37–38

Methodologically Pêcheux apprehends meaning effects via correlations of interdiscourse, intradiscourse, preconstruction, and transverse-discourse in given social structures.[23] Effects of preconstruction – via the assumptions of 'subjectivity' – are found in particular discursive formations where ideological mis/recognition is sustained in types of explication associated with syntactic and semantic beliefs.[24]

> Indeed, interdiscourse is the locus for a perpetual 'work' of reconfiguration in which a discursive formation ... is led to absorb *preconstructed* elements produced outside it, linking them metonymically to its own elements by *transverse-effects* which incorporate them in the *evidentness of a new meaning* ...
>
> ibid.: 193; emphasis added

Meaning generation, then, relies upon a subject's intradiscourse vis-à-vis interdiscourse to preconstruct objects for enunciation in imaginary instances of self-evidence (i.e., ideology). Intradiscourse designates the operation of discourse with respect to the subject's 'own' discourse, for example: what I have

---

23   Broadly defined, interdiscourse denotes speech acts between subjects, intradiscourse designates the subject's 'own speech', the preconstructed represents the instituted system of possible speech acts and transverse-discourse (the transverse-effect) registers the linearisation of syntagma in graphic or phonetic forms (Pêcheux, 1982). Furthermore, 'transverse-discourse' attempts to characterize the transformation from text (spoken or written) to 'meaning'.

24   By applying Saussure's research to explain the genesis of meaning effects Pêcheux begins to outline how a given social formation will exhibit specific linguistic norms which 'govern' particular forms of subjection sustained in certain forms of speech activity.

said, what I am saying, and what I will say. This 'co-reference' phenomenon sustains intradiscursive meaning (i.e., the continuity of 'consciousness'). Between reference and meaning, according to Pêcheux, a sustaining effect connects propositions via the continuous embedding of intradiscourse syntactically. "I shall call this the *sustaining effect*, to mark the fact that it is this relation that realises the articulation between the constituent propositions ... a kind of *return of the known in thought*" (ibid.: 73–74). Syntax agentically generates intra-verbal apprehension of the always-already-there by embedding certain forms of coreference *in* discourse (this may be a form of 'pretext'). "Coreference designates the overall effect by which the stable identity of the 'referents' – what is at issue – comes to be guaranteed" (ibid.: 117). To 'support' the co-reference of discursive formations specific semantic structures must be technically represented as non-speculative entities (e.g., the always-already-said). Type A and type B ideologies, then, guarantee the realization of the real as authoritatively empirical, however, the transmission of these ideological structures is subject to speculative assumptions. Consequently, ideology, for Pêcheux, is embedded within discursive formations determined by forms of co-reference which are preconstructed instances of linguistic mis/recognition between subjects. "Thus we find that ... the embedding effect of the preconstructed and the effect I have called articulation ... are in reality materially determined in the very structure of interdiscourse" (ibid.: 113). Interdiscourse is, therefore, structured by particular preconceptions regarding semantic *certainty*. According to Resch:

> Pêcheux focuses on the semantic element of linguistic practice because, in his opinion, semantics is a source of contradiction for both Saussurian linguistics and Chomskyan 'generative grammar'.
>
> RESCH, 1992: 262[25]

Moreover, Resch also defines the importance of the epistemological break for Pêcheux's concept of scientific practice:

---

25   Pêcheux's materialist theory of discourse attempts to overcome the theoretical contradictions found in the linguistics of Saussure and Chomsky by demonstrating that meaning is an ideology which enables speech to *appear* as the spontaneous expression of a sovereign subject. A central problem for semantic theory is that it cannot explain (or typically ignores) the material basis of meaning and seeks to obfuscate the radical exteriority of language by appealing to 'innate ideas' (cf. Chomsky, 1965; Resch, 1992).

It is the absence of the subject form that distinguishes scientific concepts from ideological representations or 'meaning' in the strict sense of
an articulation between preconstituted subjects. Concepts of science do
not have a *meaning* for Pêcheux; rather, they have a function in a process
without a subject of meaning or knowledge.

> ibid.: 267

This book that you are 'reading', then, continues Pêcheux's research regarding the epistemological break of linguistics and the possibility of a science of
meaning.

CHAPTER 2

Ferdinand de Saussure (1857–1913)

Pêcheux suggests that Ferdinand de Saussure effected a rupture in the history of theoretical ideologies by establishing linguistics as a science via the 'Saussurian break'. An examination of the *Course in General Linguistics* shows that Saussure historicized the discipline before presenting the 'facts' of his new science.[1] "The science that has been developed around the facts of language passed through three stages before finding its true and unique object" (Saussure, 1959: 1). According to Saussure the prehistory of linguistics exhibited three prototypical forms of analysis: grammar, philology and comparative philology. Each of these 'infant sciences', as Saussure calls them, evinced particular conceptual limitations. Grammar defined formal criteria for syntactic analysis based on particular lexical categories, however, it was not sufficiently objective. "It lacked a scientific approach ... Its only aim was to give rules for distinguishing from correct and incorrect forms; it was a normative discipline, far removed from actual observation, and its scope was limited" (ibid.) Philology was questioned because, like grammar, it too exhibited a normative structure. "The early philologists sought especially to correct, interpret and comment upon written texts. Their studies also led to an interest in literary history, customs, institutions, etc" (ibid.). Comparative philology attempted to juxtapose different languages using certain interpretive protocols, however, Saussure also found this discipline insufficiently scientific. "But the comparative school ... did not succeed in setting upon the true science of linguistics. It failed to seek out the nature of its object. Obviously, without this elementary step, no science can develop a method" (ibid.: 3). Grammar, philology, and, comparative philology were, then, theoretical ideologies from which Saussure's linguistic science broke away (in Pêcheux's terms this moment constitutes Saussure's epistemological break). Saussure declares that his science of linguistics concerns 'all manifestations of human speech'; 'written texts'; 'the history of all

---

1 According to Ludwik Fleck "A fact is supposed to be distinguished from transient theories as something definite, permanent, and independent of any subjective interpretation by the scientist. It is that which the various scientific disciplines aim at" (Fleck, 1979: xxvii). For Pêcheux the discipline of linguistics is *pre-scientific* due to the ideology of meaning which is assumed by the putative function of subjectivity in speech acts. Such metaphysical beliefs support subjective interpretation as a valid form of evidence. This is what Pêcheux calls the subject as the cause of itself.

observable languages'; 'the forces that are permanently and universally at work in all languages' and 'the general laws to which all specific phenomena can be reduced' (ibid.: 6). Thus conceived the Saussurian break constituted the foundation of linguistic *knowledge*.

Saussure's rupture – which Pêcheux insists requires further theoretical development – is found in the *double structure* of linguistic phenomena: syntax/ meaning; individual/social; systematic/spontaneous; synchronic/diachronic; signifier/signified; phonic/graphic; immutable/mutable; static/evolutionary; internal/external; physical/mental &c. Saussure identifies this double structure as a substantive 'dilemma' for linguistic research.[2] "Everywhere we are confronted with a dilemma: if we fix our attention only on one side of each problem, we run the risk of failing to perceive the dualities ..." (ibid.: 9). Saussure maintains that social organisation is language-dependent, and moreover, it appears that Saussure's science of signs relates conceptually to the double structure of ideological formations described by Pêcheux. As outlined in the preceding chapter Pêcheux contends that ideology can be divided into two kinds: empiricist (A) and speculative (B).[3] In consequence, a double structure (dilemma) of ideological representation affects the linguistic basis of society. Auditory or graphic structures (e.g., speech and writing) are empirical realities, however, these structures are also used speculatively (e.g., in political ideologies, mythologies, 'literature' &c). Pêcheux's type A and type B ideologies define a duality that repeats Saussure's dilemma regarding the double structure of linguistic phenomena. Saussure attempts to resolve this problem by conceptually separating language from speech and explains that language [*langue*] should not be confused with speech [*langage*]. Language is a socio-cultural practice that requires a number of tacit conventions for operation.[4] The adoption of these norms permits the exercise of speech across a given social group. Speech is only possible in so far as norms are followed by a number of individuals who 'agree' to use the language. Saussure maintains that language unifies speech. Speech sounds become 'meaningful' when phonetic and graphic

---

2 A dilemma denotes a situation where a choice must be made between two or more alternatives which may be equally unwelcome.

3 Ideology A designates the imaginary semantic assumptions of the 'always-already-there' within certain discursive formations whereas ideology B indicates the orthographic form of the assumed syntactic order/s.

4 For example, such tacit assumptions may include the following: 1) the language 'works' (i.e., the linguistic system produces the desired result); 2) the interlocutors are both competent speakers; 3) the speech activity is free from distortion or is otherwise 'true'.

structures are associated with certain social practices.[5] Moreover, language [*langue*] is not speech [*langage*] because the material characteristics of verbal articulation (e.g., phonation) can be distinguished from the ideas that are 'conveyed' by speech acts (this fact is clearly evinced by different national languages). Saussure is less concerned with *what* is said and instead seeks to know *how* a given part of *langue* functions systematically. He conceptually separates the physical (sound waves), physiological (phonation and audition), and psychological parts (word-images and concepts) of language to suggest that the 'word-image stands apart from the sound itself' (Saussure, 1959: 12).

A given social structure determines the language – via institutional conditions – that is articulated in individual acts of speech or writing. As Saussure notes: "It is both a social product of the faculty of speech and a collection of necessary conventions that have been adopted by a social body to permit individuals to exercise that faculty" (ibid.: 9). Haroche, Henry, and Pêcheux remark how Saussure had to oppose the typical assumptions of 'natural' language to begin studying the objective structures of discourse: "it is by resisting the solicitations of empirical evidence that Saussure was able to formulate the concepts of linguistics as a science" (Haroche *et al.*, 1971). The facts of *langage* are not of the same nature of those of *langue*. Speech [*langage*] is not language [*langue*], according to Saussure, because sound waves or graphic material should not be confused with strictly *linguistic* structures. Saussure's resistance to the normative self-evidence of human speech [*langage*] was expressed as the nascent science of language [*langue*]. In his analysis of the 'speaking circuit' Saussure describes phonation (i.e., speech sounds) and audition (i.e., listening) as interdependent communicative relations that are structured by the system of language [*langue*]. Individual acts of speaking and writing rely on the socially instituted recognition of associated structures: e.g., physical structures (sound waves, graphic notation, gestures) coupled with psychological structures (word-images). "We should also add the associative and co-ordinating faculty ... plays the dominant role in the organisation of language as a system" (Saussure, 1959: 13). Language [*langue*] associatively co-ordinates the various syntactic elements that are used for communicative activity. "But to understand clearly the role of the associative and co-ordinating faculty, we must leave the individual act ... and approach

---

5   Evidently, a particular transformation occurs when a sound wave becomes a 'meaning', however, this process seems to be more or less automatic due to the habitual recognition of certain 'ideas' which are reinforced by social structures. Moreover, to transform natural phenomena into ideology supposes a 'primitive' tendency to identify non-ideological objects (e.g., physical vibrations of sound) ideologically (e.g., 'meaningful beliefs').

the social fact" (ibid.: 13). *Langue, langage,* and *parole* are thus distinguished by Saussure as the system of language [*langue*], human speech in general [*langage*], and the individual execution of speech acts [*parole*]. The systematicity of language [*langue*] is exhibited in various forms of social behavior. Signs, ideas, and verbal conduct are 'linked together' to produce predictable patterns of individual and social activity. Saussure remarks how linguistic averages will then prevail which determine the likelihood of a certain speech act occurring together with a particular speech situation: 'the same signs united with the same concepts'. In such cases sound waves and/or graphic notation represent what is institutionally reinforced and thus – by associative mechanisms – the individual 'understands' the language [*langue*] via semantically co-ordinated comprehension. Saussure suggests that if we had the technical means to identify all those associated word-images that a person 'comprehends' in discourse we would be able to perceive the 'social bond' supported by instituted speech. This *ideal* bond is produced via the community of speaking subjects and their reciprocal linguistic co-ordination. Yet, the social production of language is not readily apparent in *parole* (i.e., individual speech activity), despite the fact that it is a fundamental part of the associative process realized in communicative structures. Moreover, individual speech activity, is – according to Saussure – strictly limited by social practice: a single person can neither create nor modify the language that is *generally* accepted by the social group. Saussure further maintains that language is 'a sort of contract signed by the members of the community' and individuals gradually assimilate the word-images of the speech community through an 'apprenticeship' which guides linguistic co-ordination. However, in practice, social behavior appears to be generated by assumptions of self-evident meaning.

According to Pêcheux ideology A (Technical/Empiricist) generates the 'meaning' of given linguistic structures which are, then, theoretically associated with ideology B (Political/Speculative) in so far as signification depends upon recognition (e.g., acceptability). In Saussure's terms this associative process determines the signifying structures of the 'social bond' via systems of *parole* – resulting in particular correlations of syntax and 'meaning'. Signification, and more generally language, is then a semiological – 'intersubjective' – relationship that, according to Saussure, is part of social psychology.

> *A science that studies the life of signs within society* is conceivable; it would be part of social psychology ... I shall call it *semiology* (from Greek, sēmeîon, 'sign'). Semiology would show what constitutes signs, what laws

govern them ... Linguistics is only part of the general science of semiology ....

SAUSSURE, 1959: 16

Social psychology is discussed by Pêcheux/Herbert in "Reflections on the
Theoretical Situation of Social Sciences and Especially, of Social Psychology"
where he declares that social psychology (and 'social science' in general) is
an ideological combination of political practice and technical practice in
response to a 'demand' for social cohesion and order vis-à-vis existing institutions. The social sciences, then, employ particular discursive techniques
to produce an ideology of social order. These ideo-technical practices facilitate the adaptation-readjustment of social relations towards the 'realization
of the real'. In his view psychology, sociology and social psychology have not
produced scientific knowledge – these 'social sciences' produce a repressive
ideology via liturgical myths (Herbert, 1966). The social sciences are thus
semiological systems with a dual structure – both semantic (ideology A) and
syntactic (ideology B) – and this duality permits the analysis and definition
of *parole* (i.e., individual speech acts) on the basis of social association. The
object of semiology, therefore, may appear elusive because it exhibits both
individual and social characteristics. Saussure notes that psychologists typically do not account for language as a social product and tend to study individual instances of language use rather than explaining the 'social bond' that
is produced via linguistic structures.

Language and speech are reciprocally co-ordinated in so far as language is
transmitted via speech and speech establishes language, however, for Saussure,
they are conceptually distinct as theoretical objects.

Language and speaking are then interdependent; the former is both the
instrument and the product of the latter ... Language exists in the form of
a sum of impressions deposited in the brain of each member of a community ... What part does speaking play in the same community? It is the sum
of what people say ... its manifestations are individual and momentary.

SAUSSURE, 1959: 19

In *Language, Semantics, and Ideology*, Pêcheux describes the features of 'interdiscourse' and 'intradiscourse' to account for 'coreference' and 'transverse-
effects' within discursive formations.[6] These discursive mechanisms can be

---

6 The generation of linguistic coreference – in so far as it relates to a given discursive process – seems to oblige certain subjects to function as agents of meaning via the realization of

applied theoretically to Saussure's linguistic discovery (i.e., the dilemma of linguistic double structures: individual/social &c.). If language [*langue*] is distinct from *parole* the possibility of coreference – syntactic, semantic, or pragmatic – may be explained by the realisation of intradiscourse interdiscursively. The continuity of language in social structures is determined by the recognition of 'meaning effects' intradiscursively, yet this activity is not the *immediate* result of individual *parole*. "In this sense it can indeed be said that intradiscourse, as the 'thread of the discourse' of the subject, is strictly an effect of interdiscourse on itself, an 'interiority' wholly determined as such 'from the exterior'" (Pêcheux, 1982: 117). Saussure's *langue/parole* distinction is, then, conceptually reframed in Pêcheux's interdiscourse/intradiscourse theory.

> I shall say that the subject-form (by which the 'subject of discourse' identifies with the discursive formation that constitutes him) tends to absorbforget interdiscourse in intradiscourse, i.e., *it simulates interdiscourse in intradiscourse*, such that interdiscourse appears to the be the pure 'already-said' of intradiscourse, in which it is articulated by 'coreference'.
>
> ibid: 118

The Saussurian dilemma of associating language [*langue*] with *parole* is addressed by Pêcheux in terms of 'incorporation-concealment' vis-à-vis certain conditions of ideological mis/recognition:

> I think the subject-form can be characterized as realising the incorporation-concealment of the elements of interdiscourse: the (imaginary) unity of the subject, his present-past-future identity, finds one of its foundations here.
>
> ibid.: 117–118

The subject of *parole*, i.e., the speaking subject, 'absorbs' language associatively and this induces the 'coincidence' of social and individual linguistic forms. An assumed correspondence arises between the subject and itself which is of interdiscursive origin, i.e., the subject's discourse is established as a co-ordinated result between existing signifiers that confounds the typical assumptions

---

transverse-effects. For example, the individual-agent who apparently 'reads' a text and then 'interprets' it is already involved in a form of ideological activity as soon as it begins to convey its experience in 'natural' language. "That is, we have to be aware that both author and reader of these lines live 'spontaneously' or 'naturally' in ideology, in the sense in which we have said that 'man is by nature an ideological animal'" (Althusser, 2014: 188).

regarding the apparent 'individuality' of *parole*. For example, the co-ordination of national culture and 'public' discourse (i.e., generalized speech) further corroborates Pêcheux's theory of interdiscourse in Saussurian terms. "The culture of a nation exerts an influence on its language, and the language, on the other hand, is largely responsible for the nation" (Saussure, 1959: 20). Moreover, the associative structures of language are an observable feature of the institutional discourse articulated by governments and other 'authorities':

> The internal politics of states is no less important to the life of languages ... the relations between language and all sorts of institutions (the Church, the school, etc.) ... is all the more inseparable from political history.
>
> ibid.: 20–21

Such sociopolitical conditions, according to Saussure, determine the transmission of language [*langue*] given that institutions define generalized speech acts (i.e., the material basis of language is found in graphic and phonic structures which facilitate certain forms of *parole* through interdiscourse). Pêcheux summarizes such interdiscursivity in the following way:

> The object of linguistics ... thus appears to be traversed by a discursive division between two spaces: that of the manipulation of stabilized significations, normalized by a pedagogical hygiene of thought, and that of the transformation of meaning ... grasped in an indefinite 'rebirth' of interpretations.
>
> PÊCHEUX, 1988: 646

Pecheux's theory suggests that interdiscourse functions via preconstructed and articulation-sustaining systems of incorporation-concealment (A and B ideologies). The purpose of discourse analysis is, then, to identify how interpretive practices function in certain transformations of the 'always-already-there' such that both the empirical and speculative conditions of discourse are described with reference to the genesis of signifying structures.

> Any utterance or sequence of utterances is thus linguistically describable as a series (lexico-syntactically determined) of possible points of diversion, leaving room for interpretation. It is in this space that discourse analysis claims to work ... *From this perspective, the main point is to determine in the practice of discourse analysis is the place and time of interpretation in relation to description.*
>
> ibid.: 647; emphasis added

This descriptive/interpretive schema is contextually embedded within a given 'discourse structure'. Description is contextualized vis-à-vis interpretation and such effects are linguistically defined by the objective division of language [*langue*] and individual speech acts [*parole*]. In "A Method of Discourse Analysis Applied to Recall of Utterances" Pêcheux outlines an experiment designed to assess the effect of contextual cues on retrieval performance for 'connected' utterances. According to Pêcheux the analysis of a 'discourse structure' attempts to characterize the associative mechanisms of language [*langue*] and individual speech [*parole*] via the notion of 'context' (Pêcheux, 1971). Within a given linguistic system a 'discursive string' mediates a given representation between an addresser and an addressee and such enunciations are, Pêcheux suggests, contextually defined.

> The structure of a discourse is assumed to be determined partly by a set of tacit production conditions. These production conditions represent the general social or interactional context in which the discourse takes place.
>
> PÊCHEUX, 1971: 67

To measure 'context effects' Pêcheux compares the paradigmatic proximity of utterances (i.e., enunciative 'content') to 'semantic centration' (i.e., tendential meaning).

> The method, when applied to a given sequence of discourse, therefore should allow for a systematic analysis of the relationship between specific characteristics of the observed sequence of discourse (a discourse surface) and the production conditions under which the discourse is generated.
>
> ibid.: 67–68

Pêcheux relies, theoretically, on the Saussurian rupture between *langue* and *parole* to analyze discourse as a series of contextually determined events.[7] Gadet notes that, for Saussure, language is always characterized as a double structure – an inferred duality – where it is at once 'faculty and institution, production and reception, phonic substance and thought, individual act and

---

7 Context effects represent forms of interaction where certain discourses are tacitly endorsed-accepted by situated subject-agents, and, failing to observe such norms 'in' language can also provoke particular admonitory procedures. In this respect, *contextual* cues are not indissociable from agencies of repression.

social fact, system and evolution' (Gadet, 1989: 64). According to Gadet this dual system of language vis-à-vis speech is presented as a dichotomy/dilemma in Saussure's *Course in General Linguistics*. "*Langue* is primarily defined by a series of oppositions between it and *parole* ... *Langue* is a linguistic knowledge primarily displayed in judgements of identity and difference" (ibid.: 66–68). Regarding Pêcheux's distinction between ideology A (meaning), and ideology B (syntax), it is evident that ideological mis/recognition is possible because of the double structure identified by Saussure.[8] Furthermore, the 'Marxist' base/superstructure division appears as another linguistic duality which may explain the inception of ideology via the imposition of subordinate and super-ordinate forms of discourse. Pêcheux notes, following the work of Althusser:

> The (economic) base determines the superstructure 'in the last instance';
> The superstructure enjoys a 'relative autonomy' in relation to the base;
> There is a 'reciprocal action' of the superstructure on the base.
>
> PÊCHEUX 2014: 3

Saussure's theory of double structures (e.g., individual/social, graphic/phonic, syntactic/semantic &c.) suggests how a 'dilemma' between base and super-structure could emerge in terms of language [*langue*] and individual enunci-ations [*parole*].

> Thus, the language/speech opposition, historically necessary for the constitution of linguistics goes hand in hand with a certain naivety of Saussure with regard to sociology ... The couple freedom/constraint or, if one prefers, creativity/system has the circular properties of an ideological couple, insofar as each of the two terms present presupposes the other.
>
> HAROCHE et al., 1971

The production and comprehension of a given 'discourse structure' is sys-tematically related to the description and interpretation of the social order

---

8 In addition, Althusser also appears to apprehend the magnitude of the Saussurian break for theories of unconscious subjection. Commenting on Lacan's use of Saussure's work Althusser writes: "Thus were we introduced to the paradox, formally familiar to linguistics, of a discourse both double and unitary, unconscious and verbal, having as its double field of deployment but a single field, with no beyond other than in itself: the field of the 'signi-fying chain'" (Althusser, 1996: 24). Pêcheux furthers Lacan's application of Saussure's theory by outlining how everyday discourse (i.e., natural language) incorporates and conceals the linguistic misprision stipulated by ideological state apparatuses.

where such associations are sustained by interdiscursive forms of co-reference. Consequently, the base/superstructure distinction may be usefully applied to explain the acquisition of intradiscourse. The freedom of selecting an individual utterance is constrained by the systematic conditions of a given social order and this freedom/constraint limitation is an oppositional distinction highlighted by Gadet's 'notional duality' of social fact/individual act. Saussure contends that linguistics is a science of value (i.e., an axiological system) with synchronic and diachronic forces regulating particular forms of discourse. For example, a language may be diachronically structured by certain institutional changes and, subsequently, synchronized by the 'equation' of certain significations which supposedly share the same 'meaning'. The relationship of *langue* to *parole* is – in this sense – axiologically structured in so far as the value of a given discourse is institutionally determined.

> The conceptual side of value is made up solely of relations and differences with respect to the other terms of language, and the same can be said of its material side. The important thing in the word is not the sound alone but the phonic differences that make it possible to distinguish this word from all others, for differences carry signification.
>
> SAUSSURE, 1959: 117–118

Whether these differences appear in auditory (e.g., phonation) or visual form (e.g., orthography) does not diminish the axiological aspect of language as a differential system.[9]

> Values in writing function only through reciprocal opposition within a fixed system that consists of a set number of letters ... Everything that has been said up this point boils down to this: in language there are only differences.
>
> ibid.: 120

---

9 The value of language appears to follow what Althusser calls – commenting on Lacan – 'The Law of Culture'. "Lacan has shown that the passage from (in the limit case, pure) biological existence to human existence (the child of man) is effected under the Law of the Order that I will call the Law of Culture and that this Law of Culture can be conflated in its *formal* essence with the order of language" (Althusser, 1996: 25). Culture is language-dependent i.e., for a given form of culture to continue it must exist *as a language* that can be 'followed' via training, e.g., instruction, pedagogy, and so on. Linguistic 'value' is thus attached to 'meaning' as a function of The Law of Culture, however, as both Pêcheux and Althusser demonstrate, there are considerable differences between scientific and non-scientific forms of culture and this difference marks the division of ideology/science.

Haroche *et al.* note how value and meaning are synchronically related insofar as 'value dominates meaning'.

> Saussure's fundamental position on this subject, is the idea that, from the linguistic point of view, value dominates meaning ... The principle of subordination of meaning to value can ... be considered as the core of the Saussurian rupture.
>
> HAROCHE, et al., 1971

Meaning is subordinate to value in terms of 'acceptability'.[10] The condition of acceptability contributes to the institution of a given language that is then advanced by *parole* under the freedom/constraint model of discursive production. "The community is necessary if values that owe their existence solely to usage and general acceptance are to be set up; by himself the individual is incapable of fixing a single value" (Saussure, 1959: 113). The relation of sound to meaning – as well as the graphic form of this linguistic process is – according to Saussure – arbitrary in so far as the mechanism of their identity (i.e., signifier/signified) is not a connection of strict necessity. "A word can always evoke everything that can be associated with it in one way or another" (ibid.: 126). Sound, meaning, and writing rely on *associative* systems that 'valorize' structures of language in the form of instituted norms found in material culture:[11]

> To think that there is an incorporeal syntax outside material units distributed in space would be a mistake ... A material unit exists only through its meaning and function ... Conversely ... a meaning and function only exist through the support of some material form.
>
> ibid.: 139

According to Haroche *et al.*, as noted above, meaning is subordinate to value. In Saussure's *Course in General Linguistics* this inference is confirmed by the

---

10   For example, consider how cultural norms may be uncritically accepted in various social circumstances. Certain linguistic practices are enculturated such that the 'meaning' of a speech act is defined by the practice of a given culture. Occult powers, supernatural events, and witchcraft may all be 'accepted' by a given community in this sense. This typically occurs in cultures where there is little evidence of causal analysis. "Primitive mentality does not trouble to ascend or descend the series of conditions which are themselves conditioned" (Lévy-Bruhl, 1923: 124).

11   Institutional mechanisms of semantic subjection are the object of Pêcheux's 'materialist theory of discourse' (Pêcheux, 1982). Meaning thus defines the 'always-already-given' via the assumed obviousness of natural language found in ideological practices.

fact that signifier and signified are associated by conditions of *acceptability* ('general acceptance') and not physical or 'metaphysical' necessity. "To explain means to relate to known terms, and in linguistics, *to explain a word is to relate it to other words, for there are no necessary relations between sound and meaning*" (ibid.: 189; emphasis added). Pêcheux's research challenges the 'acceptability' of a given discourse in Saussurian terms by attempting to separate speech (i.e., *parole*) from language (i.e., *langue*) via the concept of ideology. Meaning is not self-evident for Pêcheux given that it functions *associatively* and not necessarily. Using linguistic concepts Pêcheux attempts to redefine the methodology of social science by breaking epistemologically with preconstructed discourse as an 'obvious' structure of communication. According to Williams (1999) the linguistic research of Pêcheux focuses on texts or enunciations to demonstrate how certain statements are constrained by institutional conditions in so far as 'accepted' forms of interdiscourse define the social history of speech activity. The relation of signifier to signified 'realizes' the incorporation-concealment of discursive structures because 'meaning', for Pêcheux, is a speculative ideology. Gadet notes that the Saussurian sign (signifier/signified) establishes a conceptual relation between visibility and invisibility or presence and absence in so far as the signifier 'represents' the signified by certain *imaginary* associations (Gadet, 1989). Interdiscourse is actualized in *parole* whereby *langue* is invested with meaning (i.e., the discourse exhibits 'value') given that institutional structures function as an axiological 'absent cause'.

> *Parole* can be thought of as how subjects and objects are positioned in relation to each other. Within the discursive formation there are limitations on what can be said from certain subject positions ... The enonces treated within discourse analysis retain an essential relation to divergence and to memory and in that respect they are inserted into a continual process of conservation and re-use.
>
> WILLIAMS, 1999: 102

Saussure's value theory of language explains how *parole* is conserved, exchanged, and re-used in different social contexts based on certain axiological principles.[12] Pêcheux works in the tradition of Saussure's break despite the

---

12   Extrapolating from Saussure's theory of language Pêcheux appears to suggest that a given mode of production will sustain those speech acts which reproduce the 'meaning' of the social system. Thus, the value of speech acts 'corresponds' to the reproduction of the social structure. Moreover, Leroi-Gourhan, notes that tools and language are intrinsically

fact that Saussure's account of linguistic 'creativity' appears to be a theoretical ideology.

> It remains, finally, to explain what is meant by a 'dominance-effect' within the production of given discursive sequence ... I think it is possible to account for this phenomenon ... based upon the notion that the discursive process is *determined* by its conditions of production and upon a rejection of the ideological notion of 'infinite creativity'.
>
> PÊCHEUX, 1995: 105–106

Pêcheux notes that, for Saussure, the creative index of *parole* seems to somehow escape *langue* (and correlatively dominance) through indeterminate 'aestheticized' theories of linguistic activity (e.g., free speech): "it is easy to show that the conception of thought as 'creative activity' is a spontaneous extension ... of the idealism inherent in the subject-form" (Pêcheux, 1982: 119). Pêcheux appears to have identified that Saussure established a break in linguistics comparable to the example adduced by Althusser in his studies of Karl Marx's epistemological rupture with 'orthodox' economic theory. In regard to the binary ideological structure of *langue* (i.e., empirical and speculative ideologies) Pêcheux's research is, then, a continuation of Saussure's work coupled with certain Althusserian principles.

> For Pêcheux, Saussure's work was the origin of linguistic science, the affirmation of the Saussurean break being of fundamental theoretical importance. The essential ingredient of the Saussurean break – the linguistic equivalent to the Marxist epistemological break referred to by Althusser – involved viewing language as a system.
>
> WILLIAMS, 1999: 106

Parole for Pêcheux is systematically determined by language [*langue*], and for that reason, *parole* is subject to structural subordination vis-à-vis the specious ideology of self-evident 'meaning'.

---

connected in the history of technology. "Throughout history up to the present time, technical progress has gone hand in hand with progress in the development of technical language symbols" (Leroi-Gourhan, 1993: 114). Saussure's rupture may, therefore, mark the beginning of a post-semantic society given that the myth of meaning has been technically superseded by the science of language.

In fact ... I have shown that the Saussurian notion of *parole* constituted precisely the 'weakest link' of the scientific apparatus set up in the form of the concept of *langue* ... Saussure's *parole* is ... a pure ideological excipient ... a stop-gap, a plug to close the 'gap' opened by the scientific definition of *langue* as systematicity in operation.

PÊCHEUX, 1982: 174

Pêcheux is not saying that *parole* is somehow fictitious – individuals, of course, speak – he is suggesting that *parole* is structurally subordinate to *langue*. The idea of *spontaneous* speech is – for Pêcheux – an ideology. Furthermore, the concept of *parole* is not equivalent to discourse:

discursivity is not *parole*, i.e., it is not a 'concrete' individual way of inhabiting the 'abstraction' of the *langue*; it is not a matter of a use, of a utilisation or the realisation of a function. On the contrary, the expression discursive process is explicitly intended to put in their proper (idealist) places the notion of *parole* and the psychologistic anthropologism which goes with it.

ibid.: 58

The relationship of *langue* to semantics is located in the practice of 'meaningful' speech where 'spontaneous' subjectivity emerges from the absent interior of *parole*.

Thus *langue* as a system turns out be linked in contradictory fashion both to 'history' and to 'speaking subjects', and this contradiction is currently at work in linguistic researches in different forms which constitute precisely the object of what is called 'semantics'.

ibid.: 7

'Meaning' is ideologically determined by discursive formations in which 'competent' and 'coherent' enunciations are regulated by institutional authorities of the *langue*.

Pêcheux addressed the question of the theoretical place of 'discourse' within the Saussurean model ... In other words, though linguistics had established itself as a science through a 'Saussurean' epistemological break, it had 'forgotten' to develop an adequate theory of meaning production in discourse.

HELSLOOT & HAK, 1995: 11

Saussure's research initiates a theoretical break for the science of linguistics from its ideological prehistory, however, for Pêcheux this break is incomplete and further research must be done to explain *parole* in terms of *langue* in so far as *parole* is *systematically* rather than spontaneously defined.[13]

> Thus in looking to recast versions of the *langue* versus *parole* dichotomy, Pêcheux is intending to reformulate the distinction between system and event as a new one between linguistic basis and discursive processes. To support this assertion Pêcheux must first clear the way to challenge certain Saussurean precepts with an eye to emphasizing the role of discursive process itself.
>
> MONTGOMERY & ALLAN, 1992

Saussure's break is methodologically related to questions in the history of science regarding new discoveries and forms of theoretical innovation. In Pêcheux's view Saussure's theory constitutes critical step for linguistic *science*, however, the *langue/parole* distinction remains attached to subjectivism and is, consequently, incompatible with scientific practice. "A science detached from its history, such is the condition of a real history of science" (Fichant, 1969). The statement is delivered in "The Idea of the History of the Sciences" where Michel Fichant, a colleague of Pêcheux's, outlines a rudimentary theory of scientific histories with three 'consequences':

1) The history of a science can only find the concepts of its object in the science of which it is the history;
2) there is no initial definition of a science ... but its real history, the real conditions of the production of its concepts;
3) the history of science implies an epistemology. By an epistemology we mean ... the theory of the specific production of the concepts and of the formation of the theories of each science.

      ibid.

---

13   Pêcheux supports Saussure's hypothesis regarding the objectivity of language, however, to dispense with the problem of 'subjective' language use Pêcheux attempts to establish that meaning is an ideology. Linguistic ideology is transmitted symbolically and – in many instances – this occurs via alphabetic scripts (written or spoken). Thus 'semantic' transmission is achieved by a particular technology of writing. According to Leroi-Gourhan: "For classical as well as modern thinking, the alphabet is more than just a means of committting to memory the progressive acquisitions of the human mind; it is a tool whereby a mental symbol can be noted in both word and gesture by a single process" (Leroi-Gourhan, 1993: 212). In this sense ideology is 'in' the alphabet given that certain arrangements of alphabetic cognition are assumed to possess meaning.

Saussure differentiates his research from philology and grammar to found the science of linguistics. This important theoretical development occurs by virtue of epistemological innovation in so far as physical (e.g., phonation, audition &c.) concepts are used to explain *langue* scientifically: the history of the science of linguistics is a history of recognized error. Yet, Pêcheux finds that Saussure regresses theoretically by positing that 'analogy' is a creative force in language without explaining how *parole* is determined by material conditions vis-à-vis 'value'. According to Saussure: *"Meaning plays no part in phonetic changes, but it must intervene in analogy"* (Saussure, 1959: 165; emphasis added). Semantic self-evidence is expressed analogically to 'create' new, spontaneous, acts of *parole*, however, the outcome of this ideological process dismisses the evidence of *langue* as an objective system.

> Analogy, then, is one more lesson in separating language from speaking ... It shows us that the second depends on the first ... Any creation must be preceded by an unconscious comparison of the materials deposited in the storehouse of language, where productive forms are arranged according to their syntagmatic and associative relations.
>
> ibid.: 165

Although analogy may appear to separate *parole* from *langue*, for Pêcheux the 'analogical' dimension of language continues to function as an ideology for the explanation of spontaneous speech acts.[14] As Saussure declares: "We must go further and say that analogy is grammatical" (ibid.: 165). In this sense analogy is the syntax of creative *parole* (i.e., Saussure's work returns to a pre-scientific normative theory of grammar). So – by *analogy* – subjectivity re-enters *langue* and Saussure regresses behind the epistemological break of his linguistic science.

---

14   In Althusser's terms analogy appears to function as a 'spontaneous ideology' of linguistic science. Because Saussure could not overcome the problem of subjective speech acts the notion of analogy enabled him to suggest that sound waves may be analogically related as 'word-images' *after* they have been invested with 'meaning'. This problem is also addressed by Chomsky as a theoretical issue for 'transformational grammar'. The spontaneous ideology of linguistics thus established questions that cannot be resolved without fundamentally altering the assumptions governing the discipline (hence the importance of Saussure's rupture). For further discussion of 'scientific ideology' see Althusser's *Philosophy and the Spontaneous Philosophy of the Scientists* (Althusser, 1990).

Noam Chomsky (1928–)

Zellig Harris[1] taught Noam Chomsky linguistics at the University of Pennsylvania (Barsky, 2011). Chomsky consolidates much of his teacher's thought in the composition of *Syntactic Structures* (1957).

> During the entire period of this research I have had the benefit of very frequent and lengthy discussions with Zellig S. Harris. So many of his ideas and suggestions are incorporated in the text ... and in research on which it is based that I will make no attempt to indicate them by special reference.
>
> CHOMSKY, 1957: 6

Chomsky – following Harris – finds that semantic categories are theoretically problematic for linguistic science and he proposes various answers to account for the problem of 'meaning' in language (e.g., competence, performance, and transformation). Pêcheux, however, suggests that Chomsky's notional solutions are systematically related to the speculative presuppositions of linguistic idealism (i.e., Chomsky's solutions are theoretical ideologies).[2]

> Since the advent of Chomskyism, semantics ('interpretative' or 'generative') has been at the centre of linguistic controversy, especially in respect to its relationship with syntax ... These controversies depend, as we shall see, on *philosophical* questions which themselves involve the problem of universality and ideal language.
>
> PÊCHEUX, 1982: IX; emphasis added

---

1 Genealogically the research of Zellig Harris was of great importance for Pêcheux's vision of non-subjective social science. Harris sought to eliminate subjective considerations from structures of language and Chomky appears to have followed this scientific principle to some extent. Yet, Chomsky regresses behind the theoretical advances of both Saussure and Harris when he represents meaning syntactically in cases of 'generative grammar'.

2 For Pêcheux 'philosophical questions' within linguistics are ideological obstacles for the science of language. Much of his research in *Language, Semantics, and Ideology* is directed towards describing how the discipline of linguistics is *really* a branch of philosophy that permits subjective explanations of language use. In this sense, the concepts and categories that are used to study language (e.g., philosophies of language and grammar) function as theoretical ideologies closely aligned with ideological state apparatuses.

According to Pêcheux the Chomskyan school of linguistics follows a "formal-logicist tendency ... a critical development of linguistic structuralism via 'generative' theories'" (ibid.: 6). Chomsky's account of linguistics, in this view, attempts to explain transformations in a given linguistic structure *without* recourse to the category of 'meaning', i.e., semantic change ostensibly occurs via syntactic mechanisms. Chomsky states "[t]here is no aspect of linguistic study more subject to confusion and more in need of clear and careful formulation than that which deals with the points of connection between syntax and semantics" (Chomsky, 1957: 93). Syntactic and semantic objects are theoretically distinct, according to Chomsky, however, he notes that certain linguistic correlations between the two do, in fact, occur. Chomsky suggests that grammar is best formulated as 'a self-contained study independent of semantics' because 'grammaticalness cannot be identified with meaningfulness', yet, between syntactic structures and meaning 'we do find many correlations' (ibid.: 106–108). Chomsky suggests that syntax acts to 'embed' meaning within speech acts:

> In describing the meaning of a word it is often expedient, or necessary, to refer to the syntactic framework in which this word is usually embedded ... This is not surprising; it means that the syntactic devices are being used fairly systematically.
>
> ibid.: 104

The linguistic process Chomsky defines to explain the integration of semantics via syntax is 'generative grammar'. Generative grammar functions *tacitly* in so far as phonetic and semantic structures are performatively realized in speech situations subject to a framework of syntactic 'competence'. In *Cartesian Linguistics* Chomsky writes:

> By a 'generative grammar' I mean a description of the tacit competence of the speaker-hearer that underlies his actual performance in production and perception (understanding) of speech. A generative grammar, ideally, specifies a pairing of phonetic and semantic representations ... abstracting away from many factors that interweave with tacit competence to determine actual performance.
>
> CHOMSKY, 1966: 75

Pêcheux is critical of Chomsky's theory because generative grammar appeals to the 'creative subjectivity of *parole*' (found in Saussure's research) via certain performative presuppositions (Pêcheux, 1982: 37–38). Grammatical structures thus generate semantic effects in a way that appears *automatic*. In *Aspects of the Theory of Syntax* such 'automatic' discourse is presented by Chomsky in the following terms:

> Obviously, every speaker of a language has mastered and internalized a generative grammar that expresses his knowledge of his language. *This is not to say he is aware of the rules of the grammar or even that he can become aware of them*, or that his statements about his intuitive knowledge are necessarily accurate.
>
> CHOMSKY, 1965: 8; emphasis added

Tacit competence and actual performance are conceptual corollaries of *langue* and *parole*, however, Chomsky's appeal to subjective explanation is, in Pêcheux's view, theoretically inadequate for a linguistic science.[3] Chomsky's generative grammar, in Pêcheux/Herbert's terms, is an instance of syntactic ideology, i.e., an ideology which empirically generates the 'always-already-there'. Chomsky's *Cartesian Linguistics* is directly referenced in Pêcheux's *Language, Semantics, and Ideology* and in *Automatic Discourse Analysis* there are bibliographic entries for Chomsky's *Syntactic Structures* and *Aspects of the Theory of Syntax*. Darian A. Wallis discusses the connection between Chomsky's notion of 'linguistic competence' and discourse theory in "Michel Pêcheux's theory of language and ideology and method of discourse analysis: A critical introduction" published by the journal *Text & Talk*. According to Wallis:

> Indeed, the conditions of production [for discourse] function as a principle of selection-combination on *the elements of a language to constrain or limit what a person says and is capable of saying, even if he/she has the necessary competence*. There are some utterances an individual would be ideologically incapable of producing, his/her linguistic competence notwithstanding.
>
> WALLIS, 2007: 254; emphasis added

If discursive conditions are structurally determined by syntactic transformations, then 'necessary' competence is, in fact, contingent, in so far as such competence is 'mastered and internalized'. Chomsky's work evidently represents a

---

3   The research of Harris appears more reliable in this regard as he directly describes certain methodological principles to prevent the analysis of language as a subjective phenomena.

continuation of Saussure's problematic via tacit competence and actual performance (i.e., language vs. *parole*).[4]

> We thus make a fundamental distinction between *competence* (the speaker-hearer's knowledge of his language) and *performance* (the actual use of language in concrete situations) ... The problem for the linguist, as well as for the child learning the language, is to determine from the data of the performance the underlying system of rules that has been mastered by the speaker-hearer and that he puts to use in actual performance.
>
> CHOMSKY, 1965: 4

Furthermore, the conditions of language acquisition outlined in *Aspects of the Theory of Syntax* can be applied to Pêcheux's type A (syntactic/empirical) and type B ideologies (semantic/speculative) whereby actual performance is subject to tacit competence. Chomsky writes:

> In short, the structure of particular languages may very well be largely determined by factors over which the individual has no conscious control and concerning which society may have little choice or freedom.
>
> ibid.: 59

Tacit competence and actual performance are – according to Chomsky – connected via the 'deep' and 'surface' structures of grammar:

> the syntactic component consists of a base that generates deep structures and a transformational part that maps them into surface structures ... The final effect of a grammar, then, is to relate a semantic interpretation to a phonetic representation – that is, to state how a sentence is interpreted.
>
> ibid.: 135

---

4   Linguistic competence is, of course, to a certain extent obligatory. Compulsory education ensures that most individuals can at least recognize various commonplace items, write their name, obey basic commands, and 'read' the news. Basic literacy establishes a general receptivity to social norms which may function as a tacit ideology. Indeed, the ability to identify the social order is a necessary condition for its legitimacy. Symbolic representation was crucial to the evolution of existing society given that the subordination of thought to graphic linearization became an important way to codify social strata.

Sentential transformations are examples of what Pêcheux calls 'transverse-discourse' and in Chomsky's analysis transformative mechanisms constitute a tacit interpretive schema.

> Using some recent terminology, we can distinguish the 'deep structure' of a sentence from its 'surface structure'. The former is the underlying abstract structure that determines its semantic interpretation; the latter, the superficial organization of units which determines the phonetic interpretation and which relates to the physical form of the actual utterance, to its perceived or intended form.
> CHOMSKY, 1966: 33

Robert Resch suggests Saussure is unable to conceptualise individual enunciation (*parole*) as a function of language (*langue*) and that Chomsky substitutes 'deep structures' for a social explanation of the transformation problem (Resch, 1992). In *Automatic Discourse Analysis* Pêcheux appears to adopt Chomsky's deep/surface distinction to describe the structural effects of discursive systems.

> Our task is therefore to work backwards from these 'surface effects' to the invisible structure which determines them; only when we have done that will it be possible to realize a general theory of processes of discursive production as *theory of the rule-governed variation of 'deep structures'*.
> PÊCHEUX, 1995: 96

Discursive surfaces (e.g., 'texts') are, in Pêcheux's analysis, realized via specific conditions of production.

> Given a dominant state of conditions of production of discourse, there is a corresponding dominant process of production which we can reveal by comparing different empirical discursive surfaces resulting from that dominant state. The intersection-points defined by metaphoric effects allow us to extract the *semantic domains* determined by the dominant process and the relations of *logical-rhetorical dependency* it induces between those domains.
> ibid.: 106

According to Pêcheux discourse analysis leads to the identification of meaning effects by 'reading' surface structures as interpretations of tacit production conditions.[5]

> The ultimate purpose of this undertaking is, then, to provide the preconditions for a practice of *reading*, defined as the systematic detection of symptoms representing meaning-effects within the discursive surface.
>
> ibid.: 118

While Pêcheux incorporates Chomsky's theory of rule-governed variation in forms of discourse he does not assume that these rules correspond to a universal subject *a priori*. Chomsky, however, supports the idea of universal grammar as an *a priori* (innate) structure that can be identified in natural languages:

> ... the main task of linguistic theory must be to develop an account of linguistic universals ... A theory of substantive semantic universals might hold for example, that a certain designative must be carried out in a specified way in each language. Thus it might assert that each language will contain terms that designate persons or lexical items referring to certain kinds of objects, feelings, behavior, and so on.
>
> CHOMSKY, 1965: 27–28

Pêcheux and his colleagues find that semantic universals are a potential obstacle for linguistic science:

> the very notion of the immanent universe of meaning poses the question of semantic universals, that is to say of a metalinguistic system capable of describing 'reality'... like a net ... explicitly organized in the form of an administrative practice ... or implicitly structured as a system of representations.
>
> HAROCHE et al., 1971

---

5 Pêcheux's theoretical aim is to generate a critical method of reading that is not limited by the existing reading codes which function as philosophical and literary systems, i.e., myths. Thus he attempts to discover how meaning is produced in materialist terms without recourse to ideological explanations. Pêcheux generally follows Althusser's attempt to extirpate the reading subject from the activity of encoded recognition. "Clearly grasp what follows, we must bear firmly in mind that both he who is writing these lines and the reader who is reading them are themselves subjects, and therefore ideological subjects ... As St. Paul admirably puts it, it is in the 'Logos', in other words, in ideology, that we 'live move and have our being'" (Althusser, 2014: 188–189).

Needless to say 'universality' is not a universal concept: the idea of universality arose under specific historical circumstances in the works of Plato and Aristotle and found further expression in the Port-Royal school of logic and numerous other scientific and philosophical treatises. Both Pêcheux and Chomsky comment on the Port-Royal school with reference to linguistic criteria:

> Summarizing the Port-Royal theory in its major outlines, a sentence has an inner mental aspect (a deep structure that conveys its meaning) and an outer, physical aspect as a sound sequence ... The deep structure is, however, represented in the mind as the physical utterance is produced.
>
> CHOMSKY, 1966: 40

Innate ideas, for Chomsky, are *analogous* to 'deep structure' and through this supposed connection he suggests that language acquisition involves the recognition of 'linguistic universals'.

> As a long-range task for general linguistics, we might set the problem of developing an account of this innate linguistic theory that provides the basis for language learning ... A theory of linguistic structure that aims for explanatory adequacy incorporates an account of linguistic universals, and it attributes tacit knowledge of these universals to the child.
>
> CHOMSKY, 1965: 25–27

Pêcheux evidently finds Chomsky's research useful, yet, he is critical of Port-Royal logic in so far as it adheres to certain theological precepts.

> Such then, for the Port-Royal grammarians ... the action of the relationship between comprehension and extension, is concerned exclusively with the order of being, the world of essences, without any addition from thought: we are on a level at which being itself designates itself.
>
> PÊCHEUX, 1982: 23–24

The preceding statement, by Pêcheux, statement generally agrees with the religious ontology found in Port-Royal logic:

> Since we cannot have any knowledge of *that which is without us*, save through the medium of *ideas which are within* us, the reflections which may be made on our ideas form perhaps the most important part of logic, since it is that which is the foundation of all the rest.
>
> ARNAULD & NICOLE, 1850: 29

The 'ideas within us' are, for Chomsky, the deep structure of language and the surface structure constitutes the relations of meaning that reflect this inner truth.[6] "It is the deep structure underlying the actual utterance, a structure that is purely mental, that conveys the semantic content of the sentence" (Chomsky, 1966: 35). If, following Pêcheux, linguistic surfaces are determined by the deep structure of discursive production Chomsky's 'purely' mental account of innate linguistic structures seems implausible when accounting for historical change in forms of discourse. Chomsky's rationalism succumbs to the same problem that the Port-Royal school reveals: 'being itself designates itself'.

> To my knowledge, the only substantive proposal to deal with the problem of acquisition of knowledge of language is the rationalist conception that I have outlined. To repeat: suppose that we assign to the mind, as an innate property, the general theory of language we have called 'universal grammar'... The theory of universal grammar, then, provides a schema to which any particular grammar must conform.
>
> CHOMSKY, 2005: 77

Thus, the external world (knowledge of that which is without us) is prescribed or in some way conforms to 'universal grammar' (the medium of ideas which are within us). In *Language and Mind* Chomsky explains the conceptual basis of language philosophically (via rationalism), however, he does not appear to consider the ideological presuppositions of language use in certain social systems. Yet, such issues are raised by Chomsky and Herman, in *Manufacturing Consent: The Political Economy of the Mass Media* using a 'propaganda model'.

> This book centers in what we call a 'propaganda model'... It is our view that, among their other functions, the media serve, and propagandize on behalf of, the powerful societal interests that control and finance them.
>
> CHOMSKY & HERMAN, 1988: XI

Manufacturing Consent goes some way towards describing the theory of pragmatics that is absent from Chomsky's generative grammar. Chomsky and

---

6 Surface structures and deep structures are supposedly connected – as Saussure's research also suggests – via associations of sound and meaning. Chomsky maintains that such associations exist 'in the mind' *a priori*. Chomsky, therefore, appears to implicitly support the Munchausen effect as a 'dimension' of his metalinguistic system.

Herman clearly state that the *language* of the 'masses' is subject to manipulation by various agencies of the 'media'.[7]

> The mass media serve as a system for communicating messages and symbols to the general populace. It is their function to amuse, entertain, and inform, and to inculcate individuals with the values, beliefs, and codes of behavior that will integrate them into the institutional structures of the larger society. In a world of concentrated wealth and major conflicts of class interest, to fulfil this role requires systematic propaganda.
>
> ibid.: 1

This model suggests that particular aspects of linguistic competence and performance are structurally determined by external – social – effects of 'propaganda'.

> Structural factors are those such as ownership and control, dependence on other major funding sources (notably, advertisers), and mutual interests and relationships between the media and those who make the news and have the power to define it and explain *what it means*.
>
> ibid.: XI; emphasis added

In Pêcheux's terms propaganda constitutes a 'meaning effect' specific to certain discursive conditions that are socially constructed. According to Chomsky and Herman the 'propaganda machine' shapes and manipulates public opinion, however, they note it is not always successful.

> These structural factors that dominate media operations are not all-controlling and do not produce simple and homogeneous results ... The beauty of the system ... is that such dissent and inconvenient information are kept within bounds and at the margins ... it does not imply that any propaganda emanating from the media is always effective.
>
> ibid.: XII

---

7 While the audio-visual system of the media diseminates information to great numbers of people this process simultaneously presents potential dangers. According to Leroi-Gourhan: "From the social point of view, the audiovisual indisputably represents a valuable gain inasmuch it facilitates the transmission of precise information and acts upon the mass of people receiving it in ways that immobilize all their means of interpretation ... The situation now apparently becoming generalized may therefore be said to represent an improvement in that it eliminates the effort of 'imagining'... But imagination is the fundamental property of intelligence, and a society with a weakened property of symbol making would suffer a concomitant loss of the property of action" (Leroi-Gourhan, 1993: 213–214).

Systematic propaganda is a pragmatic solution to issues raised by differences in linguistic value. Linguistic value – in the Saussurian sense – is what propaganda attempts to define:

> As we have already said, the concept of value is closely related to the idea of language as a system and what we will agree to call the principle of the unity of language ... As we know the implementation of this principle in the constitution of the particular theory or syntax of such and such a language involves semantic criteria.
>
> HAROCHE, *et al.*, 1971

The generation of linguistic value – in so far as it determines social power via mechanisms of 'acceptability' – is a 'pragmatic' practice of semantic control. If meaning is subordinate to value – as Haroche *et al.* suggest – propaganda is a vehicle to inculcate new 'values' or sustain those which are currently valorized.[8] In an interview entitled "On the nature of pragmatics and related issues" Chomsky notes that his studies of syntax are informed by a 'use theory of meaning' (influenced in part by Wittgenstein and Austin).

> The study of such uses of language is 'pragmatics' in a conventional terminology. Whether there is also a semantics of natural language in the traditional sense ... seems to me an open question ... In any event, it is a matter for discovery, not stipulation. From this point of view, 'pragmatics' must be a central component of any linguistic theory that aims to be comprehensive.
>
> CHOMSKY, 1999

Chomsky's 'propaganda model' marks an attempt to theorize the meaning effects of propaganda in terms of pragmatic conditions, i.e., instances of language use. The process of 'manufacturing' meaning via consent is conceivably an ideological process for legitimizing certain kinds of linguistic competence and performance in relation to particular social norms. Norman Fairclough writes:

---

8 Following the work of Pêcheux – and Althusser – ideological state apparatuses provide the necessary propaganda to support state power, however, the apprehension of such inculcation may bypass awareness because 'meaning' exists in the very means of cognition, e.g, speech sounds, writing, the alphabet and so on. The graphic representation of speech sounds in writing produces the interior-exterior of phoneticized graphism that Pêcheux calls intradiscourse.

Ideologies are closely linked to linked to language, because using language is the commonest form of social behavior ... If, as I shall argue,
ideology is pervasively present in language, that fact ought to mean that
the ideological nature of language should be one of the major themes of
social science.

FAIRCLOUGH, 1989: 2–3

Discourse – for Pêcheux – is an intermediary zone between language (*langue*)
and individual speech (*parole*) articulated via pragmatic structures (e.g.,
'contextual cues') which are specified in the conditions of production for a
given enunciation.[9] Pêcheux theoretically differentiates the linguistic basis
from the discursive process to find that ideological effects develop through
the imposition of meanings which are represented by the subjective 'use' of
discourse. Pêcheux maintains that self-evident meaning is a pre-Saussurian
ideology for the field of linguistic science, however, given that certain conditions of language use are ostensibly 'pragmatic' the ideological problem
of semantics must be explained objectively and not, he posits, by relying on
the 'subject-form of discourse'. Hence, Pêcheux's theory of discourse studies
how the embedding/articulation of 'meaning' is ideologically defined by linguistic processes. His materialist theory of discourse attempts to deconstruct
the always-already-given in terms of empirical and speculative ideologies. In
his view, semantic (ideology A) and syntactic (ideology B) beliefs function as
imaginary mechanisms for the embedding/articulation of 'self-evident' forms
of discourse (Pêcheux, 1982). "A meaning effect does not pre-exist the discursive formation in which it is constituted" (ibid.: 187). Consequently, when a
speech act is 'realized' the performative framework of a given statement is
pragmatically dissimulated by existing discursive norms:

> a word, expression or proposition does not have a meaning '*of its own*'
> attached to it in its literalness; its meaning is constituted in each discur-
> sive formation, in the relationships into which one word, expression or
> proposition enters with other words, expressions or propositions of the
> same discursive formation.
>
> PÊCHEUX, 1982: 112

---

9 For example, a subject's 'meaningful' discourse may appear as a spontaneous response to
   interdiscursive prompts, yet, such activity could, in fact, be the result of certain unconscious
   forms of mis/recognition. Pêcheux's notion of transverse-discourse attempts to establish how
   'meaning' is a quasi-automatic behavior to which individual-agents respond via speech acts
   without perceiving the material history of symbolic devices such as alphabetic characters.

Empirical ideologies implicate meanings which are assumed to be real: therefore 'meaning effects' constitute a tacitly accepted linguistic reality. Chomsky, in *Language and Mind*, initiates an attempt to isolate the formal structures that differentiate linguistic competence from performance, and he also suggests that 'pragmatic' phenomena require further investigation.

> So far, the study of language has progressed on the basis of a certain abstraction: namely, we abstract away from conditions of use of language and consider formal structures and the formal operations that relate them ... It may be that the next great advance in the study of language will require the forging of new tools that permit us to bring into consideration a variety of questions that have been cast into the waste-bin of 'pragmatics'....
>
> CHOMSKY, 2005: 98

Nicos Poulantzas – a contemporary of Pêcheux and Althusser – presents 'state writing' as a formal, pragmatic, structure that supports 'the institutional materiality of the state' (Poulantzas, 1978). Chomsky's 'propaganda model' suggests how State discourse could function as a general syntax for political power. Poulantzas notes that the capitalist State determines its legitimacy via certain forms of discourse and, in this way, 'self-selects' the appropriate agents and organisations to achieve such ends. Furthermore, this orthographic authority, according to Poulantzas, encodes its own criteria for 'appropriate' scientific research.[10]

> Today, it is clear that the State tends to incorporate science itself by organizing its discourse ... The capitalist State regiments the production of science in such a way that it becomes, in its innermost texture, a *state science* locked into the mechanism of power; and as we know, this is not just true of the so-called human sciences.
>
> ibid.: 57

---

10   Althusser suggests that scientific practice occurs within the ideological conditions of a given society and, in this sense, scientists produce a 'spontaneous philosophy' of their social practice. "There is within the 'consciousness' or 'unconsciousness' of scientists such a thing as a *spontaneous philosophy of scientists* (SPS)" (Althusser, 1990: 120). SPS represents how scientists attempt to syncretize their vocational work with the extra-scientific ideology of the existing social order.

State discourse, then, determines the syntax which sustains the performance of 'legitimate' forms of institutional materiality (in Chomskyan terms this appears to be the formal basis for linguistic 'competence'). According to Poulantzas:

> The discourse must always be *heard* and *understood*, even if not in a uniform manner: it is not enough that it be uttered as an incantation. This presupposes that, in the various codes of thinking, the State itself is *overcoded* ... Through a process of measured distillation, this overcoding is inculcated in the totality of subjects.
>
> ibid.: 58

In Chomsky's terms the State exhibits a generative grammar which governs the existing forms of 'institutional materiality' via certain statements, i.e., state semantics is the realization of linguistic value.[11] In *The Social Sciences: A Semiotic View* Algirdas Julien Greimas presents linguistic structures in terms of 'transcoding'. The process of transcoding sustains meaning across different linguistic objects resulting in the continuity of sense and reference via signifying structures:

> Signification is simply this transposition of one level of language into a different language, and meaning is simply possibility of *transcoding* ... If therefore we reduce the problem of meaning to its minimal dimensions (i.e., to transcoded significations)... we can ask if scientific activity in this domain should not consist in working out *techniques of transposition* ... By a different route we have returned to the problem of the relations between the models of description and the elementary structure of signification, as it can be apprehended and clarified at its source.
>
> GREIMAS, 1990: 7–8

State writing appears to transcode, or in Poulantzas' lexicon 'overcode', social structures with a meaning represented by certain ideological conditions. To determine the required meaning effects of state discourse such 'transcoded significations' are assumed to be always-already-there (i.e., function as pre-structured forms of social interaction).[12]

---

11 According to Haroche *et al.* (1971) meaning is subordinate to value. Such subordination may then support the proposition that the State effectively guarantees what society 'means' vis-à-vis its ideological apparatus.

12 Transcoding does not necessarily require that the system of language is objectively verified via scientific practice. For example, one ideology may be transcoded into another

> Translated into linguistic language, meaning is identified with the ori-
> ented process of actualisation that, like every semiotic process is presup-
> posed by – and presupposes – a virtual or realised system or program.
>
> ibid.: 9

Furthermore, Greimas notes that:

> Semiotics now counts as one of its urgent tasks, the study of discursive
> organisations of signification. Linguistics, for its part, being the most
> developed of semiotic systems, is recognized among the social sciences
> as having the greatest claim to the status of science.
>
> ibid.: 12

Transcoding and the scientificity of linguistics, in this view, generally follows
the Saussurian double structure of system (*langue*) and process (*parole*), however, Saussure's research presents certain theoretical issues for techniques of
discursive 'transposition'. According to Greimas:

> use of the Saussurian *langue/parole* distinction does pose some prob-
> lems, if only because it requires us to conceive of and put in place an
> *instance of mediation* that allows for the movement to and from these two
> forms of semiotic existence.
>
> ibid.: 12

Chomsky's work is cited by Greimas in "On Meaning" where he refers to 'deep
versus surface structures' with Greimas further explaining that the scientific
project for semiotics 'is generative – not exactly in the Chomskyan sense, but
as a coherent description of the generation of signification not as it is but as
signifying objects which are produced' (Greimas, 1989: 540). Conceptually
Greimas's research continues the Saussurian break between reference and
meaning – with the effects of syntax and semantics functioning as generative mechanisms for discursive interaction. 'Transcoding' follows a generative

---

without any indication that such change is, in fact, a function of imaginary mis/recogni-
tion. Pêcheux suggests that semantic and syntactic ideologies 'represent' in language particular illusory processes which subjects typically accept as accurate – all misconceptions
nothwithstanding.

schema (via Chomsky's theory) due to the apparent linguistic continuity of institutional systems that produce syntax and meaning discursively:

> what is obvious today, but was once difficult for people to accept, is that the generative apparatus produces discourses, that is to say, totalities of meaning in terms of words or sentences.
>
> ibid.

Generative transcoding perpetuates particular modes of signification by pre-supposing the speculative mediation of system and process in the form of 'syntactic actants'. Such generative structures virtually transcode the connection from *langue* to *parole* and vice versa:

> the subject of discourse is no more than a virtual instance, an instance constructed in linguistic theory in order to account for the transformation of language ... Further, this mediating instance shows a syntactic subject, an actant ... realised as a discursive program.
>
> GREIMAS, 1990: 12

Generative grammar, according to Greimas, relates individual subjects to social structures in terms of *programmatic* discourse.[13]

> We could note ... that at the level of the individual practice, locally concentrated competencies are acquired and added to, thanks to discursive practice. We can also note that on the social level, syntactic structures are susceptible of transformations and that as a result ... the competent subject of discourse, while being an instance that is presupposed by the functioning of a discourse, can be considered as a *subject in the process of formation*, constant formation.
>
> ibid.: 13

---

13   Particular discursive formations program the 'subjectivity' of the subject given that its culture is the product of social inscription. Systems of writing prescribe the content of such programming via disciplines. According to Althusser: "Behind the literary disciplines there is a long heritage: that of the humanities. To understand the humanities, we must seek out the meaning of the 'culture' they dispense *in the norms* of the *forms of behavior* that are *dominant* in the society under consideration: religious, moral juridical, political, etc., ideology – in short, in *practical ideologies*" (Althusser, 1990: 94). I note that the media apparatus provides the 'main body' of literature that circulates in society today and consequently facilitates discursive programming informally for certain 'consumers'. Thus the reception of such 'broadcasting' generates popular culture as a specific form of programmed behavior.

Linguistic performance is – for Chomsky – a function of generative competence. The structure of generative grammar specifies the rules of 'formatives'
(well-formed strings of syntax) (Chomsky, 1965: 3). Formatives structure cognition via certain acts of linguistic performance, however, this does not imply
direct knowledge of their generative mechanisms on the part of those individuals 'using' such syntax.

The generative grammar of the State determines social practice via
'accepted' forms of discourse given that its *authority* is legitimated by certain
structures of institutional materiality. According to Poulantzas the different
functions of the state apparatus are all directed towards the qualification/
subjugation of individual subjects and the 'school mechanism' is an integral
part of ideological process (Poulantzas, 2008: 253). In Saussure's terminology
a 'language-state' is generated by means of syntagmatic and associative co-
ordinates that remain fixed, i.e., static. 'Static linguistics or the description of
a language-state is *grammar* ... where it is a question of a complex and systematic object governing the interplay of existing values' (Saussure, 1959: 134).
Saussure maintains that linguistic structures exhibit static (synchronic) and
evolutionary (diachronic) histories, i.e., periods of relative immobility or
mobility of linguistic form.

> Immobility – the relative fixation of an idiom – may have an external
> cause (the influence of a court, school, an academy, writing, etc.) which
> in turn is positively favored by social and political equilibrium. But if
> some external upheaval that has affected the equilibrium of the nation
> precipitates linguistic evolution, this is because language simply reverts
> back to its free state and follows its regular course.
>
> ibid.: 150

Language in a 'free state' represents relatively unstructured relations between
phonetic, graphic, and semantic elements.

> Everything that relates to the static side of our science is synchronic;
> everything that has to do with evolution is diachronic. Similarly, syn-
> chrony and diachrony designate respectively a language-state and an
> evolutionary phase.
>
> ibid.: 81

Synchronic and diachronic linguistic structures suggest how Chomsky's
'formatives' are subject to generative variation. Formatives are, in this sense,
determined by conditions of production that facilitate the inscription of

institutional discourse wherein meaning is 'automatically' generated via social structures of accepted 'competence' (e.g., the ideological state apparatus) Pêcheux, however, finds that Chomsky's account of meaning cannot explain discursive transformations without presupposing an innate grammar of deep structures.

> Note in passing that the spontaneous hermeneutics that characterizes the subject-effect in respect of language is reproduced, without any fundamental change in its nature, by the theoretical elaborations in Chomskyan and post-Chomskyan conceptions of semantics ... As we have just seen, discursive processes, as conceived here, cannot originate in the subject. Yet they are necessarily realized in the same subject. This apparent contradiction relates to the question of the constitution of the subject and to what we have termed its subjection.
>
> PÊCHEUX, 1995: 130–131

Chomsky's generative theory assumes syntax functions to relate interiority to exteriority via linguistic universals of the 'always-already-there' (i.e., self-evident meaning). Yet, discursive sequences (i.e., elements of a given corpus) are pre-structured by surfaces of enunciation (e.g., passages or phrases of text/ speech) and, according to Pêcheux's theory of discourse, this anterior signifying procedure is typically forgotten by the subject who 'uses' such discourse 'freely'.[14]

> The relative exteriority of an ideological formation with regard to the discursive formation necessarily finds expression within that discursive formation itself ... the process whereby a concrete discursive sequence is produced or recognized as having a meaning for a subject disappears from the subject's view.
>
> ibid.: 129

In consequence, the associative and syntagmatic structures of discourse are not readily apprehended by the subjects who simply relay a given language

---

14   In Althusser's research this problem is broached in a discussion of how reality is 'read'. What a subject sees in a reading of reality is an effect of its apparatus of 'vision', yet this perceptual system may produce the illegibility of ideological mis/recognition. "The oversight, then, is not to see what one sees, the oversight no longer concerns the object, but

which has been produced 'automatically' via generative mechanisms.[15] Chomsky notes 'generative grammar' may – in some cases – escape awareness however, Pêcheux does not reduce language acquisition to a form of 'spontaneous' meaning in so far as the subjection/qualification of agency is apparently legitimated by 'self-evident' forms of discourse.

> This fact that any sequence 'has meaning' necessarily belongs to a discursive formation that is repressed for (and perhaps by) the subject is concealed from the subject by the illusion that he himself is at the source of meaning, that he can grasp anew a pre-existing universal meaning (this explains among other things, the eternal duality between individuality and universality that characterizes the subject's discursive illusion).
>
> PÊCHEUX, 1995: 130

Indeed, Pêcheux finds that the theory of 'generative semantics' represents the theological dogma of meaning *syntactically*.

> Remember that, in generative semantics, the idealism of a universal theory of ideas is, as I have said, 'openly admitted', for example in the project of a grammar consisting of a set of transformations leading from each conceptual structure to the wider set of surface structures that may be used to express that concept. *In other words, in the beginning was the meaning ....*
>
> PÊCHEUX, 1982: 208; emphasis added

---

the sight itself. The oversight is an oversight that concerns *vision*: non-vision is therefore inside vision; it is a form of vision and hence has a necessary relationship with vision. We have reached our real problem, the problem that exists *in* and is posed *by* the actual identity of this organic confusion of non-vision in vision" (Althusser, 1970: 22).

15   Self-generating subjectivity then appears as the effect of such automatic discourse, however, this process typically remains mystified due to the functioning of ideological state apparatuses.

John Searle (1932–)

In *Speech Acts: An Essay in the Philosophy of Language* John Searle outlines a *philosophical* account of various types of speech activity.

> How do words relate to the world? ... How do words stand for things? What is the difference between a meaningful string of words and meaningless one? ... Such questions form the subject matter of the philosophy of language.
>
> SEARLE, 1969: 3

Although he thanks Noam Chomsky in the preface Searle asserts that *Speech Acts* does not represent a linguistic theory. "It is not an essay in linguistics. Linguistics attempts to describe the actual structures – phonological, syntactic, and semantic – of natural human languages" (ibid.:4). After stating this, however, Searle then proceeds – in subsequent sections of *Speech Acts* – to describe what are usually considered elements of linguistic theory: rules of language use, context, and meaning (i.e., syntax, pragmatics, and semantics).

> Speaking a language is engaging in a (highly complex) rule-governed form of behavior. To learn and master a language is (*inter alia*) to learn and to have mastered those rules. This is a familiar view in philosophy and linguistics, but its consequences are not always fully realized.
>
> ibid.: 12

For Pêcheux, the research of Searle and the 'Oxford school' (*viz.* J. L. Austin and P. F. Strawson) combines both philosophy and linguistics to express a spontaneous ideology of enunciation and implicature (i.e., an ideology of 'speech acts') (Pêcheux, 1982: 6). The philosophy of language is an ideological solution to real questions regarding the science of language. Pêcheux suggests that the *philosophy* of language represents an *inter-mediate* discourse between linguistics and ideology. By definition a philosophy of language is exactly that, i.e., a *speculative* account of linguistic phenomena and Searle apparently regards the 'intuitions of the speaker' as the 'evidential' basis for his *philosophical* study of speech acts:[1]

> So, in our era of extremely sophisticated methodologies, the methodology of this book must seem naively simple. I am a native speaker of a language. I wish to offer certain characterizations and explanations of my use of elements of that language ... This method, as I have been emphasizing, places heavy intuitions on the native speaker. But everything I have ever read in the philosophy of language, even work by the most behaviourist and empirical of authors, relies similarly on the *intuitions of the speaker*.
>
> SEARLE, 1969: 15; emphasis added

Pêcheux outlines a theory of reading codes in his work on automatic discourse analysis whereby semantic 'transformations' are theoretically related to certain modes of ideological 'reading' (i.e., 'interpretations' which are pre-structured by philosophies of language).[2]

> We must assume the existence of an explicit or implicit consensus between the coders as to the modalities of reading; in other words, the text can only be analyzed within *a shared system of values which has a meaning for the coders and which constitutes their mode of reading* ... The ultimate danger is therefore that the results of the analysis will reproduce the reading-grid that made it possible ... because of the phenomenon of participatory reflection that occurs between the *object* and the *method* designed to apprehend that object.
>
> PÊCHEUX, 1995: 67–68

Searle appears to affirm the spontaneous self-evidence of the speaking subject – by virtue of the 'intuitions of the speaker' – as criteria for the 'naively simple'

---

1 Pêcheux – by contrast – does not assume the intuitions of the speaker constitute the basis of speech acts. Speech acts are, according to Pêcheux, indexed to the discursive formations associated with given speech situations. His materialist theory of discourse suggests that every speech act is issued in relation to existing structures of language which may be traced to particular institutional conditions, for example, academic 'disciplines'.

2 Althusser anticipates such a theory of reading in *Reading Capital*. "We have now reached the point we had to reach in order to discover from it the reason for this *oversight* where a *sighting* is concerned: we must completely reorganize the idea we have of knowledge, we must abandon the mirror myths of immediate vision and reading, and conceive knowledge as production" (Althusser, 1970: 24).

assumptions of his speech act theory. In consequence, Searle's reading protocol appears to support a tacit ideology of speech activity. Semantic ideologies, according to Pêcheux, typically accept that the speaking subject is the bearer of 'its own meaning' via enunciation (i.e. speech acts).[3]

> In other words, enunciation designates both the fact that the subject is the support for his enounced *and* the set of subjective effects (different psychological contents) which underlie that enounced. It is sufficient for my purposes to emphasize the fact that the ideological circle system/ speaking-subject constitutes the invariant of the different forms taken by 'semantics' today.
>
> PÊCHEUX, 1982: 39

Describing his methodology for the study of speech acts Searle contends that the 'meaning' of a given speech act is realized in accordance with such an issuance conforming to contextual rules.

> The speech act or acts performed in the utterances of a sentence are in general a function of the meaning of the sentence ... the meaning of sentences is not in principle distinct from a study of speech acts. Properly construed, they are the same study ... the study of the meaning of sentences and the study of speech acts are not two independent studies but one study from two points of view.
>
> SEARLE, 1969: 18

In Searle's account meaning is, principally, determined by the pragmatic conditions of a given speech situation, i.e., a subject's 'intended' meaning will thus conform to the contextual rules of a specific speech act. When a given meaning is specified via a speech act it appears there is a consensus (explicitly or implicitly determined) regarding the issuance (i.e., enunciation) and its contextual ramifications. Some comparable theories are also discussed by Pêcheux and his colleagues in *Social Contexts of Messages* (1971) with regard to the circumstances of enunciative implicature and the mechanisms by which extralinguistic conditions are attributed to intradiscursive processes (e.g., 'situational' causes).

---

3   The intutitions of the speaker are an example of what Pêcheux calls the Munchausen effect whereby the subject is attributed the cause of its own discourse and apparently realizes a meaning which is pre-constructed by existing discursive formations.

Contexts ... operate as factors which arouse and determine superordinate semantic states. These semantic states, in turn, affect subordinate perceptual processes and determine which referential potentialities will be activated in any particular case. Both the immediate intralinguistic context and the particular extralinguistic frame in which a given segment of discourse is embedded affect the choice or determination of referential meaning potentialities.

CARSWELL & ROMMETVEIT, 1971: 9

Furthermore, Pêcheux is not convinced that speech act theory can adequately apprehend the conditions of production for given ideologies of 'context'.[4]

I insist on this point because Anglo-Saxon analytic philosophy today easily lends itself to a theory of language which, via the notions of presupposition, performative and speech act (*énonciation*), tends to 'explain' legal-political and ideological relationships as a word game in which subjectivities confront one another *in actu*, each trying to catch the other, in all senses of the term: in a word, the struggle to the death of speaking-subjects.

PÊCHEUX, 1982: 182

Searle, *actually*, uses a baseball analogy to liken speech acts to other kinds of rule-governed activity:

I know that in baseball after hitting the ball fair, the batter runs in the direction of first base, and not in the direction, say, of third base or the left field grand stand ... My knowledge is based on knowing how to play baseball, which is *inter alia* having internalized a set of rules. I wish to suggest that my knowledge of linguistic characterizations is of a similar kind.

SEARLE, 1969: 14

---

4   Searle's philosophy of speech acts appears to represent what Althusser calls a 'practical ideology'. Practical ideologies (moral, religious, juridical, political and aesthetic) denote those practices which are not scientific but function as a means to legitimate certain forms of 'culture'. The philosophy of speech acts constitutes a practical ideology regarding the 'self-evidence' of speech activity. "It is true that all the great philosophical currents we have briefly analysed are subordinated to the 'values' of the practical ideologies which exist in a conjuncture: to the values, let us say, of the dominant ideology (and, beneath it, the dominated ideologies)" (Althusser, 1990: 130).

'Linguistic characterizations', according to Searle, represent the rules governing speech acts and these are supposedly verified by the 'intuitions of the speaker'. Pêcheux, however, finds that such 'intuitive' descriptions of speech activity do not adequately reveal the effects of embedded ideological conditions:

> the notion of 'speech acts' in fact conveys a miscognition of the determination of the subject in discourse, and that *taking up a position* is really by no means conceivable as an 'originary action' of the speaking-subject: on the contrary, it must be understood as an effect, in the subject-form, of its determination by interdiscourse as transverse-discourse, i.e., an effect of 'exteriority' of the ideologico-discursive real, in so far as it 'returns upon itself' and crosses itself.
>
> PÊCHEUX, 1982: 121–122

Norman Fairclough notes:

> Anglo-American pragmatics is closely associated with analytical philosophy, particularly with the work of Austin and Searle on 'speech acts'. The key insight is that language can be seen as a form of action: that spoken or written utterances constitute the performance of speech acts ... and implicating meanings which are not overtly expressed.
>
> FAIRCLOUGH, 1989: 9

Searle addresses the question of meaning in relation to the kinds of speech acts that are often encountered in ordinary language. Assertions, questions, and orders are examples of speech acts with characteristically different forms of illocution.[5]

> Stating, questioning, commanding, promising, etc. = performing *illocutionary* acts ... Correlated with the notion of illocutionary acts is the notion of the consequences or *effects* such acts have on the actions, thoughts, or beliefs, etc. of hearers.
>
> SEARLE, 1969: 24–25

---

5   The assumed meaning of an illocutionary act is typically obtained with reference to the perceived *context* of locution.

Structures of illocution determine what Pêcheux calls the specific 'meaning effects' of given discursive conditions. For Searle, illocutionary acts constitute meaning via the 'constitutive rules' that govern performative utterances.

> I have said that ... speaking a language is performing acts according to rules. The form this hypothesis will take is that the semantic structures of a language may be regarded as a conventional realization of a series of sets of underlying constitutive rules, and that speech acts are acts characteristically performed by uttering expressions in accordance with these sets of constitutive rules.
>
> SEARLE, 1969: 36–37

In this Searlean presentation meaning is a result of realized constitutive rules and, if the rules are not recognized, the speech act will be ineffective.[6] Searle revises the work of Paul Grice to formulate an account of illocutionary meaning that depends on the intentional recognition of constitutive rules (e.g., 'accepted' linguistic norms). Pêcheux's objection to 'rule-governed' meaning is that performative acceptability typically *assumes* illocutionary competence. Thus certain speech acts can implicitly convey ideological miscognition of the subject-form of discourse (e.g., the Munchausen effect: subject as cause of itself). If the rules of semantic structures are contextually delimited by superordinate and subordinate states of illocution certain interpretations of what reality 'means' may predominant in particular social situations. An example of this hypothesis is discussed by Pêcheux and his colleagues in "Processing of Utterances in Context" from *Social Contexts of Messages*:

> Different linkages between context and utterance will most likely make for different patterns of information processing ... Context and utterance then are related at the level of cognitive representations as consecutive

---

6 I note here that Searle's general approach to the philosophy of language broadly concerns *rules* of linguistic use. Thus his 'method' is really an exercise in stipulating norms of application for semantic ideologies. Searle offers an imaginary solution to what a given statement might 'mean', i.e., speculative conventions of linguistic interaction are 'supported' by his suppositions regarding the normative principles of meaningful utterances. Searle produces an imaginary solution to an ideological problem. "Every imaginary (ideological) posing of a problem (which may be imaginary, too) in fact carries in it a determinate problematic, which defines both the possibility and the form of the posing of this problem. This problematic *recurs* as its mirror-image in the solution given to this problem by virtue of the mirror action peculiar to the ideological imagination" (Althusser, 1970: 129).

events ... *The context restricts the range of possible interpretations of the utterance.*

ROMMETVEIT *et al.*, 1971: 33; emphasis added

Linguistic information is processed according to this model by context-utterance linkages: cognitive representations are elicited via stimulus events which affect the interpretation of messages in specific situations. The representation of a context is connected to stimuli in so far as an utterance functions as a vehicle for message transmission. 'Meaning effects' are thus generated via context-utterance linkages where context, stimulus, and utterance, are aligned in a given enunciation. An 'appropriate context' is one that assumes the greatest probability of correlation of superordinate linkages to utterances whereas an 'inappropriate context' reduces information processing to subordinate forms. In unidirectional enunciations a given representation is structurally guaranteed by presuppositions that are linked to the decoding and retrieval of linguistic information (i.e., existing beliefs). Linguistic stimuli, also appear to be synchronically related in illocutionary acts through context-utterance linkages within associated structures of discourse. Pêcheux notes that 'semantic centration' in discursive structures is proximally defined by certain conditions of production, e.g., socially structured context-utterance linkages. Each 'discourse structure' is part of a superordinate linguistic system L in which a discursive string D_x represents R (referent or subject-matter of discourse) between an addresser A and addressee B (Pêcheux, 1971: 67). This simple schema of discourse does not explicitly account for the imaginary effect of E (enunciation) in which a subject experiences its discourse self-referentially.

> If enunciation is defined as the necessarily ever-present relationship between the subject of enunciation and its utterance, then this clearly introduces a new form of the illusion that meaning originates in the subject or that the subject can be identified with the origin of meaning.
>
> PÊCHEUX, 1995: 135

Searle, adapting Grice's work, suggests that an enunciation (utterance) is meaningful when a statement is recognized as an intentional act that corresponds to certain illocutionary conditions. Whether or not the subject is the origin of meaning, for Searle, seems to be a subordinate question that is resolved by an appeal to 'expressibility': 'But even in cases when it is in fact impossible to say exactly what I mean it is *in principle* possible to come to be able to say exactly what I mean' (Searle, 1969: 19; emphasis added).[7] The 'principle of expressibility' notionally defines the superordinate features of a given language in terms of rules that – in principle – determine the structure of meaning-effects:

> it enables us to equate rules for performing speech acts with rules for uttering certain linguistic elements, since for any possible speech act there is a possible linguistic element the meaning of which (given the context of the utterance) is sufficient to determine that its literal utterance is a performance of precisely that speech act.
>
> ibid.: 20–21

Here Searle states that a meaningful utterance is defined by performative conditions which are equal to the 'rules' which determine the norms of expressibility. The speaking subject, in this sense, is identified with its statements by virtue of conforming to the rules that govern speech acts in so far as these events are contextually understood via interdiscourse.[8] Yet, the principle of expressibility cannot definitively explain the illusion of semantic mis/recognition due to the interpretive structure of context-utterance linkages and speaker 'position' that Pêcheux outlines:

> the discourse of the subject is organized by a direct or deferred reference (or by the absence of a reference) to the situation of enunciation as experienced subjectively by the speaker – the speaker's 'I here and now': his points of origin on the axes of person, tense, and localization.
>
> PÊCHEUX, 1995: 136

---

7   Searle appears to assume that his principle of expressibility is in no need of objective verification. Indeed, to do so would controvert the ideological presuppositions of his philosophy of language. Consequently, Searle seems to espouse a broad description of contextual performativity which is, in practice, a kind of literary criticism. What is generally proposed in *Speech Acts* does not attain the status of scientific knowledge. Hence his philosophy of language is not altogether indissociable from fiction. Searle 'establishes' – philosophically – a particular description of speech activity which is 'appreciated' by those who are suitably 'informed'. "The relation between literary disciplines and their object ... has as its *dominant* function not so much the knowledge of this object but rather the definition and inculcation of rules, norms and practices designed to establish 'cultural' relations between the 'literate' and these objects" (Althusser, 1990: 92).

8   The rules of discourse that speakers exhibit transactionally may be unknown to those individuals who are speaking 'freely'. As Chomsky, Althusser, and Pêcheux, maintain syntax is assimilated unconsciously, therefore, the speaking subject is perhaps only vaguely aware that its speech activity is the product of habitual rule-following.

Yet, the study of speech acts, Searle notes, permits the separation of 'brute facts' from 'institutional facts' (Searle, 1969: 50–53). Brute facts are the object of the natural sciences and are broadly 'physical'.

> The model for systematic knowledge of this kind is the natural sciences, and the basis for all knowledge of this kind is generally supposed to be simple empirical observations recording sense experiences.
>
> ibid.: 50

Institutional facts, on the other hand, are broadly social.

> A marriage ceremony, a baseball game, a trial ... Such facts ... I propose to call institutional facts. They are indeed facts; but their existence, unlike the existence of brute facts, presupposes the existence of certain human institutions.
>
> ibid.: 51

Speech acts are institutionally structured in accordance with particular rules that legitimate certain utterances within a given situation.

> Every institutional fact is underlain by a (system of) rule(s) of the form 'X counts as Y in context C'. Our hypothesis that speaking a language is performing acts according to constitutive rules involves us in the hypothesis that the fact that a man performed a certain speech act, e.g., made a promise, is an institutional fact. We are not, therefore, attempting to give an analysis of such facts in terms of brute facts.
>
> ibid.: 51–52

The question, naturally, remains how brute facts (e.g., physical vibrations) become institutional facts (e.g., speech acts) and Searle attempts to resolve such concerns by appealing to 'intentionality'.[9]

---

9 While Searle suggests that 'intentionality' can explain the generation of meaning effects his discussion does not address how discursive formations determine the object of intention. Furthermore, I find that 'intentional meaning' seems to constitute – what Althusser calls – a practical ideology via 'institutional facts'. "Practical ideologies are complex formations which shape notions-representations-images into behavior-conduct-attitude-gestures. The ensemble functions as practical norms that govern the attitude and the concrete positions men adopt towards the real objects and real problems of their social and individual existence, and towards their history" (Althusser, 1990: 83).

The obvious explanation for the brute regularities of language (certain human made noises tend to occur in certain states of affairs or in the presence of certain stimuli) is that the speakers of a language are engaging in a rule-governed form of intentional behaviour.

ibid.: 53

Here are two objections to Searle's 'obvious explanation' regarding the correlation of brute facts and institutional facts in forms of intentionality: one from Pêcheux's research and the other from B. F. Skinner's. Pêcheux states:

The 'acts of the speaking subject' in a given 'situation' and in the presence of given 'interlocutors' – in other words, the subjective illusion which certain theories of enunciation take at face value – are in reality an *effect of relations between discursive processes*.

PÊCHEUX, 1995: 182

A person does not intentionally 'choose' what it will 'freely' say: what is said – for it to be intelligible to others – is structurally determined by forms of discourse which pre-exist individual enunciations.

The fact that one specific (graphic or phonic) sequence – rather than another – is constantly being 'filtered' or 'selected' is not the result of an *act of choice on the part of the speaker* ... This point – and we can do no more than outline it here – seems to enable us to overturn the problematic which sees 'literal meaning' as a natural link between 'language' and 'thought'.

ibid.

For Skinner, intentionality is an unnecessary and potentially ideological presumption of verbal behavior. One should not assume that institutional facts convey 'meaning' instead linguistic regularities should be viewed as particular correlations of stimuli and responses within a strict causal structure (see the next chapter). However, Pêcheux, in *Automatic Discourse Analysis* finds that the behaviorist model (S-O-R: stimulus-organism-response) does not sufficiently explain how discourse is socially embedded.

In an experiment on 'verbal behavior'... the experimenter is part of the *apparatus*, whatever the modality of his *presence* – physical or otherwise – within the conditions of production of the response discourse; in other words, the stimulus is a stimulus only in so far as it refers to the 'verbal communication' situation in which a provisional pact is established between experimenter and subject.

ibid.: 83

Yet, further research indicates that the S-O-R model could, with some theoretical improvements, be applied to the study of preconstructed discursive formations.[10] Searle, paradoxically, suggests that speech acts constitute 'intentional behavior' – but speaker intentionality is, for Pêcheux, an imaginary occurrence simulated by certain institutional ideologies (e.g., phantasies of self-evident meaning). In *The Construction of Social Reality* Searle deploys his theory of speech acts to consider the intentional basis of social phenomena.

> The theory of speech acts is in part an attempt to answer the question, How do we get from the physics of utterances to meaningful speech acts performed by speakers and writers ... This book extends the investigation to social reality ....
>
> SEARLE, 1995: XI

Searle contends that the relationship of speech acts to social reality has been neglected because the classical thinkers of sociology (Weber, Simmel, and Durkheim) did not possess the correct conceptual apparatus. 'That is ... they lacked an adequate theory of speech acts, of performatives, of intentionality, of collective intentionality, of rule-governed behavior, etc.' (ibid.: XII).[11] Searle posits that speech act theory has clear relevance to the theoretical foundations of social science in so far as speech acts generate social norms, i.e., institutional facts.

> This book is about a problem that has puzzled me for a long time: there are portions of the real world, objective facts in the world, that are only facts by human agreement. In a sense there are things that exist only

---

10   Skinner provides the rudiments for such a theory in his book *Verbal Behavior* (1957). Verbal behavior, according to Skinner, is basically a form of interpersonal technology and, as such, is subject to control by various technical processes. Verbal activity is, then, predictable due to the formal structure of operant conditioning. Hence, Skinner's work on the technology of behavior may also further explain – in materialist terms – how sound and meaning are connected as 'associations' in Saussure's research.

11   Karl Marx's name is conspicuously absent from Searle's list of eminent sociologists. This omission may be due to Marx's methodological rejection of philosophy and other imaginary systems (e.g., religion).

because we believe them to exist. I am thinking of things like money, property, governments, and marriages.

ibid.: 1

The practice of interpersonal agreement is determined by certain subjective conventions and, as a result, Searle suggests that institutional facts are not reducible to 'brute facts', furthermore, the 'invisible structure of social reality' is based on a *belief* system that is not immediately perceptible.

To give you a feel for the complexity of the problem, I want to begin by considering the metaphysics of ordinary social relations ... the complex structure of social reality is, so to speak, weightless and invisible.

ibid.: 3–4

Performative utterances (speech acts) define social relations by means of legitimating 'institutional facts' in particular contexts.

Performatives are members of the class of speech acts I call 'declarations'... Institutional facts can be created with the performative utterance of such sentences as "The meeting is adjourned", ... "War is hereby declared", etc. These utterances create the very state of affairs that they represent; and in each case, the state of affairs is an institutional fact.

ibid.: 34

Searle further suggests that performative utterances can only produce institutional facts successfully if their constitutive conditions are in agreement with the 'Background'.

Intentional states function only given a set of Background capacities that do not themselves consist in intentional phenomena ... I have thus defined the concept of the 'Background' as the set of nonintentional or preintentional capacities that enable intentional states to function ... It is important to see that when we talk about the Background we are talking about a certain category of neurophysiological causation.

ibid.: 129

The Background appears to function via individuated forms of situational automaticity which delimit non-intentional systems of causality (e.g., 'spontaneous' speech activity).

The key to understanding the causal relations between the structure of the Background and the structure of social institutions is to see that the Background can be causally sensitive to the specific forms of the constitutive rules of the institutions without actually containing any beliefs or desires or representations of those rules.

  ibid.: 141

The Background, then, generates a superordinate context that does not necessitate direct – immediate – knowledge of the purportedly *invisible* system that determines its rules.[12]

I have said that the structure of human institutions is a structure of constitutive rules. I have also said that people who are participating in the institutions are typically not conscious of these rules ... and even the very people who create the institution may be unaware of its structure.

  ibid.: 127

Hence, the appearance of intentional behavior is, in fact, pre-structured by the Background in which a given social context is realized by inadvertently following certain rules (e.g., institutional norms).

To explain how we can relate to rule structures such as language ... in cases where we do not know the rules and are not following them either consciously or unconsciously, I have to appeal to the notion ... I have called 'the Background'.

  ibid.: 129

Pêcheux's colleague Paul Henry presents a theory of language processing in *Social Contexts of Messages* that is informed by a study of how referents are connected to contexts that is of particular significance for Searle's 'Background' theory. Henry writes:

The referent is often considered to be the pivot of the relation between a message and the 'extralinguistic reality'. Therefore, the notion of referent would appear to be essential in the study of language in contexts.

---

12   Searle's 'Background' may then represent – in light of Skinner's research – an 'unseen' system of conditioning in which operant behavior is tacitly reinforced by effects of the social environment. In this sense the social order may be likened to a 'Skinner box' (operant conditioning chamber).

Unfortunately, this notion remains very imprecise and is, more or less, related to a conception of language in which words are thought of as labels applied to real or fictitious entities.

HENRY, 1971: 77

Searle notes in his theory of speech acts 'X counts as Y in context C'. C, in this sense, appears to function as the 'Background' in which X is 'realized' as Y, however, C may also affect the performative mis/recognition of X 'intending' Y categorically and/or conditionally (e.g., Pêcheux's Munchausen effect). Henry finds that a given context (i.e., the Background in Searle's terms) is an effect of relations *between* discursive processes.

The present conception is rooted in a theoretical analysis of communication processes which implies that the relationships (1) between a message and the language and (2) between a message and contexts, involve other messages or discourses not involved in the contexts in the usual sense.

ibid.

An assumed context is not infallibly free from instances of ideological mis/recognition, and for this reason, Henry suggests how terms of reference ('the object or event about which something is said') are defined by certain messages embedded in communicative activity (e.g., superordinate and subordinate speech acts).

The functioning of a message in relation to other messages in production or interpretation will be called a *discursive process* ... Now the notion of context will be analyzed so that it will be possible to differentiate among the various relations between a message and the communication it covers.

ibid.: 77–78

A context, then, associates or dissociates an agentic position and a locus via customary forms of illocution. "As defined here, the *position* is always related to messages, discourses or behaviors, whereas the *locus* is determined by the social structure" (ibid.: 79). Speech acts both shift and constrain discourse within a given locus in so far as individual positions are articulated in relation to the background context.[13]

---

13   A context may also be used to include or exclude certain discursive behaviors via norms of acceptability. Once the context of a speech act is disclosed its 'meaning' then, apparently,

As the process of shifting and the constraints to which it is submitted are very important from our point of view, it is necessary to discuss it in greater detail. An important idea which must be introduced is that, given the locus a person occupies in the social structure and given the situation in which he is embedded, he cannot adopt the discourse and conduct of every other possible locus.

ibid.: 80

The associative or dissociative mechanisms of discursive processes are structurally differentiated by the subject positions related to a given locus. Furthermore, such loci are directly integrated by the discursive practices which regulate such 'meaning effects'.

Now, what we suggest is that economic, institutional and ideological factors are intimately tied to a locus occupied by an individual in the social structure. These factors constitute the conditions of production of the individual's discourses and the conditions of interpretation of those he receives. Through these conditions of production, the range and types of positions a given individual can adopt are determined.

ibid.: 81

In "What is language: some preliminary remarks" Searle asserts that the development of language involves both individual intentions *and* social conventions. According to Searle:

The speaker intentionally produces an utterance, and he intends that the utterance should have conditions of satisfaction ... then there has to be some *social recognized conventional device* ... which can be regularly and conventionally taken by his interlocutors to convey the message ... the first phenomenon is essential to the performance of speech acts, and the second ... consists typically of words and sentences of a language.

SEARLE, 2007: 32

---

makes sense – when it was previously 'out of place'. Thus, linguistic norms may also implictly govern forms of morality that function as practical ideologies within a given social formation. For example, the workplace, the school, and the home evince particular structures of authority regarding who says what and when they may say it.

Searle suggests that speaker intentionality is 'logically prior' to convention, yet, he does not *objectively* explain how speech acts are intelligible without antecedent comprehension of existing linguistic structures.[14] Henry's research appears to suggest that 'speaker intentionality' is strictly limited by the subject positions associated with a given locus, or, in other words, a linguistic shift (e.g., an interpretation) is bound by social constraints. "It is evident that everybody cannot behave in every possible way or say everything possible" (Henry, 1971: 80). Moreover, Searle maintains that language is a creative force because representation permits the 'composition' of reality, however, the contextual constraints of existing linguistic structures associated with a given locus seem to predetermine intentional acts.

> None is more remarkable than this: in human languages we have the capacity, not only to represent reality, both how it is and how we want it to be, but we have the capacity to create a new reality by representing that reality as existing. We create private property: money, property, government, marriage, and a thousand other such phenomena by representing these phenomena as existing.
>
> SEARLE, 2007: 41

Despite Searle's creative vision of intentional representation, the question remains how 'institutional facts' are generated via performative utterances. Henry attempts to address this problem using his concept 'conditions of production' for such 'meaning effects'.

> What are termed conditions of production are the complete set of economic, institutional, and ideological factors tied to given locus and involved in message production and interpretation. In a given situation, only some of the factors constituting the conditions of production are relevant and involved in the processes. Thus, we will have to consider *different states of the conditions of production*.
>
> HENRY, 1971: 83

---

14   According to Pêcheux such an assumption would constitute an ideological representation of the 'always-already-there' given that speech activity cannot realize the intitutions of the speaker without the support of existing discursive formations. Furthermore, Searle's spontaneous philosophy of speech acts does not attempt to engage with what Foucault calls 'archaeology'. Archaeology – in Foucault's terms – is the study of 'archives'. Archives represent the 'enunciative regularities' of discursive formations in their historical specificity. These systems of statements constitute the real history of discursive practice.

Searle remarks that pragmatic components of language limit how language is *used* by setting 'certain constraints' via formal linguistic structures (Searle, 2007: 17). Searle thus outlines the structural elements of language without describing a theoretical equivalent of what Henry calls 'conditions of production of discourses'. In this sense Searle's research appears to represent another example of the ideological lacunae that Saussure's research attempts to displace: self-evident meaning. According to Searle: "The relation of syntax to semantics is ... crucial. Syntax organizes semantics according to three principles: discreteness, compositionality, and generativity" (ibid.: 18). Discreteness designates the continuity of grammatical elements within a given speech act, compositionality combines syntactical and semantic functions via particular rules, and generativity facilitates the expression of new 'meaningful' speech acts.[15] There is, in addition, a fourth principle: 'commitment'.

> That is, we will not understand an essential feature of language if we do not understand that it necessarily involves social commitments, and that the necessity of these social commitments derives from the social character of the communication situation, the conventional character of the devices used, and the intentionality of speaker meaning. It is this feature that enables language to form the foundation of human society in general.
>
> ibid.: 37

Commitment is what gives language its social character whereby the verbal activity of a speaker is 'meaningfully' understood throughout the speech community: 'we have to see that the speech act is more than just the expression of an intention or the expression of a belief. It is above all a public performance' (ibid.: 39). Searle's account of linguistic interaction overlooks ideological aspects of speech activity by assuming that all those who use a given language are equally committed to its veracity, and, that the language is, naturally, free from distortion. As Pêcheux notes above speech act theory mis/recognizes the transmission of 'meaning effects' by guaranteeing the 'conventional' continuity of language against a background (context) of assumed intentionality: "enunciation designates both the fact that the subject is the support for his enounced and the set of subjective effects (different psychological contents)

---

15   Searle – in some cases – seems to suppose that meaning is 'obvious' and the function of syntax is to deliver it. This metaphysics of meaning is thus the corrolary to his spontaneous philosophy of speech acts. Yet, without examining the history of semantic production Searle's research cannot perceive its own history as a form of discursive practice.

which underlie that enounced". Such ideological presuppositions are evinced by Searle in the following summary:

> In evolving a language we found that we needed a speaker meaning, conventions, and internal syntactic structure. But if we understand these as relating in a certain way to human intentionality ... we already get the commitments that typically go with those types of illocutionary acts. *Nothing further is necessary to guarantee that speakers will be committed by their utterances.*
>
> SEARLE, 2007: 39; emphasis added

The production and transmission of discursive regularities, including speech acts, are not – for either Pêcheux or Henry – reducible to individual – intentional – guarantees of what Searle calls 'commitment'. "The state of the conditions of production is dependent upon the connections between the locus of the speaker and the locus of the addressee, as well as upon the environment" (Henry, 1971: 83). Instead, a given social formation appears to determine an individual's discursive position relative to its superordinate or subordinate locus in so far as each subject assumes discrete representations of meaning which are 'automatically' realized via particular conditions of production (cf. Pêcheux, 1982; Henry, 1971).

> Conditions of production and interpretation of the discourses are tied to the different loci assigned to people by social structures. In a given situation, only some elements of these conditions are dominant, and the latter make up a state of the conditions of production. In messages or discourses, people take positions according to the state of their conditions of production.
>
> HENRY, 1971.: 83

Searle undoubtedly strives to couple speech act theory with a social explanation of language, yet, his description of institutional facts remains a spontaneous philosophy of intentionality. Moreover, Searle's account of intentionality pays little attention to the material basis of linguistic structures in so far as institutional facts define social reality by means of preconstructed discourse. By contrast Henry finds that illocution (i.e., the performative conditions of an utterance) should be analyzed in terms of the referential structures embedded within loci. "What we will call *referent is considered to be constructed in discourses which are tied to specific conditions of production*" (Henry, 1971: 83). Tied information limits interpretations by ideological forms of of self-reference whereas free information refers to objective definitions of reality.

> Free information refers to other discourses or messages (in the present case, to scientific discourses) whereas tied information appears to be constructed in the actual message itself and thus does not implicitly involve other messages.
>
> ibid.: 90

If intentionality is attributed exclusively to the individual speaking subject this typically appears as an effect of tied information. As Searle declares: "Nothing further is necessary to guarantee that speakers will be committed by their utterances" (Searle, 2007: 39).[16]

---

16   For Pêcheux and, relatedly, Althusser, ideology is an elementary form of tied information which functions as a guarantee for certain instituted (i.e., preconstructed) forms of existence. Indeed, the purpose of ideology is to 'commit' individuals to the belief that the meaning of a given social order is legitimate.

CHAPTER 5

B. F. Skinner (1904–1990)

As I noted in the preceding chapter Pêcheux – in *Automatic Discourse Analysis* – evinces rudimentary knowledge of certain behaviorist concepts associated with B. F. Skinner's research programme. Pêcheux additionally makes a critical remark in *Language, Semantics, and Ideology* regarding the philosophical opportunism of 'Marxist' Pavlovism.[1] In fact, Pêcheux did not devote much space to behaviorist psychology in either of these texts, however, he does demonstrate cognizance of the basic principles of the S-O-R (stimulus-organism-response) model. I find that these principles can further elucidate the theoretical relationship between meaning production and the 'process without a subject'. According to Pêcheux the spontaneous philosophy of linguistics assumes the subject functions as the foundation of discursive interaction. He further attempts to describe how such subjective assumptions are incompatible with a scientific account of meaning generation. Meaning is *immediately* 'realized' by the subject-form as a structure of language that is self-evidently 'self-generating'. According to Pêcheux a materialist theory of discourse begins by challenging the spontaneous existence of the subject as origin or cause of itself. The illusion of spontaneous subjectivity is manifest when individuals accept as evident the 'obvious' meaning of what they hear, say, read, write, and know. The origin of meaning is mis/recognised as the subject of discourse.

In *Automatic Discourse Analysis* Pêcheux contrasts two 'rival families of schemata' to evaluate certain 'structural elements' as potential vehicles for meaning effects in discourse: 1) reaction and 2) information. The reaction schema derives from psycho-physiological and psychological theories of behavior such as the 'stimulus-organism-response' [S-O-R] schema. The information schema denotes 'sociological and psycho-sociological theories of communication' e.g., 'the sender-message-receiver' schema (Pêcheux, 1995: 82). After a relatively limited comparison of the two theories Pêcheux indicates the information schema – rather than the reaction schema – is better suited to his theory of discourse. "... In other words, the S-O-R schema implies too many theoretical 'forgettings' for it to be retained in its present form" (ibid.: 84). Yet, the S-O-R model

---

1   Ivan Petrovich Pavlov (1849–1936) received the Nobel Prize for research in physiology. He also developed an account of classical conditioning which has been subsequently applied to behaviorist theories of learning.

appears more relevant to Pêcheux's theory of discourse than he initially proposed. Skinner's theory of behaviorist psychology is directly opposed to explanations that involve, what Pêcheux calls, the ideology of the subject-form. In *Beyond Freedom and Dignity* Skinner outlines a 'technology of behavior' that – to some extent – accounts for the problem Pêcheux seeks to explain in his materialist theory of discourse: the Munchausen effect. The Munchausen effect denotes the 'fact' that subjects are the authors of their own intentionality within pre-structured forms of meaning.

> We are here dealing with a causality which effaces itself in the necessary effect it produces in the form of the relationship between subject, centre and meaning, something I have called in condensed fashion the 'Munchausen effect'.
>
> PÊCHEUX, 1982: 191

Skinner identifies what Pêcheux calls the 'Munchausen effect' – a result of pre-scientific ideologies of human behavior – in terms of 'indwelling agents' and other personified beliefs.

> There is a sense in which it can be said that the methods of science have scarcely yet been applied to human behavior ... It has to do with the treatment of the causes of behavior ... Intelligent people no longer believe that men are possessed by demons ... but *human behavior is still commonly attributed to indwelling agents.*
>
> SKINNER, 1972: 7–8; emphasis added

The more scientific explanation prevails over 'indwelling agents' and other imaginary causes of behavior the less likely an individual is to be 'possessed' by the subject-form and its inner meaning (i.e., the Munchausen effect). Skinner – as does Pêcheux/Herbert – finds that indwelling agents and occult theories of subjectivity, are still promulgated by the humanities, social sciences, and other religious/ideological orders.

> Almost everyone who is concerned with human affairs – as political scientist, philosopher, man of letters, economist, psychologist, linguist, sociologist, theologian, anthropologist, educator, or psychotherapist – *continues to talk about human behavior in this prescientific way.*
>
> ibid.: 9; emphasis added

In Pêcheux's analysis scientific research is a process without a subject, yet, individuals are 'always-already-subjects' and thus continue to identify with specious forms of 'information', i.e., as *subjects* they are repeatedly confronted by prescientific ideologies.[2] Pêcheux notes, however, that such subjection is *necessarily* questioned by the practice of scientific research.

> The paradoxical result of this repercussion of the process without a subject of knowledge on the individuals who are its agents is therefore that it realises in the subject-form a challenging of the subject-form.
>
> PÊCHEUX, 1982: 195

Indwelling agents and other fictions are, in Pêcheux's terms, 'phantasies' of the Munchausen effect whereby the subject appears as the cause of itself. "One of the consequences ... within the subject as 'cause of himself'... is a series of what one might call metaphysical phantasies. ... the 'Munchausen effect'" (ibid.: 108). Evidently, Skinner sought to avoid metaphysical phantasies (e.g., indwelling agents) by defining psychology as a science of behavior. Pêcheux's Munchausen effect appears closely related to what is called 'introspection' as an 'internal' phantasy: the subject as cause of itself becomes aware of itself by reflecting on its own internal reality.

> Many psychologists, like the philosophers before them, have looked inside themselves for explanations of their own behavior. They have felt feelings and observed mental processes through introspection. Introspection has never been very satisfactory, however.
>
> SKINNER, 1990: 1206

Introspection is methodologically problematic, for Skinner, because it assumes the result of an internal process (i.e., 'reflective thought') which has been generated by external conditions, (i.e., a subject's thoughts are not the 'source' of reflection but, rather, the effect of antecedent training). John B. Watson who was an important precursor to Skinner's research writes:

> Psychology as the behaviorist views it is a purely objective experimental branch of natural science. Its theoretical goal is the prediction and control of behavior. Introspection forms no essential part of its methods, nor

---

2 This issue is given detailed analysis by Althusser in *Philosophy and the Spontaneous Philosophy of the Scientists*. "Scientific ideology (or the ideology of scientists) is inseparable from scientific practice: it is the 'spontaneous' ideology of scientific practice" (Althusser, 1990: 88).

is the scientific value of its data dependent on the readiness with which they lend themselves to interpretation in terms of consciousness.

WATSON, 1994: 248

The Munchausen effect depends on the mis/recognition of meaning as a self-evident structure for consciousness with 'introspection' apparently providing access to this datum.[3] In Pêcheux's terms, this inner process of 'reflective thinking' would determine the phantasies made possible by ideology in so far as such *beliefs* are supported by the experience of introspection (i.e., subjective self-evidence).[4]

> I shall say that the material character of meaning, masked by its transparent evidentness for the subject, lies in its constitutive dependence on what I have called the 'complex whole of ideological formations'....
>
> PÊCHEUX, 1982: 111

What an individual 'means' in a given situation does not originate from the depths of subjective interiority: it is constituted by external factors, i.e., from the material conditions that legitimate 'meaning' via preconstructed forms of discourse:

> the meaning of a word, expression, proposition, etc., does not exist 'in itself' (i.e., in its transparent relation to the literal character of the signifier), but is determined by the ideological positions brought into play in the socio-historical process in which words, expressions and propositions are produced (i.e. reproduced).
>
> ibid.

In Skinner's research verbal behavior is a product of reinforcement, in this sense, 'meaning' is a reinforced behavior.

---

3 Introspection is a form subjective training in which an individual is taught to 'look inwardly' to find an experience which is mediated by certain symbolic structures of social origin. After being conditioned to view reality using particular symbols (e.g., the alphabet) introspective activity then appears to furnish the belief that the subject is the source of its own meaning.

4 Mohamed Elhammoumi notes "Pêcheux's research framework is of continuing relevance to experimental social psychology, psycholinguistics, possessing as it does much potential for analyzing concrete instances of human higher mental function, rue-governed [sic] behavior, disidentification, ideology, and discursive speech analysis" (Elhammoumi, 2012: 772).

The verbal stimuli we call advice, rules or laws describe or allude to contingencies of reinforcement. People who have been advised or who follow rules and obey laws behave for either of two very different reasons:
their behavior has been directly reinforced by its consequences, or they
are responding to descriptions of contingencies.

SKINNER, 1987: 782

As noted above Pêcheux makes some superficial remarks regarding the limited
applicability of the S-O-R (Stimulus-Organism-Response) model to speech
activity in *Automatic Discourse Analysis*. I find, however, that the S-O-R model
requires greater elaboration in relation to discourse theory because it advances
the basic principles of Saussure's epistemological break. In Skinner's terms
the meaning of a given discourse is determined by the reinforced behavior
that is associated with it, thus, the connection between a phonetic structure
and a semantic structure is, in effect, an operant that has been conditioned
recursively. An individual 'inhabits' its meaning through contingent structures of verbal reinforcement. Behaviorist psychology, therefore, rejects theories of psychological subjectivity that rely upon 'indwelling agents' or other
imaginary causes of mental functioning. Skinner's behavioral theory, in light
of Saussure's science of language, appears to suggest that the relationship of
langue to *parole* is structured by operant conditioning (i.e., *langue/parole* vis-
à-vis operant/reinforcement). According to Pêcheux the epistemological rupture that separates a science from its ideological past always displaces, in its
own domain, the imaginary interpretations previously assumed to evince the
real phenomena. The evidentness of meaning – derived from a speculative
ideology – is supplanted by the body of concepts and experimental method
which represents the objectivity of science empirically via the material process of knowledge production (Pêcheux, 1982). By applying Skinner's research
to advance Saussure's epistemological break in linguistics, a given speech act,
subsequently, appears as the *effect* of discursive contingencies that function
via reinforced behavior/s. According to Skinner 'subjectivity' (or for that matter, 'consciousness') is, in fact, a verbal operant which has been reinforced to
facilitate what is called self-observation.[5] However, it is not the self – as an
indwelling agent – that is observed but, rather, the contingencies of interdiscourse which occur in forms of reinforced behavior.

---

5 Introspection facilitates diverse forms of 'internal' surveillance. Moreover, after the subject
   has 'learnt' to accept introspective forms of conditioning it may then be 'corrected' if state
   apparatuses find that a given individual does not met certain expectations regarding the
   established norms of personal conduct.

All behavior, human or nonhuman – is unconscious, it becomes 'conscious' when verbal environments provide the contingencies necessary for self-observation ... Other verbal contingencies generate the behavior called self-management or thinking, in which problems are solved by manipulating either contingencies (as in practical problem solving) or rules (as in 'reasoning').

SKINNER, 1987: 782

Verbal behavior, according to Skinner, exhibits different characteristics depending on what type of language is used within a given situation. The most common – and least specialized – is the vernacular language of 'everyday life':

we use a language that came into existence long before there were philosophers or scientists of any kind. It is properly called a vernacular ... the language of the household, of daily life. We all speak it. It is the language of newspapers, magazines, books, radio, and television.

SKINNER, 1990: 1209

Such 'natural' language may be analyzed as verbal behavior, i.e., as forms of linguistic interaction subject to reinforcement and contingency. Colloquial communication generally assumes that the mind or 'self' is the source of choices and intentions, however, for Skinner such errors are due to the unwitting use of vernacular language, i.e., the verbal environment has not been adequately apprehended in terms of operant behavior.

The vernacular refers to many feelings and states of mind ... It is easy to suppose that the references are to an initiating mind, but ... the useful allusions are prior to contingencies of selection or to the beginnings of action ... We do not see the histories of selection responsible for what is done and therefore infer an internal origination ... *There is no place in a scientific analysis of behavior for a mind or self.*

ibid.: 1209; emphasis added

Pêcheux's 'Munchausen effect', in principle, corresponds to Skinner's theory of verbal behavior in so far as meaning is not subjectively defined but, in fact, the product of pre-existing discursive formations.[6]

---

6   A subject's verbal repertoire is, for Skinner, the effect of certain modes of training. Operant conditioning and reinforcement construct the systems of perception through which a subject identifies itself and 'its own' activity. Both Skinner and Pêcheux indicate that subjects

I shall say that the subject-form of discourse, in which interpellation, identification and the production of meaning coexist indissociably, realises *the non-sense of the production of the subject as cause of himself in the form of immediate evidentness.*

PÊCHEUX, 1982: 191

The Munchausen effect (i.e., subject as cause of itself) is a quasi-mystical belief where the subject of discourse appears to be self-caused by indwelling agency. Because speech functions as mode of operant conditioning, a given vernacular language effectively reinforces, via contingent consequences, the 'internal' thought-behavior of an individual subject. Without the objective apprehension of this process – such as the research outlined by Skinner – 'natural' languages, which are the effect of reinforcement, appear as a cause of behavior. The mind or self is then, for both Pêcheux and Skinner, an ideology that has been perpetuated by psychological theories mis/recognizing the source of 'subjectivity'.

What, then, are we to make of the fact that for 100 years psychologists have tried to build just such a science of mind? ... Have these been parts of a search for something that does not exist? It appears that we must say so ... psychologists have unwittingly been analyzing contingencies of reinforcement, the very contingencies responsible for the behavior mistakenly attributed to an internal originator.

SKINNER, 1990: 1209

Skinner suggests that 'thought' evolved in conjunction with speech when the control of this verbal faculty was conditioned by reinforcement.

The [human] species underwent ... unique evolutionary change when its vocal musculature came under operant control and when vocal behavior began to be shaped and maintained by its reinforcing consequences. People could then prime the behavior of others by telling them what to do as well as by showing them.

ibid.: 1206

Structures of social control could then be realized by operant conditioning:

---

may assume that they view themselves and the world 'directly', yet, such assumptions neglect to ascertain that such 'immediacy' is the product of historically specific forms of symbolic mediation (e.g., natural language, ideological state apparatuses &c.).

The laws of governments and religions describe the contingencies of (usually negative) reinforcement maintained by those institutions. They have the effect of warnings: By obeying the law a person avoids behaving in ways that would be punished.

ibid.: 1206–1207

Human culture is, for Skinner, the result of operant conditioning in which behavior is regulated by forms of reinforcement.[7] "Modeling, telling, and teaching are the functions of the social environments called cultures" (ibid.: 1207). When individuals are taught that the self is the origin of behavior they are conditioned to verbalize in a vernacular form and thus, according to Skinner, begin to confuse the effects of operant conditioning with an indwelling agent (i.e., the self). Furthermore, language – as a culturally reinforced structure of communication – is reproduced by individuals conforming to existing conventions.

Rules of grammar and spelling bring certain verbal contingencies of reinforcement more forcefully into play. Society codifies its ethical, legal, and religious practices so that by following a code the individual may emit behavior appropriate to social contingencies without having been directly exposed to them. Scientific laws serve a similar function in guiding the behavior of scientists.

SKINNER, 1963: 513

Verbal behavior is reinforced socially by mechanisms of operant conditioning. "Verbal behavior ... can be defined just in terms of its contingencies: Its special characteristics are derived from the fact that reinforcement is mediated by other organisms" (ibid.: 514). Speech acts, then, appear to follow the S-O-R [stimulus-organism-response] model whereby contingencies of reinforcement are culturally determined and, consequently, the ideological issue

---

7   According to Leroi-Gourhan human culture is comprised of numerous 'operating sequences'. "A group's body of knowledge is the basic constituent of its unity and personality. The transmission of this intellectual capital is the necessary precondition for the group's material and social survival. Transmission is effected through the same hierachy as operating sequences" (Leroi-Gourhan, 1993: 258). Skinner's research suggests how such 'operating sequences' are maintained in behavioral repertoires which are the product of particular forms of conditioning. The extinction of a given repertoire indicates that a specific activity is no longer reinforced.

of 'internal origination', for a given response, can be viewed as a conditioned assumption regarding the 'mental' characteristics of indwelling agency.

> We see the effect in casual discourse. If we ask someone, 'Why did you go to the theater?' and he says, 'Because I felt like going,' we are apt to take his reply as a kind of explanation. It would be much more to the point to know what has happened when he has gone to the theater in the past ... and what other things in his past or present environment have induced him to go.
>
> SKINNER, 1972: 12–13

Colloquial expression, for Skinner, does not represent verbal behavior as a product of operant conditioning. Moreover, the internal originator 'inner man' is, for Skinner, a verbal allusion/illusion that is used to conceal insufficient knowledge of behavioral contingencies (i.e., existing forms of operant conditioning).

> Unable to understand how or why the person we see behaves as he does, *we attribute his behavior to a person we cannot see ... The function of the inner man is to provide an explanation which will not be explained in turn* ... He initiates, originates, and creates, and in doing so so he remains ... divine. We say that he is autonomous – and, so far as the science of behavior is concerned, that means miraculous.
>
> ibid.: 14; emphasis added

'Inner man' (i.e., the self) thus seems incorporeal and, therefore, outside material reality, in other words, inner man is supernatural (i.e., metaphysical).

> Autonomous man serves to explain only the things we are not yet able to explain in other ways. His existence depends upon our ignorance ... The task of a scientific analysis is to explain how the behavior of a person as a physical system is related to the conditions under which the human species evolved and the conditions under which the individual lives.
>
> ibid.: 14

Skinner spurns the pre-science that is disseminated (and uncritically accepted) throughout the humanities and social sciences (and in vernacular language more generally).[8] In Pêcheux's terminology Skinner seeks to dismantle the

---

8 Pêcheux suggests the discipline of linguistics may serve as a theoretical ideology that is used to support spontaneous theories of the speaking subject which aim to ideologically

Munchausen effect and follow the scientific method as a 'process without a subject'.

> Physics did not advance by looking more closely at the jubilance of a fall-
> ing body, or biology by looking at the nature of vital spirits, and we do not
> need to try to discover what personalities, states of mind, feelings, traits
> of character, plans, purposes, intentions ... are in order to get on with a
> scientific analysis of behavior.
>
> ibid.: 15

Personalities, states of mind, and feelings are forms of verbal behavior which are subject to operant conditioning, i.e., the use of these words is contingently reinforced by the cultures which transmit such 'knowledge' (e.g., schools, universities, families &c.).[9] According to Skinner: "Behavior is shaped and maintained by its consequences. Once this fact is recognized, we can formulate the interaction between organism and environment in a much more comprehensive way" (ibid.: 18). 'Meaning' in Skinner's terms is a certain form of verbal behavior, subject to reinforcement, and may 'represent' what Pêcheux calls the 'always-already-there' as a preconstructed, ideological, reality. Along with the 'always-already-there' is – in prescientific belief – usually coupled Skinner's 'inner man' or Pêcheux's 'subject-form of discourse'. Pêcheux – as does Skinner – finds that *subjectivity* is used to denote something that has not been explained in materialist terms.

> I can now assert that it does not suffice for the constitution of a materi-
> alist theory of discursive processes for it to reproduce as one of its the-
> oretical objects the ideological 'subject' as 'always-already-given'... such
> a theory, if it genuinely intends to fulfill its claims, cannot do without a
> (*non-subjectivist*) *theory of subjectivity*.
>
> PÊCHEUX, 1982: 90

---

separate speech activity from the social history of language (e.g., the Munchausen effect). In this sense Pêcheux's characterization of the linguistic field appears to indicate that the science of language is not entirely detached from the fictional domain of literature (Pêcheux, 1982: 110–129).

9 Certain 'genres' of verbal behavior are – quite simply – acts of literature. Such speech activity is derived from literary culture which is comprised of preconstructed textual material derived from fictional sources. "Fiction is determinate illusion, and the essence of the literary text is to establish these determinations" (Macherey, 1978: 64).

A non-subjectivist theory of subjectivity could thus account for both Pêcheux's 'Munchausen effect' and Skinner's 'indwelling agents'. Such a research programme, according to Pêcheux, would involve the conceptual articulation of three areas of enquiry:

> With the result that the theoretical domain of this work is ultimately defined by three inter-linked zones which can be designated respectively as *subjectivity*, *discursivity* and the *sciences/ideologies discontinuity*.
>
> ibid.

Skinner's technology of behavior marks an attempt to replace theories of subjectivity with a science of behavior in which organism and environment are contingently related via operant conditioning.[10]

> The contingencies under investigation have become steadily more complex, and one by one they are taking over the explanatory functions previously assigned to personalities, states of mind, feelings, traits of character, purposes, and intentions.
>
> SKINNER, 1972: 18

Once the subjectivity of inner man has been represented as behavior regulated by reinforcement the 'autonomy' of the subject is identified as an effect of operant conditioning, however, Skinner notes, this fact has been met with ideological resistance from established *authorities*.

> We have moved forward by dispossessing autonomous man, but he has not departed gracefully. He is conducting a sort of rear-guard action in which, unfortunately, he can marshal formidable support. He is still an important figure in political science, law, religion, economics, anthropology, sociology, psychotherapy, philosophy, ethics, history, education, child care, linguistics, architecture, city planning, and family life ... in almost every theory the autonomy of the individual is unquestioned.
>
> ibid.: 19

---

10   Skinner's behaviorist programme suggests that subjects are selectively reinforced to see the 'reality' of fiction, i.e., structures of reinforcement establish the operation of certain 'reading' protocols which sustain the imagined basis of literary disciplines. After a certain period of conditioning the subject begins to see what really cannot be seen. In Pêcheux's terms these forms of interdiscourse are realized as meaning-effects which guarantee the truth of a given illusion. The apparent veracity of a literary allusion/illusion, then, produces an *impression* of reality.

Pêcheux directly challenges autonomous man, and its institutional support system, by examining how conditions of discourse structure forms of ideological agency via assumed characteristics of subjectivity (e.g., freedom, responsibility, intention, self-consciousness &c.).

> I shall say that the mark of the unconscious as 'discourse of the Other' ... makes every subject 'work', i.e., take up positions 'in full awareness and full freedom', take initiatives for which he is 'responsible' as the author of his actions, etc., and the notions of *assertion* and *enunciation* are there to designate in the domain of 'language' the subject's actions in taking up positions as a speaking subject.
>
> PÊCHEUX, 1982: 121

The 'discourse of the Other' – translated into Skinner's terminology – represents verbal behavior which has been reinforced by operant conditioning. According to Skinner one commonly reinforced ideological attribute of 'autonomous man' is that he is 'free'.

> *In the traditional view, a person is free. He is autonomous in the sense that his behavior is uncaused.* He can therefore be held responsible for what he does and justly punished if he offends. That view, together with its associated practices, must be re-examined when a scientific analysis reveals unsuspected controlling relations between behavior and environment.
>
> SKINNER, 1972: 19–20; emphasis added

As noted above Pêcheux outlines a comparable account of autonomous subjection where the ideological subject is the author of its actions 'in full awareness and full freedom'. In another formulation of this theory he writes:

> The material conditions under which the human animal is reared and trained, including the specific materiality of the imaginary (the family apparatus as an ideological apparatus) thus represent the way ... in which the determinations that subject the physiological individual as an ideological subject are necessarily realised in the body of an animal belonging to the 'human species' in the biological sense of the term.
>
> PÊCHEUX, 1982: 121

Autonomy is thus, for both Pêcheux and Skinner – imagined – if it is thought to arise from the self causally (i.e., self-caused causality). Rather 'autonomy' is the result of specific kinds of training which, for Skinner, are defined by forms of operant conditioning. An individual should be neither denigrated nor glorified for its deeds if these are supposed to arise from an 'indwelling agent' (e.g., the subject as cause of itself):

> By questioning the control exercised by autonomous man and demon-strating the control exercised by the environment ... scientific analysis shifts the credit as well as the blame to the environment, and traditional practices can then no longer be justified. These are sweeping changes, and those who are committed to traditional theories and practices natu-rally resist them.
>
> SKINNER 1972: 21

Autonomous man – Skinner's 'inner man' – persists, however, to function as an imaginary construct that is used to explain the always-already-given structure of ideological experience.[11]

> One difficulty is that almost all of what is called behavioral science con-tinues to trace behavior to states of mind, feelings, traits of character, human nature, and so on. Physics and biology once followed similar prac-tices and advanced only when they discarded them.
>
> ibid.: 24

The phantom of subjectivity appears to invoke certain verbal behaviors that have been reinforced as imaginary explanations of unperceived environmen-tal factors which determine the real actions of individuals. Skinner suggests that such imaginary explanations of behavior (e.g., ideologies of inner man) will exhibit less prevalence with increasing scientific knowledge.

> As the interaction between organism and environment has been under-stood ... effects once assigned to states of mind, feelings, and traits are beginning to be traced to accessible conditions, and a technology of behavior may therefore become available. It will not solve our problems, however, until it *replaces traditional prescientific views*, and these are strongly entrenched.
>
> ibid.: 25; emphasis added

---

11   Gatian de Clérambault posits that certain forms of delusion may be attributed to the experience of mental automatism. In such cases the subject is unable to stop performing particular automatic actions and, consequently, experiences itself passively. Ideology – in this sense – appears to generate a syndrome of passivity in which subjects display illusory forms of autonomy.

The interior 'qualities' of autonomous man are, in fact, trained physiological responses to reinforced contingencies: an imaginary cause (subjective agency) has been associated with a real stimulus. Pêcheux/Herbert suggests that the illusion of subjectivity (i.e. the subject as cause of itself) arises via certain kinds of verbal behavior where 'meaning' is generated by the mis/recognition of imaginary effects.[12]

> This is how the subject's identification with political and ideological structures which constitute *subjectivity* as origin of what the subject says and does ... conceals from the agent his position within the structure.
> HERBERT, 1968

For Pêcheux/Herbert such imaginary effects conceal-disguise the fact that every subject's discourse is materially determined by external conditions. The illusion of subjectivity is promoted, authorized, and disseminated by many social institutions that support the ideology of 'inner man' (e.g., ideological state apparatuses). Furthermore, Skinner maintains that 'negative reinforcers' may be applied to certain individuals who challenge the beliefs stipulated by a given social order. Negative reinforcers are a form of aversive control which may be used to curb particular behaviors (e.g., 'inappropriate' speech acts).

> In one form or another intentional aversive control is the pattern of most social coordination – in ethics, religion, government, economics, education, psychotherapy, and family life.
> Skinner, 1972: 28

Not all control is necessarily aversive: positive reinforcers can be used for operant conditioning that is not punitive in nature. "What is overlooked is control which does not have aversive consequences at any time" (Skinner, 1971: 41). In this sense, what is called 'personal freedom' is, in fact, a structure of reinforced behavior that has been generated via operant conditioning. "Freedom is

---

12   The experience of subjectivity corresponds to various modalities of fiction and, with it, grammar. Indeed, the idea of an 'autonomous' subject is supported by certain imaginary assumptions required for the staging of literary performances (e.g., fictitious characterizations of reality). Fictional objects are 'attached' to grammatical forms via beliefs which do not require empirical evidence to be effective instances of a given narrative. Therefore, the practice of narration, and literary production more generally, will manifest various pre-scientific ideologies.

a matter of contingencies of reinforcement, not of the feelings the contingencies generate" (ibid.: 37–38). The 'feeling' of freedom, should not, in Skinner's view, be confused with the forms of operant conditioning which may induce such 'feelings' via verbal repertoires.

> We learn to perceive in the sense that we learn to respond to things in particular ways because of the contingencies of which they are a part ... The perceiving and knowing which arise from verbal contingencies are ... products of the environment.
>
>   ibid.: 188

Hence, the notions of 'personality', 'character', and 'self' are conveyed by verbal techniques which have been socially reinforced to promote the apparent utility of 'self-awareness'.

> The verbal community specializes in self-descriptive contingencies. It asks questions such as: What did you do yesterday? What are you doing now?... And it is because such questions are asked that a person responds to himself and his behavior in that special way called knowing or being aware. Without the help of a verbal community all behavior would be unconscious. Consciousness is a social product.
>
>   ibid.: 191–192

The S-O-R (stimulus-organism-response) model represents how a 'self' is the product of material contingencies reinforced by responses to certain stimuli between the human organism and its environment.[13]

> A self is a repertoire of behavior appropriate to a given set of contingencies ... The picture which emerges from a scientific analysis is not a body with a person inside, but of a body which *is* a person in the sense that it displays a complex repertoire of behavior.
>
>   ibid.: 199

Skinner's behaviorist psychology represents the 'death' of autonomous man: the end of an explanatory fiction historically reinforced by prescientific descriptions of human interaction.

---

13   Ideological state apparatuses appear to deliver the structural contingencies that secure the reproduction of the relations of production. Ideology is the 'stimulus' that elicits the prescribed responses from subjects via systems of self-regulating mis/recognition.

He has been constructed from our ignorance and as our understanding increases, the very stuff of which he is composed vanishes ... An experimental analysis shifts the determination of behavior from autonomous man to the environment – an environment responsible both for the evolution of the species and for the repertoire acquired by each member.

ibid.: 200–214

The subject of speech – as a repertoire of contingent behaviors – is given comprehensive analysis in Skinner's book *Verbal Behavior*. Speech activity is shaped and maintained by reinforcing consequences: specific repertoires are the result of predictable environmental conditions. In his 'functional analysis' Skinner questions both meaning and intentionality in so far as these notions reproduce theoretical ideologies that obfuscate the real mechanisms of verbal conditioning. For example, paraphrase does not establish *how* a particular statement 'means something' – as a given form of verbal behavior – it is simply the repetition of particular speech acts and not an explanation of semantic, syntactic, or pragmatic 'causality'.

The difficulty is that the ideas for which sounds are said to stand as signs cannot be independently observed. If we ask for evidence of their existence we are likely to be given a restatement ... One has not accounted for a remark by paraphrasing 'what it means'... *The only solution is to reject the traditional formulation of verbal behavior in terms of meaning.*

SKINNER, 1957: 6–10; emphasis added

For both Pêcheux and Skinner meaning is an ideology used to 'demonstrate' speaker intentionality in the absence of a real analysis investigating the behavior of speech activity (i.e., meaning is a subjective *belief*).

There is obviously something suspicious in the ease with which we discover in a set of ideas precisely those properties needed to account for the behavior which expresses them. We evidently construct the ideas from the behavior to be explained. There is, of course, no real explanation ... These terms ['meaning', and 'information' &c.] all have the same effect of discouraging a functional analysis and of supporting, instead, some of the practices first associated with the doctrine of ideas.

ibid.: 6–7; emphasis added

Skinner does not attempt to determine the 'intrinsic' meaning of verbal behavior: his scientific method hypothetically correlates variables (dependent/

independent) to establish probability of response for a given speech act. If 'meaning' appears to be 'obvious' this is not due to a given speech act denoting an innate idea for the subject. For Skinner 'meaning' is a specific instance of environmentally reinforced verbal behavior repeating with historically observed probability.[14]

> It is usually asserted that we can *see* meaning or purpose in behavior and should not omit it from our account. *But meaning is not a property of behavior as such but of the conditions under which behavior occurs* ... When someone can say that he can see the meaning of a response, he means that he can infer some of the variables of which the response is usually a function.
>
> ibid.: 13–14; emphasis added

Pêcheux's notions of empirical ideology and the 'always-already-there' suggest that meaning functions as a socially prescribed discursive structure and Skinner's functional analysis of meaning supports the hypothesis that preconstructed discursive interaction (the 'always-already-there') is a predictable correlation of particular verbal operants. The always-already-there of empirical ideology can, in this sense, be viewed as a historically determined repertoire of behavior in which individuals 'adopt' social norms which are typically deemed obvious, however, as Skinner indicates, a given repertoire is subject to operant conditioning and, therefore, contingently defined by existing agencies of authority.

> We observe that a speaker possesses a *verbal repertoire* in the sense that responses of various forms appear in his behavior from time to time in relation to identifiable conditions ... We are concerned here not only with the fact that certain specific forms of verbal behavior are observed but that they are observed under specific circumstances.
>
> ibid.: 21–22

Skinner finds that meaning is a prescientific belief and he appears, in certain respects, to corroborate the Saussurian break between *langue* and *parole*, yet, his research furthers this apparent disjunction by establishing that operant conditioning is the real basis of verbal behavior.

---

14   Skinner's research on verbal behavior suggests that if a given meaning is no longer reinforced subsequent 'unlearning' may result in extinction, i.e., a meaning (contingently reinforced S-O-R) is 'extinct'. Hence the associations (in Saussure's terms) that connect a semantic structure to graphic or phonic form are deactivated by disuse.

J. L. Austin (1911–1960)

The broad assumptions of Austin's ordinary language philosophy are problematic, for Pêcheux, because they exhibit ideological tendencies of subjective self-evidence vis-à-vis language use (i.e., Austin implicitly supports the Munchausen effect of self-caused subjectivity as a vehicle for discursive preconstruction).[1]

> In other words, a pure logico-linguistic theory of discourse is perfectly possible (cf. some aspects of the work of Austin, Ducrot, etc.) but such a theory must remain blind to the question of the subject as 'always-already-given'. That is why it is a matter of idealism.
>
> PÊCHEUX, 1982: 90

In another citation, however, Pêcheux finds that Austin's work may further the analysis of institutionally structured discourse.[2]

> We might evoke the concept of the 'performative' introduced by Austin to underline the necessary relationship between a discourse and its position within an extra-linguistic institutional mechanism.
>
> PÊCHEUX, 1995: 80

According to Pecheux individual verbal performances can be attributed to institutional factors, hence, speech acts are, in general, predictable.[3]

---

1 The subject as a cause of itself is 'built-in' to Austin's performative theory of speech acts. Simply by virtue of speaking the subject realizes certain intentions, yet, linguistic norms establish its discourse, therefore, such acts of intentionality are circumscribed by the prevailing definitions of 'natural' language.

2 Following the research of Pêcheux and Saussure the philosophy of speech acts outlined by Austin seems to evince a double structure. Austin's performative ideology appears to represent 'spontaneous' speech activity, however, such spontaneity is only possible via certain linguistic norms. Moreover, this double structure, in Pêcheux/Herbert's terms defines various forms of 'automatic' subjection via the state apparatus. In other words, performative mis/recognition may serve to establish certain theoretical ideologies by means of 'ordinary' linguistic practice.

3 Skinner attempts to demonstrate how verbal behavior is subject to operant conditioning. Verbal performances are the result of particular modes of reinforcement which elicit

The ability to predict what the other will think appears to be a constituent element of all discourse, with variations that depend as much on
possible states of mental pathology pertinent to verbal behavior as on
the reactions that are institutionally allowed to the listener: a rambling
conversation and a sermon 'function' differently in this respect.

ibid.: 81

Austin's essay "How to Talk" delivers some pronouncements regarding speech
acts under the rubric of 'ordinary language' philosophy where his semantic
speculations are framed in terms of how language is 'situated' via certain utterances. "We shall consider a simplified model of a situation in which we use
language for talking about the world. This model we shall call by the name
'Speech-situation S_0'"(Austin, 1979: 2). Austin's speech situations are denoted
by the simple formula: 'I is a T'. The formula I is a T denotes two nominal conventions which are 'connected' to produce the phrase: I (item) is a T (type).
Thus, I is a T, represents the reference and sense of a given speech act.

In order for this language to be used for talking about this world, two sets
of (semantic) conventions will be needed. I-conventions, or conventions
of *reference*, are needed in order to fix which item it is that the vocable
which is to be an I-word is to refer to on each occasion of the uttering ...
T-conventions, or conventions of *sense*, are needed in order to associate
the vocables which are to be T-words.

ibid.: 2–3

Speech situation S_0 is, then, comprised of an I-convention and a T-convention
in which the copula 'is a' connects reference and sense (Austin calls the copula
an 'assertive link').[4] I and T specify the referent and the sense of such connected utterances:

---

probable occurrences of linguistic behavior. Indeed, Skinner posits that ordinary language
(what he calls 'the vernacular') is a prescientific (i.e., ideological) representation of linguistic activity because it does not establish the real mechanisms of verbal interaction (see the
preceding chapter).

4 A copula serves a grammatical function by connecting parts of speech (e.g., between subject
and object) however, such connections are, *ipso facto*, ideological guarantees to support the
mis/recognized structure of ordinary language. In the first instance a copula is a normative
device used to distinguish between 'correct' and 'incorrect' speech acts. Following the work
of Saussure sound and meaning may be *associated* by such performative norms. In 'truth'
ordinary language prompts subjects to 'work by themselves' via self-evident grammatical
assumptions (cf. Althusser, 2014; Pêcheux, 1982).

> Name-giving ... consists in allotting a certain vocable to a certain item-type as its 'name'. Sense-giving ('defining' in the sense of 'ostensive definition'...) consisting in allotting a certain item-type to certain vocable as its 'sense'.
>
> ibid.: 3

Regarding such nominal procedures Austin notes, "we shall not concern ourselves here with the nature or genesis of these conventions ..." (ibid.: 3). Where Pêcheux and Skinner (see the preceding chapter) both attempt to discern the nature and genesis of linguistic conventions objectively, Austin, for *philosophical* reasons, does not, however, he does suggest that verbal conventions may be presupposed in ordinary use. "We shall not go into the 'metaphysical status' of types and senses (nor of items). If we went back to the rudiments of speech theory, both might appear as 'constructions'" (ibid.: 3). Moreover, if Austin did, in fact, specify the historical origins of such conventions that analysis may compromise the coherence of model S_0, especially when addressing misnamed and/or misidentified utterances. Yet, cases of *conventional* mis/recognition are, to some extent, acknowledged by Austin in so far as inferences may be incorrect or 'wrong' in relation to speech situation S_0 (I is a T):

> Misidentifying must be carefully distinguished from what we have called 'misnaming'. There, the name is 'wrong' even though, and whether or not, the sense, wrongly allotted to it, does not match the type of the item: whereas here the name is 'wrong' because the sense, rightly allotted to it, does not match the type of the item.
>
> ibid.: 8

The possibility of lexical misadventure leads Austin to consider additional models to define speech situations: S_1, S_2 and so on, where reference and sense may be correctly stipulated. A verbal context apparently specifies the accepted semantic and syntactic structure of given speech situation S_0, however, Austin declares that conventions of reference and sense may be subject to contextual slip-ups via certain linguistic 'mistakes' (e.g., misrepresentations, abuses of language, illocutionary errors, misleading utterances, and other aberrations) that are – on occasion – found in speech acts. Austin's "How to Talk", then, suggests that representations of sense and reference are relative to a given context (i.e., speech situations – spoken or written – are determined via

particular institutional norms).[5] Without, however, specifying the metaphysical assumptions of 'accepted' speech situations Austin's theory, is, in some
respects, an example of what Pêcheux calls speculative ideology (see chapter
one). Pêcheux's colleague Paul Henry attempts to delimit conceptual problems
of this sort in his article "On Processing of Message Referents in Contexts" from
Social Contexts of Messages where he describes how forms of discourse will
vary vis-à-vis speech situations:

> Differences between representations indicate differences in the analy-
> sis of the real, assumed, or imagined, events, situations, states of affairs
> which the message is about, as well as differences in the positions of the
> speakers. They can also indicate differences in the loci occupied by dif-
> ferent speakers within the social structure and hence also differences in
> their economic, political, and ideological positions.
>
> HENRY, 1971: 91

When Austin finds speech situations differ in relation to performative assumptions, he remarks that some enunciations do not correspond to expected
outcomes, or in other words, an utterance does not fit the context. Hence the
conditions of S_0 are revised to 'realize' S_1 and so on. A given sense must correspond to or 'match' a given referent for a speech situation to be appropriately
'understood' otherwise misidentification may result, however, Austin notes,
this implies a seemingly infinite process of adjustment between a speech act
and its 'situation'.

> This sort of investigation of the nature of speech-acts might go on more
> or less indefinitely ... Moreover, we seem bound to use a whole series of
> different models, because *the difference between one named speech-act
> and another often resides principally in a difference between the speech-
> situations envisaged for their respective performances.*
>
> AUSTIN, 1979: 12–13

The successful execution of a particular speech act is, therefore, dependent,
Austin maintains, on how a speech situation is performatively enacted in

---

5   For example, while an individual may correctly articulate a sentence with respect to standard
    speech sounds this will not suffice to 'realize' a speech act that is defined by strict perform-
    ative procedures (e.g, the ruling of a judge or a military order). In such cases a successful
    speech act requires phonetic/graphic structure *plus* context (situation) to bring about the
    intended effect.

terms of certain conventions. To ensure that a speech act does not misrepresent a given situation the 'context' must be appropriate to the performance.

> In both stating and identifying our utterance is intended to fit a name to, to pin a label to, the item ... nothing is achieved to the purpose by the *production of a sense* which does not match the type.
>
> ibid.: 13; emphasis added

Henry explains how 'conditions of production' determine the representations that are conveyed in various kinds of speech activity in so far as messages are realized according to the 'perceived' context of a given speech situation.

> The different representations a speaker uses in his messages would correspond to the different states of his conditions of production ... We must then assume that in order to interpret the messages he receives, the addressee must elaborate representations in connection with those messages. If the addressee is not able to build up such representations, the message is meaningless for him.
>
> HENRY, 1971: 91

A meaningless speech act, following Austin, is one in which reference and sense do not concur. Henry suggests speech *situations* determine speech acts vis-à-vis conditions of discursive production (i.e., the social 'genesis' of messages is represented in forms of discourse).

> It enables us to differentiate between the empirical objects which can be associated with a message and the referents which are constructed in messages and discourses ... The construction of such referents involves the conditions of production of discourse and the locus in the social structure to which these conditions of production are tied.
>
> HENRY, 1971: 93

Austin, as noted above, accepts that the conventions of reference and sense are not infallible, however, in "How to Talk" his intention is to model speech situations for 'ordinary language' without presenting the historical genesis of such verbal behavior. According to Henry a given context, i.e., a speech situation, 'ties' a referent to a message within certain social parameters which define its *conventional* interpretation. Hence, 'meaningful' linguistic norms may dissimulate how discourse is *really* determined. A referent ostensibly 'means' that what is represented by a word is 'tied' to the object of which it is a representation. Austin in "The Meaning of a Word" contends that lexical questions regarding 'meaning' should be avoided as much as possible to avert problems of *nonsense*, i.e., verbal activity in which meaning does not 'make' sense. "I try to make it clear that the phrase 'the meaning of a word' is, in general, if not always, a dangerous nonsense-phrase" (Austin, 1979a: 2). One should not, Austin suggests, try to define the meaning of a word in isolation from the sentence that ostensibly expresses it, i.e., semantics (meaning) is apparently – 'tied to' – syntax: "to a say a word or a phrase 'has a meaning' is to say that there are sentences in which it occurs which 'have meanings': and to know which meaning the word or phrase has, is to known the meanings of the sentences in which it occurs" (ibid.: 2).[6] Nonetheless, Austin appears to overlook the rhetorical implications concerning the preceding *belief* in favour of a discussion in terms of 'ordinary' usage. Ordinary language supposedly demonstrates – via speech situations – how 'meaning' is realized by certain pronouncements, however, when a speech act is 'out of the ordinary' it may be disputed due to a lack of agreement between reference and sense. "Ordinary language breaks down in extraordinary cases. (In such cases, the cause of the breakdown is semantical)" (ibid.: 10). Speech situations are differentiated in terms of the referents that are used within given discursive formations and Austin suggests that meaning is, in essence, subordinate to syntax.[7] Extrapolating from this assumption appears to suggest that the less formal syntax a discourse exhibits the more likely it is to be what Austin calls a 'specimen of nonsense'. Moreover, the structure of a science exhibits strict formal necessity when dealing with law-governed phenomena whereas an ideology functions via imaginary effects within 'ordinary language'. According to Henry:

> A scientific concept is associated with a word having a regulated function in discourses produced under conditions which enable the production of scientific theories; an ideological notion is associated with words which function in specific ways in discourses tied to specific loci in the social structure.
>
> HENRY, 1971: 94

---

6 Evidently Austin endeavours to 'tie' standard grammar to meaning generation (as do Chomsky and Jakobson), however, as Saussure's research in his *Course in General Linguistics* demonstrates grammar belongs to the ideological pre-history of linguistic science.

7 The use of correct grammar provides important support for the operation of ideological state apparatuses. For example, the notion of agency (personhood) is performed using grammatical conventions.

For Pêcheux and also Skinner, the question of 'meaning' is directly related to that of intentionality, and, consequently, ideologies of agency. Michel Plon, whose work Pêcheux cites in *Language, Semantics, and Ideology*, finds that ideology appears as a 'spontaneous' experience of subjectivity that is, in fact, the result of certain social structures which subject the individual to *illusory* forms of oppression.

> By ideology we mean the sum of material and discursive effects of the immediate and spontaneous relationship that human subjectivity maintains with external reality (economic and political), this relationship being one of misunderstanding of that reality ... to such an extent that the reality in question loses all autonomy, all primacy, and becomes subordinated to thought (essential and fundamental characteristic of the idealist approach)... entirely attributable to structure of human subjectivity.
>
> PLON, 1974: 395

A theoretical corollary of such spontaneous misunderstanding is what Pêcheux calls the 'responsible subject' (Pêcheux, 1982: 107). As a result of the Munchausen effect – the responsible subject – agrees with the 'sense' of a given speech situation that has been spontaneously articulated (i.e., it 'responsibly' agrees to subjection in Plon's terms).[8] Such spontaneous mis/recognition is normalized throughout ideological speech situations in which the subject is attributed the cause of itself within the always-already-there. According to Pêcheux:

> Through 'habit' and 'usage', therefore, it is ideology that designates both *what is* and *what ought to be* ... It is ideology that supplies ... the evidentness that makes a word or utterance 'mean what it says' and thereby masks in the 'transparency of language' what I shall call the *material character of the meaning* of words and utterances.
>
> PÊCHEUX, 1982: 111

---

8 The responsible subject is the 'author' of its utterances in so far as such speech acts are 'its own', however, social history confirms certain forms of linguistic behavior are transmitted via institutional structures inter-generationally (e.g., the family apparatus). Therefore, an individual's discourse is typically prescribed by existing discursive formations which tacitly constitute the expected forms of verbalization authorized by institutions (e.g., the state apparatus). For further discussion of institutionalized forms of speech see Basil Bernstein's research in *Class, Codes and Control*.

Austin's philosophy of excuses found in "A Plea for Excuses" is a speculative presentation of culpability via 'ordinary language'. If 'ordinary language' is tendentially ideological Austin's plea for excuses appears to forgive such presumptive misunderstandings in routine cases of exoneration. Broadly considered excuses attempt to resolve whether a subject 'meant' to bring about a specific – and typically undesirable – state of affairs. Here Austin attempts to specify under what conditions an excuse can be accepted to exculpate blame:

> When, then, do we 'excuse' conduct, our own or somebody else's? When are 'excuses' proffered? In general, the situation is where someone is *accused* of having done something which is bad, wrong, inept, unwelcome, or in some other of the numerous possible ways untoward. Thereupon he, or someone on his behalf, will try to defend his conduct or to get him out of it.
>
> AUSTIN, 1979b: 2

Evidently excuses are a kind of speech act in which a claim is made for reasons of vindication. To be excused from responsibility also involves the question of 'free choice' whereby justification is provided for activity committed under duress and hence unfree (i.e., an involuntary effect). If one is deemed responsible for the event an attribution of intentionality is made to the actant who is thus held accountable for the deed. When an individual 'gets out of it' responsibility has been evaded and an excuse has been accepted for the blame 'incorrectly' attributed to the allegedly irresponsible act. A defence for the purported offence may be ascribed to compulsion, duress, intimidation or other consequences of 'unfreedom'.

> If ordinary language is to be our guide, it is to evade responsibility, or full responsibility, that we most often make excuses, and I myself have used the word myself in this way above.
>
> ibid.: 5

Personal responsibility supposes that a given act was freely undertaken and Austin cites two domains of social science that are replete with examples for the study of excuses: law and psychology. Regarding legal excuses Austin writes:

> practising lawyers and jurists are by no means so careful as they might be to give our ordinary expressions their ordinary meanings and applications. There is special pleading and evasion, stretching and strait-

jacketing ... Nevertheless, it is a perpetual and salutary surprise to discover how much is to be learned from the law ....

ibid.: 10

Psychology – Austin notes – furnishes the example of 'compulsive behavior' in
which an individual is internally 'compelled' to do some thing or other and is
thus somehow found unfree (excused) via a psychological diagnosis. Forensic
psychology examines the combination of these two domains (i.e., law and
psychology) in so far as excuses apparently permit both legal and psychological justification. Pêcheux is critical of the 'responsible subject' in so far as it is
'pinned down' by the effects of preconstructed reality whereby one is always-
already-a-subject within the always-already-there.[9] A subject's discourse
appears voluntary, however, because discursive formations pre-exist speech
acts, discourse is, in at least one sense, *involuntary* – a subject 'selects' from
the range of pre-defined meanings available – which will vary across speech
situations and levels of speaker competence. According to Pêcheux:

> [the] evidentness of meaning is ... strictly coeval with the discursive for-
> mation that dominates him where he is 'pinned down' as subject, and
> this 'pinning down' shifts along with this dominance itself during the
> 'formation' of the subject. Hence it is a question of an *imaginary identi-*
> *fication* ....
>
> PÊCHEUX, 1982: 190

Such imaginary associations are established via contingencies of imputation
and responsibility whereby subjective self-evidence is symbolically represented in discursive formations that a subject 'freely' accepts. "This symbolic
identification dominates the imaginary identification through which each verbal representation, and hence each 'word', 'expression' or 'utterance' acquires
a meaning of its own which 'absolutely evidently' belongs to it" (ibid.: 125).
Austin's plea for excuses, in certain respects, appears to defend ordinary

---

9   According to Althusser subjects 'work by themselves', however, such intentional autonomy is
actually the result of the ideological inculcation attributed to the state apparatus (Althusser,
2014). The State functions to sanction responsibility via the notion of legal personality.
According to Smith: "To confer legal rights or to impose legal duties, therefore, is to confer
legal personality ... Predictabililty of societal action, therefore, determines rights and duties
and rights and duties determine legal personality" (Smith, 1928: 283). In other words: "Legal
responsibility is exactly equivalent to liability to punishment" (Taylor, 1898: 276).

language as a useful vehicle for colloquial communication, however, he is quite aware of its limitations regarding matters of fact:

> In spite of the wide and acute observation of the phenomena of action embodied in ordinary speech, modern scientists have been able, it seems to me, to reveal its inadequacy at numerous points, if only because they have had access to more comprehensive data and have studied them with more catholic and dispassionate interest than the ordinary man, or even the lawyer, has had occasion to do.
>
> austin, 1979b: 20

Is Austin's speech act theory, therefore, a pre-scientific ideology of ordinary language? Evidently performative utterances, as conceived in *How to Do Things with Words*, provide a speculative start for scientific explanations of verbal activity and can also suggest how ideas like 'responsibility' and 'freedom' are used as normative descriptions of linguistic events, however, it appears that Austin's work is, in principle, a 'contextual' grammar.[10]

> The term 'performative' ... is derived, of course, from 'perform', the usual verb with the noun 'action': it indicates that the issuing of the utterance is the performing of an action – it is not normally thought of as just saying something.
>
> AUSTIN, 1962: 6–7

The *actual* issue of performativity is neatly encapsulated by Austin in the following interrogative sentence: "Can saying it make it so?" In other words, is the mere uttering of words, in fact, the enactment of particular deeds? To this Austin answers – with certain qualifications – yes. "When I say, before the registrar or altar, &c., 'I do', I am not reporting on a marriage: I am indulging in it" (ibid.: 6). The necessary pragmatic conditions for performative utterances to be effective are situationally defined: if the words are uttered without the

---

10   Grammar, following the research of Foucault, is a form of disciplinary power that provides a general social syntax over which the State retains authority. When the family fails to adequately socialize individuals with respect to the dominant social norms via 'ordinary language' the State holds the power to provide disciplinary correction for these *literal* deficiencies. Austin's work may be read in conjunction with Foucault's disciplinary schema to describe how speech acts support the various illocutionary exigencies of 'discipline'.

given institutional requirements being met the speech act is not binding or legitimate.

> The uttering of the words is, indeed, usually a, or even *the*, leading inci-
> dent in the performance of the act ... but it is far from being usually, even
> if it is ever, the *sole* thing necessary if the act is to be deemed to have been
> performed ... Speaking generally, it is always necessary that the *circum-
> stances* in which the words are uttered should be in some way, or ways,
> be *appropriate* ....
>   ibid.: 8

For a given speech act to be performatively instantiated it must be suitably situated, i.e., the speech act must 'fit' the situation. When an utterance is suc-cessfully enacted this, according to Austin, is an instance of 'felicity', and those instances unsuccessful, are deemed 'infelicitous'. To achieve felicity (i.e., a happy instance of performativity) there are a number of conditions (i.e., con-textual qualifications) to be met and these are satisfied by adherence to con-ventional protocols.

> There must exist an accepted conventional procedure having a certain
> conventional effect, that procedure to include the uttering of certain
> words by certain persons in certain circumstances ... The procedure must
> be executed by all participants correctly and ... must actually so conduct
> themselves subsequently.
>   ibid.: 14–15

The participants of a speech act, then, follow a kind of rite in which all fulfil their conventional obligations as its followers. In this sense, academic disci-plines such as the 'social sciences and humanities' are effectively systems of institutionalized speech acts in which certain conventions are legitimated for the purpose of reproducing particular ideas.[11] These discourses are sustained by the reproduction and transmission of certain enunciations which are approved by particular structures of authority. Austin's work can, thus, further

---

11   Speech acts (spoken or written) determine the *authority* of ideological performances
      (e.g., lectures, speeches, publications, conversations &c.). In the work of Althusser and
      Pêcheux/Herbert the social sciences serve to represent 'in ideas' certain forms of social
      domination. Hence the close connection between dominate forms of ideology and the
      educational apparatus. "In reality, no ideology is purely arbitrary. It is always an index
      of real problems, albeit cloaked in a form of misrecognition and so necessarily illusory"
      (Althusser, 2006: 283).

the understanding of how a social context determines felicitous or infelicitous utterances in a variety of speech situations associated with ideological per-formativity. For example, Plon suggests that social psychology (and the social sciences more broadly) deliver certain meaning effects via instituted forms of discourse:

> Although it is no less true of the majority of disciplines group under the label 'social sciences', social psychology constitutes a sort of organiza-tion, a cataloguing of certain types of *representation* of capitalist social relations, especially socio-political relations, forms of representation in which individuals become subjects, which is to say that they think their relations – in believing that their ideas are their own – according to their real conditions of existence.
>
> PLON, 1974a: 464

The institutional legitimacy of academic discourse (e.g., social psychology, his-tory, sociology, philosophy, literature &c.) is, following Plon, determined by the socio-political relations it incorporates as 'content' and 'knowledge'. In conse-quence, there must exist conditions of performativity which legitimate both a given discourse and its institutional support structures, moreover, these ideo-logical forms of representation – in so far as they are socio-political procedures – are synchronically articulated by the individuals who are subject to such discursive effects, i.e., in Plon's terms 'they think their relations – in believing their ideas are their own'. Rituals of performativity enable the reproduction of certain contexts (e.g., speech situations) which exist conventionally for those who are involved in their realization via particular speech acts. The discourse of social science is, for this reason, represented by the performance of a par-ticular repertoire which structures the accepted (and pre-given) socio-political relations by which the field is administered. According to Plon:

> Social psychology thus constitutes a repertoire, among others, of catego-ries and of ideological forms in which capitalist social relations may be considered by individuals. The field is thus an element of the ideological superstructure, the functioning of which contributes to the reproduction of capitalist relations of production.
>
> ibid.

Such ideologies are performatively generated in accordance with the condi-tions of enunciation adopted by those who are obligated to satisfy the appro-priate discursive protocols of institutional authority. Should such procedures

not be followed to the letter various 'issues' arise following a 'questionable' performance which – by definition – failed to meet the assumed expectations of a
given ideology.[12] According to Austin performative acts will not succeed if they
are subject to flawed delivery: misfires, misinvocations, misapplications, and
misexecutions, all induce infelicitous consequences. "When the utterance is a
misfire, the procedure which we purport to invoke is disallowed or is botched;
and our act ... is void and without effect, &c" (Austin, 1962: 16). Evidently, when
a received notion (i.e., an accepted belief) is disproven, or otherwise disre-
garded, it is no longer convincing, and 'misfires' ideologically, without induc-
ing the customary agentic response. Austin in "How to Talk" (as noted above)
defines speech situation S_0 as a specific procedure for presenting sense and
reference in accordance with certain rules (I is a T) and if the the conditions
of sense and reference change – due to contextual circumstances – a renewed
statement of the terms for subsequent speech situation S_1 will be necessary.
In such cases of restatement, for example from S_0 to S_1, the performative conditions of the act are altered which could, in certain circumstances, lead to
further infelicities (misapplications, misfires &c.). The issuance of a speech act
is therefore, in Austin's account, determined by performative conditions which
conditionally guarantee its felicity. Performative success implies that reference and sense are associated in such a way that the utterance is acceptable
to all those 'taking part' in the speech act. Subject, verb, and complement of a
phrase, thus correspond, with the result being that the sentence is appropriate
to the context. Austin's theory of 'speech situations' appears to further the discursive analyses formulated by Pêcheux given that various speech acts may be
related to the 'ideological' mechanisms of ordinary language. Speech acts convey 'meaning effects' via social relations – due to this – Austin's descriptions of
performativity are useful for outlining the rules which such utterances *ordinarily* conform to (Searle also attempts a rule-governed analysis of meaning – see
chapter four). Performative utterances are usually effective under 'ordinary'
conditions, yet, Austin's discussion of infelicity indicates that speech acts are
subject to 'misfiring' in so far as S_0 is no longer appropriate for a given situation.
What is revealed – as a result of such analysis – is how sense and reference are
established via procedures which participants appear to *enact* so that certain

---

12   According to Althusser the education system is the 'number-one' ideological state appa-
     ratus (Althusser, 2014). The educational apparatus permits the ongoing realization of the
     'always-already-there' via accepted forms of inculcation. Thus 'ordinary language' may
     convey particular pre-scientific notions regarding linguistic norms within the relations
     of production that serve to realize State control of speech activity (e.g., grammar vis-à-
     vis law).

contextual effects may be realized in speech situations. In Poulantzas' research ideological speech activity appears to function as a modality of state power that represents – in 'ordinary language' – the existing forms of social order. As a result the State makes provision for certain repertoires of 'meaning':

> The ideological apparatuses include the churches, the educational sys-
> tem, the bourgeois and petty bourgeois political parties, the press, radio,
> television, publishing, etc. These apparatuses belong to the state system
> because of their objective function of elaborating and inculcating ideol-
> ogy ... It is this sense that we can talk of a relative autonomy (a) of the
> various apparatuses and branches vis-à-vis each other within the state
> system and (b) of the ensemble of the state vis-à-vis the hegemonic class
> or fraction.
>
> POULANTZAS, 2008: 210–211

By applying this theory of illocutionary subjection to Herbert's description of type A and type B ideologies it is, then, possible to describe the relative auton-omy of the ideological state apparatus as an effect of state semantics (i.e. the instituted 'meaning' of state power is defined by relatively autonomous ideo-logical systems).[13] One one hand these systems specify the 'vocabulary-syntax' for 'state language', and, on the other, such apparatuses present certain 'argu-ments' concerning the legitimacy of the state's meaning (i.e., state politics) (cf. Pêcheux, 1982; Poulantzas, 2008). There is no doubt that the State needs a 'stable' language to convey its constitutive role and this linguistic mandate is enacted by the operation of its *authority*. According to Poulantzas:

> the State really does exhibit a peculiar material framework that can by
> no means be reduced to mere political domination ... Rather political
> domination is itself inscribed in the institutional materiality of the State
> ... *state power* (that of the bourgeoisie, in the case of the capitalist State)
> *is written into this materiality*. Thus, while all the State's actions are not
> reducible to political domination, their composition is nevertheless
> marked by it.
>
> POULANTZAS, 1978: 14; emphasis added

---

13   In Pêcheux's terms the institutional materiality of the State may represent an empirical
      ideology regarding the 'facts' of the always-already-there (i.e., a pre-constructed 'reality').
      The real conditions of state power are obfuscated by the *meaning* of a language which is
      instituted under the aegis of ideological state apparatuses in illocutionary acts.

Austin's plea for excuses would then appear to mitigate 'misapplications' of state power in the course of its functioning in so far as blame for any alleged wrongdoing could be evaded by limiting the ascription of direct political responsibility. Moreover, this process appears to occur – ideologically – within 'ordinary language': a language which has been defined by the State (e.g., national language). Austin lists five 'families' of speech acts with specific illocutionary conditions that are particularly useful for describing certain performative acts (including those associated with state power): verdictives, exercitives, commissives, behabitives, and expositives. Verdictives: "are typified by the giving of a verdict, as the name implies, by a jury, arbitrator, or umpire" (Austin, 1962: 151). Exercitives: "are the exercising of powers, rights, or influence. Examples are appointing, voting, ordering, urging, advising, warning, &c" (ibid.). Commissives "are typified promising or otherwise undertaking; they *commit* you to doing something, but include also declarations or announcements, which are not promises, and also rather vague things which we may call espousals, as for example, siding with" (ibid.:151–152). Behabitives "are a very miscellaneous group and have to do with attitudes and *social behavior*. Examples are apologizing, congratulating, commending, condoling, cursing, and challenging" (ibid.: 152). Expositives "are difficult to define. They make plain how our utterances fit into the course of an argument or conversation ... Examples are 'I reply', 'I argue', 'I concede', 'I illustrate', 'I postulate'" (ibid.: 152). The institutional materiality of the state permits the exercise of speech acts that are in accordance with its institutional norms: verdicts, rights, legal orders, and so on, comprise such forms of illocution. For example, a verdict may be reached by the State in so far as an individual committed an act which has been understood in an ordinary sense, however, such a 'fact' assumes that illocution is institutionally regulated by certain conditions of enunciation (e.g., a national language). Austin summarizes his classification of the aforementioned speech acts in the following statement:

> To sum up we may say that the verdictive is an exercise of judgement, the exercitive is an assertion of influence or exercising of power, the commissive is an assuming of an obligation or declaring of an intention, the behabitive is the adopting of an attitude, and expositive is the clarifying of reasons, arguments, and communications.
>
> AUSTIN, 1962: 163

In this sense 'ordinary' speech acts regarding freedom, responsibility, and excuses are determined in relation to institutional materiality of the state. In consequence, I find that Austin's work presents a new method to apprehend the base/superstructure distinction via performative utterances.

> As with any study of the superstructures, the important thing here is the *specificity* of the juridical and state superstructure ... What analysis can set out from is, on the one hand, the specificity of the superstructure in general and its fundamental dialectical division – from the base; and, on the other, the specificity of a *certain* law or state, a *certain* art, a *certain* morality, situated in time and space.
>
> POULANTZAS, 2008: 25

There are specific performative conditions which must be met for statements to be deemed legitimate by the institutional materiality of the state and such exercitives are ordinarily conveyed via speech acts.

> An exercitive is the giving of a decision in favour or against a certain course of action, or advocacy for it ... Arbitrators and judges make use of exercitives as well as issuing verdictives. Its consequences may be that others are 'compelled' or 'allowed' or 'not allowed' to do certain acts.
>
> AUSTIN, 1962: 155

Ideological state apparatuses – as agencies of the superstructure – guarantee legitimate speech acts in so far as these are 'accepted' vis-à-vis state authority. Austin's account of verdictives can be used to illustrate how legitimate utterances are defined via a 'verdict' regarding the rules which govern such decisions.

> Verdictives consist in the delivering of a finding, official or unofficial, upon evidence or reasons as to value or fact, so far as these are distinguishable ... Verdictives have obvious connexions with truth and falsity, soundness and unsoundness and fairness and unfairness ... Verdictives have an effect, in the law, on ourselves and on others.
>
> ibid.: 153–154

Verdictive utterances, Austin notes, may also be associated with certain behaviors: "in one sense of 'blame' which is equivalent to 'hold responsible', to blame is a verdictive, but in another sense it is to adopt an attitude towards a person and is thus a behabitive" (ibid: 155). The illocutionary force of authority underwrites prescribed judgements in regard to personal obligations, i.e., a subject is committed to a particular action by the strength of a specified verdict.[14]

> Verdictives commit us to actions in two ways: (a) to those necessary for consistency with and support for our verdict, (b) to those that may be, or may be involved in, the consequences of a verdict.
>
>   ibid.: 159

Thus the state apparatus possesses the authority to proclaim verdicts in terms of the 'always-already-there' and the performative recognition of these decrees is determined via the institutional materiality of speech acts (oral and written).

---

14   An individual may thus be subjected to particular forms of social domination simply by 'using' language, i.e., unbeknowst to the user its language is realized in terms of the state apparatus.

CHAPTER 7

Jacques Lacan (1901–1981)

I commence this discussion of Lacan's research vis-à-vis Pêcheux's theory of discourse with reference to Lacan's psychiatric spur Gatian de Clérambault (1872–1934). Clérambault's research was an important theoretical precursor to Lacan's psychoanalytic studies in certain respects. "... I will remind the reader by what doorway this entry occurred ... It stems from the work of Gatian de Clérambault, my only master in psychiatry" (Lacan, 2006: 65). Lacan cites two concepts employed by Clérambault: 1) 'mental automatism' and 2) ideogenesis: 'the ideic'.

> His [Clérambault's] notion of 'mental automatism', with its metaphorical, mechanistic ideology, which is assuredly open to criticism, seems to me, in its attempt to come to grips with the [patient's] subjective text, closer to what can be constructed on the basis of structural analysis than any other clinical approach in French psychiatry.
>
> ibid.

Pêcheux's research in *Automatic Discourse Analysis* and *Language, Semantics, and Ideology* considers particular theories of language which yield 'automatic' results.[1] A computer program outlined in *Automatic Discourse Analysis* was conceived to produce automated findings for discursive corpora and some of the hypotheses in *Language, Semantics, and Ideology* suggest that a subject's discourse is – more or less – the automatic articulation of the always-already-there. Lacan notes that Clérambault's theory of the ideogenic is a 'search for the limits of signification' via the imaginary structures of mental *automatism.*

> Clérambault's constant reference in his analysis to what he calls ... 'the ideogenic,' is nothing but a search for the limits of signification. Employing a method involving nothing but comprehension, he paradoxically manages to display the magnificent range of structures that runs

---

1   Subjective speech acts are generated vis-à-vis the institutional materiality of the State, yet this ideological relationship of 'ordinary' language to speech activity appears matter-of-fact because 'accepted' forms of linguistic behavior are automatically (i.e., unconsciously) articulated in terms of preconstructed discourse.

the gamut from the so-called *'postulates'* of the delusions of passion to
the so-called *basal* phenomena of *mental automatism*.

LACAN, 2006: 137

Clérambault used the term 'mental automatism' clinically to determine cases
of behavioral automaticity he observed in psychiatric patients. In some examples, 'mental automatism' is described in relation to subjective effects of 'psychic splitting' whereby the 'self' experiences 'ideic' automaticity, whereas in
other cases, it is defined in relation to sensory and motor functions.

> Under the heading of automatism I included such classic phenomena as
> the preceding thoughts, the enunciation of acts, the verbal impulsions,
> the tendency towards psycho-motor hallucinations ... The mental autom-
> atism thus defined is an autonomous process ... We have described the
> processes of mental automatism separately. However, we can compare
> them to two other types of automatisms which are both related and sim-
> ilar to the mental automatisms and which can enlighten us on the very
> nature of the mental automatisms. These other types are the *sensory
> automatism* and the *motor automatism*.
>
> CLÉRAMBAULT, 2002: 163–165

In another diagnostic description he writes:

> We have widely used the term mental automatism. Lacking a better term,
> we provisionally use it in a strictly restricted sense to better describe a
> certain clinical syndrome containing automatic phenomena of three
> different orders: motor, sensory and ideo-verbal. This syndrome includes
> all the well-known types of hallucinations. As we will later see, the term
> mental automatism is more comprehensive than the term hallucination.
>
> ibid.: 212

Lacan maintains that 'repetition automatism' (a concept that appears to be
derived, in part, from Clérambault's research on mental automatisms) is a
psychoanalytic symptom revealed by the insistent recurrence of particular signifiers exhibited in the speech of the analysand (e.g., automatic ideo-verbal
behavior).

> My research has led me to the realization that repetition automatism ...
> has its basis in what I have called the *insistence* of the signifying chain ...
> As we know, it is in the experience inaugurated by psychoanalysis that we

can grasp by what oblique imaginary means the *symbolic* takes hold even in the deepest recesses of the human organisms ... I posit that it is the law specific to this chain which governs the psychoanalytic effects that are determinant for the subject ....

LACAN, 2006: 6

Pêcheux cites Lacan's work to explain how the material conditions of a given ideology are typically effaced by the adoption of 'automatic' speech acts articulated by the 'discourse of the Other':

this subject ... is precisely what Jacques Lacan calls the Other ... in Lacan's formulation ... 'the unconscious is the discourse of the Other' one can begin to see how *unconscious repression* and *ideological subjection* are materially linked, without being confounded, inside what could be called *the process of the Signifier* ....

PÊCHEUX, 1982: 92

The 'repetition automatism' and its relation to the Other's discourse is addressed in Lacan's "Seminar on 'The Purloined Letter'".

Having thus established the intersubjective module of the action that repeats, we must now indicate in it a *repetition automatism* in the sense that interests us in Freud's work ... *the unconscious is the Other's discourse* ... What interests me today is the way in which the subjects, owing to their displacement, relay each other in the course of the intersubjective repetition.

LACAN, 2006: 10

Lacan's 'letter' of intersubjective signification is a source of unconscious ideation constituted by the discourse of the Other which, in some circumstances, may induce certain automatisms.[2] I will not present an analysis here of the theoretical differences between Clérambault and Freud suffice to say that mental automatisms appear to be manifestly unconscious to the subject in certain cases. Returning to the question of subjective 'meaning', as developed by Pêcheux, it seems that verbal automatisms may indicate 'insistent' semantic structures (e.g., the self-evidence of practical ideologies) found in discursive

---

2   In this sense ideology may function as an unconscious automatism in which subjects fail to identify the symbolic basis their own subjection. The involuntary diction of the Other's discourse, then, appears as a consequence of perceiving an imaginary reality automatically.

loci represented by the discourse of the Other. According to Lacan repetition automatism results from a kind of 'possession' by signifying structures in which a given 'meaning' is insistently repeated within a subject's discourse. "This is what happens in repetition automatism ... By coming into the letter's possession – an admirably ambiguous bit of language – its meaning possesses them" (Lacan, 2006: 21). This 'letter' is used metaphorically by Lacan to represent intersubjective acts of communication.

> But as for the letter itself, whether we take it in the sense of a typographical element, of an epistle, or of what constitutes a man of letters, we commonly say that what people say must be understood à la lettre (to the letter or literally) ....
>
> ibid.: 17

Each 'letter' of meaning is determined by the institutions which support structures of literacy (e.g., the educational apparatus), yet, there are many examples of unreal literation: mythology, fiction, 'narratives', symptoms of psychosis &c. In one of Clérambault's clinical commentaries he writes:

> The patient presents a split in her personality which tends to objectivate her own 'self'... she is subjected to a sub-continuous automatic ideation ... The patient perceives the internal nature of the voices (voices coming from her chest and belly) as her own, but they occur as a result of exogenous inspiration. *She demonstrates this concept by way of locutions that are full of imagery.*
>
> CLÉRAMBAULT, 2002: 100; emphasis added

Automatic ideation appears to manifest sustained subjective meaning which is, quite literally – unreal – in fictive, mythic, and/or pathogenic forms that may function as relays for the discourse of the Other.[3] Pêcheux notes that subordinate forms of discourse typically represent 'phantasmagoric' subjective beliefs in so far as symbolic subjugation is determined by ideological systems in which imaginary significations are unconsciously 'perceived-accepted-suffered' (Pêcheux, 1982: 113). In relation to such imagined oppression Pêcheux references Lacan's 'field of the Other': "The subject is subject only from being subjected to the field of the Other, the subject proceeds from his synchronic

---

3 According to Lacan: "The unconscious *is* a concept founded on the trail [*trace*] left by that which operates to constitute the subject" (Lacan, 2006: 703).

subjection in the field of the Other" (Lacan, 1977b: 188 cited in Pêcheux, 1982: 114). Pêcheux, however, maintains that Lacan's theory is idealist because it typically ignores the material conditions of discursive production associated with unconscious subjection.[4]

> Hence in the use I am making here of concepts elaborated by Lacan, I am severing them from the idealist inscription of that elaboration ... Let me just say that formulations such as 'the subject of the unconscious', 'the subject of science', etc., partake of this idealist inscription.
>
> PÊCHEUX, 1982: 92

In *Language, Semantics, and Ideology* Pêcheux does not appear to address Lacan's example of structural subjection found in "A Theoretical Introduction to the Functions of Psychoanalysis in Criminology" which is inconsistent with such accusations of 'idealism'. According to Lacan: "Neither crime nor criminals are objects that can be conceptualized apart from their sociological context" (Lacan, 2006: 103). Pêcheux's research suggests that a subject is made responsible for its discourse by the operation of ideological state apparatuses – in which a given individual's verbal behavior is determined by certain discursive structures – despite the fact that this self-same subject is not the author of state language/s (i.e., the subject is a vehicle of unconscious subjection). Evidently Lacan perceives such issues, to some extent, when he notes that "psychoanalysis, with the agencies that it distinguishes in the modern individual, can shed light on vacillations in the contemporary notion of responsibility ..." (ibid.: 104).[5] Pêcheux's theoretical dilemma regarding the 'responsible subject' concerns the automaticity of signifying structures whereby a given subject 'freely' adopts forms of discourse which are extrinsically legitimated, i.e., what is perceived-accepted-suffered 'subjectively' is maintained by the preconstructed reality of the always-already-there. To be 'possessed' by a given meaning suggests an individual's discourse is – in certain cases – 'automatic' whereby such automaticity is determined by the authority of ideological

---

4 Discourse is generated via institutional sites (e.g., family, school, and workplace), therefore, ideological representations of reality will exhibit those normative assumptions which are tacitly accepted in 'automatic' forms of social experience prescribed by the structures of authority which support such institutions.

5 The structure of super-ego is assumed to direct moral responsibility, however, if this agency functions as a practical ideology, then such moral direction will produce 'automatic' subjection via existing systems of social oppression.

state apparatuses. Lacan's 'repetition automatism' and Clérambault's 'mental automatism' are remarkable concepts to further investigation into conditions of discursive automatism whereby a given discourse is 'self-generatively' associated with subjective experience. In *My Teaching* Lacan notes three fundamental sources for the development of his research: Clérambault, Freud, and language.

> Clérambault taught me things. He simply taught me to see what I had in front of me: a madman ... So, what we have in front us is a guy who has what Clérambault called 'mental automatism', or in other words a guy who cannot make a gesture without being ordered to, without being told: 'Look, he's doing that, the little rascal'... I've naturally retained what he taught me about what he called mental automatism.
>
> LACAN, 2008: 24–25

As Lacan's example indicates mental automatism denotes ideo-verbal acts and other forms of 'intentionality' which have become in some sense automated. Such automaticity, then, establishes predictable repertoires of behavior, e.g., 'a guy who cannot make a gesture without being ordered to'. To rephrase Lacan: mental automatism is structured like a script.

> When I express myself saying that the unconscious is structured like a language, I am trying to restore the true function of everything that structures under the aegis of Freud ... if the unconscious were not language, there would be no unconscious in the Freudian sense ... it is imperative to call into question how things stand with language if we wish to begin to shed some light on what is going on with respect to the function of the unconscious.
>
> ibid.: 28–32

The subject of enunciation is, according to Lacan, circumscribed by the discourse of the Other in apparent conformity with the language defined via 'the site of speech'.

> The subject that concerns us here, the subject not insofar as it produces discourse but insofar as it is produced [*fait*], cornered even [*fait comme un rat*], by discourse, is the subject of enunciation ... To the extent that we can identify it in terms of the workings of the subject, this Other is to be defined as the site of speech. This is not where speech is uttered, but

where it takes on the value of speech, or in other words where it inaugu-
rates the dimension of truth.

ibid.: 36–37

If syntax, semantics, and pragmatics comprise three basic structural elements
of human language and if, as Lacan suggests, 'the unconscious is structured
like a language', the unconscious may exhibit a formal structure that 'automatically' organizes linguistic representations in accordance with these elements. Pêcheux cites Lacan in *Language, Semantics, and Ideology* to register
one example this notion. "It is here, I believe, that one should look for 'the
semantic effects bound up with syntax', in so far as, in Lacan's words, 'syntax,
of course, is preconscious'" (Pêcheux, 1982: 125). A subject's language may then
be defined, Pêcheux maintains, by the 'automatic' representation of preconstructed discourse, yet, he notes the imagined spatio-temporal structure of
subjective experience requires further explanation as a self-evident syntax.

For our purposes here I shall therefore say that the preconscious characterizes the reappropriation of a (conscious) verbal representation by
the (unconscious) primary process ... it is clear that any discourse is an
occultation of the unconscious ... I think this will help us understand
that the notorious problematic of 'enunciation' found so frequently in
linguistic research today ... arises in reality from the theoretical absence
of *a linguistic corollary of the Freudian imaginary and ego*: it still remains
to construct the theory of the 'verbal body' that finds a position in time
(tenses, moods, aspects, etc.) and a space (localisation, determiners, etc.)
which are the imaginary time and space of the speaking subject.

ibid.: 124–125

Hence, what is enunciated by the subject could thus exhibit forms of ideological automaticity that have been unconsciously adopted via existing linguistic
structures.[6] According to Lacan:

Speech is the mill-wheel whereby human desire is ceaselessly mediated
by re-entering the system of language. I emphasize the register of the
symbolic order because we must never lose sight of it, although it is most
frequently forgotten, although we turn away from it in analysis. *What we*

---

6 Meaning-effects may follow certain patterns of 'mental automatism'. In such cases the subject would exhibit speech behavior that is apparently 'spontaneous' without identifying that
such acts are, in fact, unconsciously preconstructed by earlier forms of language acquisition.

go on and on about, often in a confused, scarcely articulate fashion, are the
subject's imaginary relations to the construction of his ego.
      LACAN, 1988: 179; emphasis added

Pêcheux's references to Lacan's work are used to explain how the imaginary effects of ideology may be transmitted in forms of discourse. The apparent automaticity of ideological agency is thus a consequence of certain symbolic systems in which an individual's autonomy has been unconsciously subjected to illusory beliefs (e.g., the Munchausen effect). The question of imaginary mis/recognition and, relatedly, mis/identification, Lacan explains, is directly connected to what a subject 'sees' from its position in the symbolic order (i.e., its loci).

> For there to be an illusion ... in which the imaginary can include the real and, by the same token, fashion it, in which the real can also include, and by the same token, locate the imaginary ... everything depends on the position of the subject. And the position of the subject ... is essentially characterized by its place in the symbolic world, in other words the world of speech.
>
>   LACAN, 1988: 80

Lacan develops his discussion of imaginary experience by 'reflecting' on the nature of optical illusions and then suggesting how the subject's imagination is formed by real – unconscious – structures of language which are determined by certain kinds of social practice. 'Full speech', Lacan maintains, represents to subjects what they perceive as the 'truth' of their interaction with the Other via certain performative conditions.[7] Hence, full speech appears to guarantee the veracity of subjective experience, however, Lacan does not appear to demonstrate how such discourse may be preconstructed by the 'always-already-there' (see chapter one).

---

7 Althusser describes the genesis of such experience with reference to intersubjective role designation/s whereby individuals apparently 'adopt' a particular identity vis-à-vis social norms. "It would seem that ideology here functions as the image of the 'other', an image that has been brought into conformity, socially and familially [*conforme socialement et familiale-ment*], with what the family/society expects of every individual who comes into the world, beginning in infancy ... It seems that one has a psychosocial need to identify with the 'other' in order to recognize oneself as existing" (Althusser, 2006: 284). Recall that, for Lacan, the unconscious is the 'discourse of the Other'. Hence, the 'site of speech' may automatically determine subject positions within the relations of production via accepted forms of socialization (cf. Lacan, 2008; Pêcheux, 1995).

Full speech is speech which aims at, which forms, the truth as it becomes established in the recognition of one person by another. Full speech is speech which performs. One of the subjects finds himself, afterwards, other than he was before. That is why this dimension cannot be evaded in the analytic experience.

LACAN, 1988: 107

Pêcheux proposes speech acts are determined by syntactic and semantic structures which find articulation in the 'discourse of the Other' (e.g., imaginary forms of subjection). Lacan's research appears to support this view given that the 'site of speech' is established symbolically: "In other words it's the symbolic relation which defines the position of the subject as seeing. It is speech, the symbolic relation, which determines the greater or lesser perfection, of completeness, of approximation, of the imaginary" (ibid.: 141). The extent to which a subject has an imaginary relationship to the real is defined by its formative identifications in so far as these symbolic acts define the discourse of the Other.[8] Furthermore, according to Lacan, the symbolic order is typically a prescriptive structure given that discursive formations regulate social cognition by relatively strict procedures of verbal interaction.

Each time that we find ourselves within the order of speech, everything which founds another reality in reality, at the limit, only acquires its meaning and its edge in relation to this same order.

LACAN, 1988: 239

This statement by Lacan typifies many problems of ideology where a particular interpretation of reality is legitimated by the structure of language that is used to represent it (e.g. 'ordinary' grammatical interpretations of reality). Lacan notes that speech is semantically overdetermined given that it produces polysemic effects that are irreducible to *one* meaning.

Speech as such is instituted within the structure of the semantic world which is that of language. Speech never has one single meaning, nor the word one single use. All speech always possesses a beyond, sustains various functions, encompasses several meanings.

ibid.: 242

---

8   According to Lacan: "The unconscious is that part of concrete discourse qua transindividual, which is not at the subject's disposal in re-establishing the continuity of his conscious discourse" (Lacan, 2006: 214).

If, however, semantics is an ideology, as Pêcheux maintains, the apparent polysemy of language may represent a pre-scientific belief that belongs to theories of linguistics that have not followed the Saussurian break (see chapter two). In cases of psychosis, neurosis and other psychopathologies Lacan notes – following Freud – that the imaginary register appears to generate forms of derealization and misrecognition (Lacan, 1988) The neurotic refuses to recognize its symptoms psychoanalytically (i.e., as the discourse of the unconscious) and the psychotic derealizes the symbolic order. In both cases there is a problem regarding what psychosocial reality, in fact, 'means'. What is called 'mental health', in this respect, represents appropriate beliefs towards the accepted meaning of existing norms. The psychiatric patient, therefore, fails to establish the 'correct' representation of reality that is prescribed by the existing social order.[9] Furthermore, Clérambault remarks that 'ideo-verbal' automatisms such as hallucinations should be represented in terms of the mechanisms that generate such behaviors causally. "The ideic content of the ideo-verbal hallucinations constantly distracts us away from the fact that the only thing that really matters scientifically is their mechanism" (Clérambault, 2002: 213). The same observation should, I think, be applied to 'meaning', i.e., one should not resort to 'intrinsic' meaning to explain 'what something means', rather, one should adduce the mechanisms that produce 'meaning effects' for a given subject. Mental automatisms appear, according to Clérambault, as subjective beliefs which the individual uncritically accepts as real. "We will demonstrate that the abnormalities that are ideic, ideo-verbal, and sensorial ... present to the awareness of the individual as elements that are spontaneous, autonomous, and parasitic" (ibid.: 228–229). In another phrasing Clérambault calls mental automatism a 'syndrome of passivity'.

> We provisionally propose the following term: syndrome of passivity ... The term passivity also has the advantage to be even applicable to the secondary ideation which we have defined as neoplastic, because of the fact that the patient is subjected to it.
>
> ibid.: 229

---

9   This problem has received expansive and detailed study by Michel Foucault. See *Madness and Civilization* (A History of Insanity in the Age of Reason), *Psychiatric Power* (Lectures at the Collège de France), *Abnormal* (Lectures at the Collège de France). In these texts Foucault studies psychopathology in relation to social history and finds that the norms of 'mental illness' develop in relation to juridical, economic, political, and familial practices. Thus, as socio-historical practices change so does the 'meaning' of madness.

Some patients – in his analysis – experience passivity by means of ideic automatisms over which they cannot demonstrate control (i.e., the discourse of the Other). Clérambault thus discerns a connection between passivity and automatic behavior in which the patient is afflicted by spontaneous ideas which are 'self-generating'. As stated above Pêcheux posits that ideological subjection and unconscious repression are materially linked by discursive structures. The function of transference, according to Lacan, relates imaginary formations to the real in so far as the history of an individual's intersubjective speech activity constitutes the basis of its unconscious discourse. This psychoanalytic concept (i.e., transference), may, then reveal the 'automatic' forms of discourse which structure a subject's perception of reality in established forms of social interaction. "What is fundamentally at issue in transference, is how a discourse that is masked, the discourse of the unconscious, takes hold of a discourse that is apparent" (Lacan, 1988: 247).

In "Fragment of an Analysis of a Case of Hysteria" Freud defines transference as the projection of historical identifications upon the analyst by the analysand – whose previous psychological experiences are re-lived in the present – via re-imagined 'automatic' behaviors.

> What are transferences? They are new editions or facsimiles of the impulses and phantasies which are aroused and made conscious during the progress of the analysis; but they have this peculiarity, which is characteristic of their species, that they replace some earlier person by the person of the physician.
>
> FREUD, 1953: 116

A transference manifests the prior realizations of discursive conditions which have structured the history of a subject's identity.[10] "To put it another way: A whole series of psychological experiences are revived, not as belonging to the past, but as applying to the person of the physician at the present moment" (ibid.). Transference is, then, a psychoaffective symptom of the unconscious which is generated via certain imaginary forms of discourse. As Lacan notes:

> the function of the transference can only be understood on the symbolic plane ... We see it in the dream, but we also rediscover it in the slip of

---

10   Clérambault's notion of ideo-verbal automatism appears to explain the psychogenic basis of transference in terms of 'automatic' meaning generation which a subject experiences passively.

the tongue and throughout the psychopathology of everyday life. That is our starting point for listening to the person who speaks to us. And we only have to refer back to our definition of the discourse of the unconscious, which is that it is the discourse of the other, to understand how it authentically links up again with intersubjectivity in the dialogue, that full realisation of speech.

LACAN, 1988: 247

Lacan further posits that transference supports the generation of 'meaning' in forms of discourse which the subject experiences 'psychogenically':

The fundamental phenomenon revealed by analysis is this relation of one discourse to another, using it [transference] as a support. What we discover manifested in it is this fundamental principle of semantics, that every semanteme refers to the whole of the semantic system, to the polyvalence of its usages.

ibid.

Lacan, therefore, theoretically relates transference to semantic systems (i.e., systems of 'meaning') in terms of unconscious discourse.[11] Transference effects may serve as indicators for ideological subjection in terms of repressed discursive structures vis-à-vis certain *personal* projections. Moreover, following Pêcheux's research, ideology appears to represent a generalized structure of transference by socially 'reflecting' the conditions of production which determine a given individual's discursive subjection to imaginary semantic structures (cf. Lacan, 2006; Pêcheux, 1982). The psychoanalytic basis of imaginary mis/recognition is conceptually related to the discourse of the Other by particular structures of identification which symbolically structure specular effects (e.g. 'the image of the ego').

In man, the imaginary is reduced, specialized, centred on the specular image, which creates both impasses and the function of the imaginary relation ... The subject will rediscover over and over again that this image of self [image of the ego] is the very framework of his categories, of

---

11   The effects of transference are not limited to 'full speech'. Gestures, body language, eye contact (e.g., Lacan's 'gaze'), and other forms of non-verbal behavior may also be unconsciously associated with certain semantic structures. Ordinarily, non-verbal behavior is assumed to convey meaning, yet, the *conventional* process by which a physical motion becomes 'meaningful' may bypass cognition and appear as an automatic form of ideology.

his apprehension of the world – of the object, and he will achieve this through the intermediary of the other.

LACAN, 1988: 282

The relation of the subject to its discourse is mediated by the imaginary discourse of the Other and transference reveals the extent to which certain discursive 'impregnations' remain active as structures of psychogenic perception.

> This phenomenon of imaginary investment plays a pivotal role in the transference. If it is true that the transference is established in and through the dimension of speech, it only brings about the revelation of this imaginary relation at certain crucial points in the spoken encounter with the other, that is to say, in this instance, with the analyst.
>
> ibid.

Lacan suggests that transference represents the discourse of the Other to the subject in such a way that its projection is socio-historically established via the symbolic order.

> The phenomenon of transference encounters the imaginary crystallization ... This unconscious is made up of what the subject essentially fails to recognize in his structuring image, in the image of his ego – namely those captivations by imaginary fixations which were unassimilable to the symbolic development of his history ... It is through the spoken assumption of his history that the subject becomes committed to the path of bringing into being his truncated imaginary.
>
> ibid.: 283

The history of ideological subjection may be correlated with discursive events which have been repressed due to certain conditions of intersubjective mis/recognition.[12] Clérambault's notion of mental automatism suggests how the subject is 'captivated' by imaginary structures in which volition has become subordinate to psychogenic interpretations of reality, i.e., 'automatic' forms of subjection. The term 'mental automatism' is revised by Clérambault on several

---

12 According to Althusser: "Ideology, then, is the expression of the relation between men and their 'world', that is, the (overdetermined) unity of the real relation and the imaginary relation between them and their relations conditions of existence" (Althusser, 2005: 233–234). Such imaginary relations, in Lacan's terms, are constituted by the discourse of the Other and thus direct past and future instances of psycho-social transference between subjects.

occasions for purposes of conceptual clarification. He also calls it: 'the syndrome of passivity' (as noted above), 'syndrome S', 'the triple automatism' and 'syndrome of echo'. "I will avoid using the term of automatism which seems to raise too many questions. I will designate this syndrome, which is the exclusive subject of my study, by the term syndrome 'S'" (Clérambault, 2002: 291). Whichever term is used; however, these automatic operations may be used to explain various forms of self-subjection. 'The echo' is an imaginary psychogenic effect in which particular discourses are passively adopted via certain recurring chains of verbal activity (e.g., repeating intra-discourse).

> *The echo is a central phenomenon in the syndrome. Variations of the echo give rise to the enunciations.* The extension of the enunciations produces the autonomous ideation, and extension of this autonomous ideation gives rise to the secondary personality.
>
> ibid.: 294; emphasis added

An echo is an auditory reflection which functions sonically, rather than a specular reflection, which functions visually. According to Clérambault echoes may induce 'derivations' in which imaginary representations of speech acts are automatically determined by psychogenic ideo-verbal beliefs.

> The echo is a phenomenon of derivation. The derivations tend to become conjugated and progressive, and result in a systematic construction. A derivation can on one hand utilize the preformed tracks (associations, actual feelings), and on the other hand, create certain undue communications between restricted cycles (vocabulary), or more extended cycles (sets of ideas). Such are the reasons for the production of illogical and absurd outcomes.
>
> ibid.: 294

The ideic fixations that are revealed as echoic symptoms may, over time, become pathological to the subject in the form of hallucinations or other delusions.

> The echoes of thought and the nonsenses can progressively enrich themselves with verbal complications laden with ideic contents and affective charge ... The feelings attributed to the voices are those that can be explained by the intrusive character of the voice itself or by the personal feelings of the individual himself, both of which occur in various degrees ... In other words, there is an interrupted series of formulas linking the echoes to the most complex ideo-hallucinatory productions.
>
> ibid.: 298

Furthermore, what is called 'mental illness' (e.g., psychosis) appears to be, in Clérambault's analysis, the result of certain forms of imaginary discourse which 'captivate' the subject and induce certain cognitive disturbances via ideo-verbal automaticity:

> the restriction of the personal field and the passivity with regard to the invasion, do not constitute a separate internal life in the psychotic patient. As much as we can tell the demarcation between the self and the non-self seems to disappear in time, and the subject lives in a state of depersonalization which becomes a series of contradictory accounts that are superposed and monotone where subjectivity is indistinguishable from objectivity. In the established period of the illness and even in the beginning of the illness, the patient states: '*At times, I can't tell if it is their thinking or my own*'.
>
> ibid: 332

In cases of echoic auto-construction what is passively echoed by the subject is attributed to 'spontaneous' ideation (i.e., as ideogenic certainty of imaginary enunciations).[13]

> The hallucinations think ... The echo in its pure and simple form already presents the syntactic transposition of the "I" by the "He" (he goes out instead of I go out) corresponding to the personal activity of the hallucination.
>
> ibid.: 331

In such cases of ideo-verbal subjection it appears that the symbolic order has been derived from imaginary enunciations (i.e., echoes) which auto-construct the passive syndrome realized during psychohistorical transferences (cf. Freud, 1953; Clérambault, 2002; Lacan, 2006). Furthermore, speech acts may become echoic if they constitute ideogenic automatisms which convey passive acceptance of syntactic transpositions that structure the subject's experience of psychosocial reality. For Lacan, the symbolic order represents objective experience as a system of referential structures which, consequently, permits the determination of reality vis-à-vis language.

---

13 Clérambault's research suggests new ways to investigate mechanisms of ideological inculcation. His 'syndrome of passivity' indicates how ideology may lead a subject to passively accept its subjection via certain forms of intra-discourse that appear as 'echoes' of existing social relations.

> The human order is characterized by the fact that the symbolic function
> intervenes at every moment and at every stage of its existence. ... *If the
> symbolic function functions, we are inside it. And I would even say – we are
> so far into it that we can't get out of it.*
>
> LACAN, 1988a: 29–31; emphasis added

The unconscious imaginary is structured by the symbolic order in so far as it
is determined by 'intersubjective' transferences. In this sense the ego typically
re-presents the history of such discourse. "Founding speech, which envelops
the subject, is everything that has constituted him, his parents, his neighbours,
the whole structure of the community, and not only constituted him as symbol, but constituted him in his being" (ibid.: 20).[14] The ego (i.e., the subject)
represents the interaction of three forms of cognition (i.e., symbolic, real,
imaginary).

> I think I can show that in order to gain an idea of the function which
> Freud designates by the word 'ego', as indeed to read the whole of the
> Freudian metapsychology, it is necessary to use this distinction of planes
> and relations expressed in the terms, the symbolic, the imaginary and
> the real.
>
> ibid.: 36

The imaginary is realized in the founding speech which 'envelops' the subject psychosocially and the apparent predominance of this 'meaningful' process is determined by symbolic structures. "The ego, the imaginary function,
intervenes in psychic life only as symbol" (ibid.: 38). When the symbolic has
been derealized, the imaginary, may, as I think Clérambault suggests, begin
to function automatically, i.e., as an 'echo' in which derivations of the passive
syndrome are registered by certain instances of ideogenesis. According to
Pêcheux:

---

14   Founding speech or ('full speech'), then, relays certain *belief* systems that appear authori-
      tative in 'accepted' social structures (e.g., state discourse). According to Althusser: "To say
      that the unconscious produces its formations, or some of them, in concrete 'situations'
      (of everyday life, family relations, workplace relations, chance relations, etc.) thus literally
      means that it produces them in formations of ideological discourse, in formations of the
      ideological. It is in this sense that we can say that the unconscious reveals the principle of
      its *articulation* with the ideological. It is in this sense that we can say that the unconscious
      'functions' on ideology" (Althusser, 2003: 58–59).

All that we can say is that any discursive process presupposes the existence of imaginary formations ... in which the position of the protagonists
of discourse intervenes as a condition of production of the discourse. It
should again be stressed that the referent is an *imaginary object* (a subject's viewpoint), and not a physical reality.

PÊCHEUX, 1995: 85

Moreover, such discursive formations are related to superordinate systems of
enunciation where the link between the imaginary – and the exterior which
determines it (i.e., full speech) – involves practised subjection (Pêcheux, 1995).
Forms of discourse exhibit the ability to become automatic via symbolic agencies which are constitutive of 'subjective' experience (e.g. ideological state
apparatuses). Lacan remarks that the symbolic relation between subjects, in
fact, determines the perception of reality in so far as such signifying structures
determine forms of identification.

The power of naming objects structures the perception itself. The *percipi*
of man can only be sustained within a zone of nomination ... Naming
constitutes a pact, by which two subjects simultaneously come to an
agreement to recognise the same object.

LACAN, 1988a: 169

Pêcheux's research suggests that such 'agreement' is the result of imaginary
formations which structure discourse in relation to certain forms of ideological subjection.[15] Zones of nomination thus define the real via symbolic conditions of mis/recognition. The symbolic order defines the real in such a way that
we are 'inside' its definition. According to Lacan:

If the human subject didn't name ... if the subjects do not come to an
agreement over this recognition, no world, not even a perception, could
be sustained for more than one instance. That is the joint, the emergence
of the dimension of the symbolic in relation to the imaginary.

ibid.: 170

---

15 For example, semantic and syntactic modes of dominance facilitate the inscription of
    preconstructed beliefs (i.e., metaphysical 'information') based on the speculative neces-
    sity of existing ideologies. In this sense, natural language delivers the unconscious
    psycho-social structures found in 'ordinary' speech acts.

The goal of automatic discourse analysis, for Pêcheux, was not only to create an instrument for parsing various forms of text (newspapers, conversations &c.) – his automatic discourse analysis attempts to demonstrate how verbal activity (written or spoken) – under certain conditions – becomes ideology 'automatically'.

> My hypothesis is that these [subject] positions are *represented* with the discursive processes in which they are brought into play ... in other words, what functions in the discursive process is a series of imaginary formations designating the positions which A and B ascribe to themselves and to one another; the image they have of their own position and of the position of the other.
>
> PÊCHEUX, 1995: 85

Commenting on Pêcheux's research in *Automatic Discourse Analysis* Paul Henry writes: "The process whereby individuals are, so to speak, 'put in their place' remains invisible, we see only its external features and effects" (Henry, 1995: 31). In consequence, the apparently 'automatic' character of subjection facilitated by discursive formations is *systematically* mis/recognized due to the imaginary beliefs associated with certain loci (e.g., the symbolic order). According to Henry:

> Pêcheux had always been anxious to intervene within the field of the social sciences, and within that of social psychology in particular ... In making his intervention, he relied upon two theoretical resources which had, it seemed to him, already overthrown the idealist problematic which dominated the social sciences: historical materialism, as reformulated by Louis Althusser, and psychoanalysis, as reformulated by Jacque Lacan's 'return to Freud'.
>
> ibid.: 22

Lacan's working knowledge of Clérambault's research on mental automatisms further indicates how automatic discourse – as a form of ideology – may be related to the passive syndrome in terms of the symbolic subjection that is derived from the echoes (cf. Lacan, 2006; Clérambault, 2002; Pêcheux, 1995).

CHAPTER 8

Roland Barthes (1915–1980)

Pêcheux briefly mentions the work of Roland Barthes in *Language, Semantics, and Ideology* with regard to the conceptually regressive character of Barthes' semiology in so far as it assumes a pre-Saussurian model of language (Pêcheux, 1982: 174–175). While Pêcheux is critical of linguistic ideologies that do not advance the epistemological break between *langue* and *parole* Barthes' writings evince some of the speculative revamping semiology has seen since its Saussurian asseveration. Consequently, Barthes' oeuvre continues to exhibit particular relevance for Pêcheux's theory of semantic ideology. According to Pêcheux, semiology is generally construed as the study of signs whereas semantics, more specifically, is the study of 'meaning' (ibid.: IX). The locus of the Saussurian break is represented by the theoretical rupture in linguistics that separates signification (i.e., signs) from meaning (cf. Haroche et. al, 1971; Pêcheux, 1982). To a certain extent Barthes – having read Saussure's *Course in General Linguistics* – does detect this rupture, however, he does not develop it beyond Saussure's initial presentation and the ideology of meaning is retained in the form of myth. Barthes outlines this 'mythical system' in *Mythologies*. "On the plane of language ... I shall call the signifier: meaning ... on the plane of myth, I shall call it: form ... I shall call the third term of the myth the signification" (Barthes, 1972: 115). Linguistic signs become 'meaningful' in myths and, according to Barthes, this occurs in an 'ambiguous way' (ibid.: 116). Mythical systems are – at the same time – meaning and form. The realization of a given myth is presupposed by its apparent significance: hence the meaning of a myth is established via certain beliefs (in Pêcheux's terms the syntax of the myth appears to determine its semantic effects) (ibid.: 115–116). The process by which myths are subjectively sustained (i.e., the ideological persistence of mythical thought) is not, however, given detailed examination by Barthes in *Mythologies*, although, he does posit that mythology is transmitted in various forms of generalized writing (including visual and oral narratives):

> since myth is a type of speech, everything can be myth provided it is conveyed by a discourse. Myth is not defined by the object of its message, but by the way it utters this message ... It is therefore by no means confined to oral speech. It can consist of modes of writing or of representations; not

only written discourse, but also photography, cinema, reporting, shows, publicity, all these can serve as support to mythical speech.

> ibid.: 107–108

Applying Pêcheux's research from *Automatic Discourse Analysis* to Barthes' *Mythologies* suggests that the 'mythical system' presented by Barthes cannot adequately differentiate mythic (e.g., fables) from non-mythic forms of discourse (e.g., science). Barthes seems to interpret most – if not all – linguistic activity in terms of a seemingly limitless mythology. Pêcheux, however, notes that subjective methods of reading characteristically present interpretive complicities on the part of the subject who reads a given text according to pre-established modes of comprehension with the result that this *affected* reading 'agrees' or 'disagrees' with (or is perhaps indifferent to) what has been read in terms of particular normative assumptions.[1]

> It follows that the obviousness of the subjective reading ... is an illusion which is constitutive of the subject-effect in respect of language and which contributes to the effect of subjection of the subject as an ideological subject.
>
> PÊCHEUX, 1995: 130

For Pêcheux, it is – *necessary* – methodologically to discover the discrepancies which exist within and between different forms of discourse (e.g., scientific vs. ideological forms).[2]

> If it is true to say that reading a scientific text means relating it to the discourse from which it has separated, we can see that the practice of analysis requires us to reveal the element in a text D_y which produces a discrepancy – a difference ascribable to the nature of its predicates and the transformations they undergo between it and the dominant process of production Δ_x.
>
> PÊCHEUX, 1995: 120

---

1 Barthes thus produces an ideological reading of myths because he does not apply the core principle of the Saussurian break to his understanding of mythology as a form of discourse. Without separating the graphic and phonic structures from the subjective 'meaning' of the story Barthes cannot address how myths are 'realized' ideologically.

2 Such a differential method is also outlined by Althusser in "Three Notes on the Theory of Discourses" where he marks out the differences between unconscious discourse, aesthetic discourse, scientific discourse, and ideological discourse (Althusser, 2003).

Myth appears relatively homogeneous given that its reception is typically determined by yet another interpretation which is not falsified but, rather, assimilated into the next mythic iteration. "What is characteristic of myth? To transform meaning into form ... Myth can reach everything, corrupt everything, and even the very act of refusing oneself to it" (Barthes, 1972: 131–132). Barthes presents myth as a total system in which everything is subsumed without remainder by its ever-present duplicity. "What must always be remembered is that *myth is a double system*; there occurs in it a sort of ubiquity: *its point of departure is constituted by the arrival of meaning*" (ibid.: 121; emphasis added). In one form myth functions via 'literature' which supports the recurrence of its phantasmatic structure via certain acts of narration.

> A voluntary acceptance of myth can in fact define the whole of our tradi-
> tional Literature. According to our norms, this Literature is an undoubted
> mythical system: there is a meaning, that of the discourse; there is a sig-
> nifier, which is this same discourse as form or writing; there is a signified,
> which is the concept of literature, there is a signification, which is the
> literary discourse.
>
> ibid.: 133

Following Lacan and, relatedly, Clérambault, the meaning effects of myth, 'characterize' a certain predominance of the symbolic by the imaginary (see the preceding chapter). Furthermore, it seems that Barthes' 'mythical system' may be symptomatic of a 'passive syndrome' in Clérambault's terms, given that mythology is a repeating 'echo' of itself. Two years prior to the French publication of *Mythologies* (1957) by Barthes an article was published in *The Journal of American Folklore* written by Claude Lévi-Strauss entitled "The Structural Study of Myth" (1955). Barthes appears to have integrated many of the key ideas from "The Structural Study of Myth" within his *Mythologies*. "Myth is language, functioning on an especially high level where meaning succeeds practically at 'taking off' from the linguistic ground on which it keeps on rolling" (Lévi-Strauss, 1963: 210). Lévi-Strauss – as does Barthes – uses the work of Saussure to further his theory of mythology. Saussure deconstructs the apparent unity of language into its basic – formal – elements and Lévi-Strauss attempts to do the same for myths and suggests that the 'gross constituent units' of myths are what he calls 'mythemes'.

> How shall we proceed in order to identify and isolate these gross con-
> stituent units or mythemes?... each gross constituent unit will consist
> of a *relation* ... The true constituent units of a myth are not the isolated

relations but *bundles of such relations*; and it is only as a bundle that these
relations can be put to use and combined so as to produce a meaning.

ibid.: 211

The meaning of a myth is, therefore, determined by 'bundles' of mythemes.
The same ideological issue concerning 'meaning' is, then, discernible in both
Levi-Strauss' "The Structural Study of Myth" and Barthes' *Mythologies*, namely,
meaning is 'realized' in myth, or, in other words, myth 'has' meaning. For both
Barthes and Lévi-Strauss meaning is, in one way or another, a property of
myth, however, they do not definitively establish what meaning is, and instead
echoically repeat that it exists. This is why I suggest that both meaning and
myth may be conceptually related to what Clérambault calls 'mental automatism' and Lacan calls 'repetition automatism'. In fact, Lévi-Strauss does make
some remarks that confirm this view in 'The Structural Study of Myth':

> the question has often been raised why myths, and more generally oral
> literature, are so much addicted to duplication, triplication, or quadrupli-
> cation of the same sequence. If our hypotheses are accepted, the answer
> is obvious: The function of repetition is to render the structure of the
> myth apparent.
>
> ibid.: 229

Myths are *narrated* through certain acts of discursive repetition and, furthermore, their 'captivating' reiteration is typically habitual for the subjects who
accept them, hence the possibility that mythic thought is a kind of mental
automatism.[3] Eric Downing in "An Essay on Aristotle's Muthos", from the journal *Classical Antiquity*, examines the various translations that have been proposed for the word '*muthos*' in Aristotle's *Poetics*, which include: story, fable,
plot, myth, stream of events, and action. I found two noteworthy observations
in Downing's study: first, the *meaning* of *muthos* is (unsurprisingly) contested
and, second, the customary interpretation of muthos is 'story'.

> Almost every reader and interpreter of Aristotle's *Poetics* agrees that
> muthos plays a, if not the, central role in his discussion of tragedy and
> epic, *but almost no one agrees on what Aristotle means by muthos*.
>
> DOWNING, 1984: 164; emphasis added

---

3 Clérambault suggests that mental automatisms may take effect as fabulations which are
   repeated via the syndrome of passivity. Such stories are then echoed to reinforce an imaginary representation of reality.

This problem, may, simply be a consequence of mythologizing, i.e., because myths function via the imaginary, they can appear to 'express' multiple meanings. According to the *Oxford English Dictionary* the etymology of myth can be traced to Latin *'mythus'* from Greek *'muthos'*. Myth:

> a traditional story, especially one concerning the early history of a people or explaining a natural or social phenomenon, and typically involving supernatural beings or events; a widely held but false belief or idea: a misrepresentation of the truth, a fictitious or imaginary person or thing, an exaggerated or idealized conception of a person or thing.
>
> OED Online, 2020

According to Downing:

> By all accounts the most rudimentary, traditional, and, as it were, fundamental meaning of muthos is 'story', by which is intended the totality of related events about which a given work reports, and which, for the sake of greater specificity, we shall refer to as muthos, or the reconstituted story.
>
> DOWNING, 1984: 165

Clérambault finds that the auto-construction of psychosis involves a story, what he calls a 'novel', which the patient echoes (i.e., repeats) symptomatically.

> The echo represents a simple account on the patient's activities ... The voices carrying information, prophecies and fabulations would constantly throw at the awareness of the subject, certain well-elaborated notions without any relationship to his actual thinking ... This is the manner in which is formed the 'novel' of the extra-personal origin of the phenomena.
>
> CLÉRAMBAULT, 2002: 331

In a footnote to Clérambault's description of the patient's 'novel' Paul Hriso writes:

> *The so-called novel is the story* reported by the afflicted individual which involves the psychotic symptoms themselves, his attempts to explain them, the modifications in his psyche, and the behavioral reactions and subsequent ordeals that result from all the previous elements.
>
> HRISO, 2002: 331; emphasis added

This 'novel' is a kind of automatic discourse in which a story (myth) has become a symptom of psychosis. According to Lévi-Strauss, as noted above, the function of repetition is to render the structure of the myth apparent'. I am, therefore, suggesting that there may be a connection between mental automatism, ideology, and mythological systems.[4] Lévi-Strauss maintains myths have an immutable character and this *belief* supports the assumed continuity of their imaginary effects:

> But what gives the myth an operational value is that the specific pattern described is timeless; it explains the present and the past as well as the future. This can be made clear through a comparison between myth and what appears to have largely replaced it in modern societies, namely, politics.
>
> LÉVI-STRAUSS, 1963: 209

Myths enchant (i.e., captivate) the subject in so far as meaning is 'automatically' generated by the discourse posited throughout each mythological system of belief – agentic, speculative, or syntactic. Within contemporary societies repressive ideology is determined by the repetition of certain myths. These accepted narratives (i.e., socially reinforced speech acts) establish constitutional legitimacy and political order.

> A remark can be introduced at this point which will help to show the originality of myth. Its substance does not lie in its style, its original music, or its syntax, but in the story which it tells.
>
> ibid.: 210

Myths represent accepted stories which provide imaginary explanations of real events via the ideologies of meaning that typically repeat 'legitimate' interpretations of the social order (e.g., received definitions of 'rightful' rule).

> If our society is objectively the privileged field of mythical significations, it is because formally myth is the most appropriate instrument for the ideological inversion which defines this society ... What the world

---

4   The mechanism for such automatic discourse may be found in Freud's concept of the unconscious. Myths, then, generate the 'meaning' that is unconsciously acknowledged in forms of ideological discourse between subjects. In this sense ideological structures support the unconscious assumptions of a given mythical system (e.g., religious myths, ethical myths, legal myths, political myths &c.).

> supplies to myth is an [sic] historical reality ... and what myth gives in
> return is a natural image of this reality.
>
> BARTHES, 1972: 142

Evidently politics has not *replaced* myth as Lévi-Strauss suggests, rather, politics is conveyed via mythical systems which support the 'automatic' assumptions of certain ideologies. The relationship between politics and myth is
ancient: this is established in the classical works of Plato and Aristotle. Plato's
'noble lie' in *The Republic* serves as a foundational myth for social order and
Aristotle's *Rhetoric* is, in essence, a manual for persuading others to believe
such 'noble' intent.

> On the basis of the lie, the citizens can in all good faith and conscience
> take pride in the justice of their regime, and malcontents have no justi-
> fication for rebellion ... Today it is generally admitted that every society
> is based on myths, myths which render acceptable the particular form of
> justice incorporated in the system.
>
> BLOOM, 1991: 366–367

Rhetoric is a certain linguistic *technique* used to support the myths of just rule
associated with politically 'persuasive' speech acts.[5]

> Rhetoric, in the general sense of the use of language in such a manner as
> to impress hearers and influence them for or against a certain course of
> action, is as old as language itself and the beginnings of social and politi-
> cal life. It was practised and highly esteemed among the Greeks from the
> earliest times.
>
> FREESE, 1926: VII

Pêcheux notes that 'semantics' (see chapter one) constitutes a form of rhetorical practice, i.e., a means to convince or coerce: "we discover that this
branch of linguistics [semantics] has some remarkable extensions ... which
thus, via politics, involves what was classically called rhetoric" (Pêcheux,
1982: 3). According to Aristotle rhetoric is a technique for reaching 'agreement'

---

5   In Althusser's terms the ideological function of rhetoric is to support the asymmetrical struc-
    ture in dominance (*structure à dominate*) such that every subject believes in the 'truth' of
    their domination. Thus social relations appear just and obligatory. Rhetoric is an activity of
    conviction-persuasion which furnishes individuals with the appropriate beliefs to suit their
    position a given social formation (e.g., duty, morality & conscience).

regarding customary beliefs (i.e., 'common knowledge') whereby rhetorical 'success' is achieved when a 'proof' is accepted for a given belief.

> Rhetoric is a counterpart of dialectic, which it resembles in being concerned with matters of common knowledge ... it enables a man to state his case in popular, not in scientific language ... *Rhetoric may be defined as the faculty of discerning the possible means of persuasion in each particular case.* These consist of proofs ... rhetoric must be considered as an offshoot of dialectic and of politics (including ethics).
>
> ARISTOTLE, 1926: XXXI–XXXII; emphasis added

Rhetoric operates, then, by assessing the 'means of persuasion' used to establish common knowledge (e.g., popular opinion) and subsequently demonstrating the appropriate 'proofs' for such beliefs. These proofs are called 'enthymemes' and they appeal to moral, emotive, and/or logical forms of persuasion.

> Now the proofs furnished by the speech are of three kinds. The first depends upon the moral character of the speaker, the second upon putting the hearer into a certain frame of mind, the third upon the speech itself, in so far as it proves or seems to prove.
>
> ibid.: 16–17

As Aristotle states rhetoric is an 'offshoot' of politics: in effect rhetoric is used to establish the 'means of persuasion' for maintaining certain structures of social dominance. Plato's 'noble lie' in *The Republic* is an example of mythical rhetoric, where the social order is legitimated via 'matters of common knowledge'[6]. Freese maintains a comparable doctrine of coercion appears in Plato's *Gorgias*: "Rhetoric is the artificer of persuasion, and its function is to persuade the unintelligent multitude in the law courts and public assemblies in regard to justice and injustice" (Freese, 1926: XVIII). Myths persuade by establishing self-evident *meaning* (i.e., common knowledge). Such beliefs may appear as 'automatic' narratives which construct imaginary explanations to represent what is deemed socially acceptable for a given society. Pêcheux/Herbert suggests much of the 'knowledge' that is administered by the social sciences

---

6 According to Althusser ideology is a 'beautiful lie' that makes society 'go'. "Plato knew that the 'people' had to be taught, from childhood, the 'Beautiful Lies' that would 'make it go' all by itself, and that those Beautiful Lies had to be taught to the 'people' in such a way that the people would believe in them, so that it would 'go'" (Althusser, 2014: 180).

functions as a response to a social demand for myth (i.e., as ideologies to *justify* the dominant system).

> If therefore political practice produces social relations, what is the nature of the transformation that allows it to be described as a practice?... We sense that the answer to these questions requires an analysis of the demand that emanates from social relations ... whether in the form of the Myth or of the system – we understand that ultimately the political function is to transform social relations by re-formulating ... philosophical subjectivity.
>
> HERBERT, 1966

The demand for 'social justice' – to which myth replies – is fulfilled by the discourse of the humanities and social sciences where, according to Pêcheux/ Herbert, such demand is then restated as a *command* that 'keeps everything in place' (i.e, the ideology of self-evident meaning).[7] Thus "Reflections on the Theoretical Situation of Social Sciences, and Especially, of Social Psychology" appears to support the contention that – in general – 'social science' is a theoretical practice responding to the demand for noble lies (i.e., the disciplines of psychology, philosophy, linguistics, sociology &c. facilitate systemic repression via 'meaningful' discourse). The rhetoric of social science is used to persuade individuals that certain ideologies are matter of fact, i.e., 'always-already-there' (ibid.). There are two myths indispensable for the continuity of present-day society: 1) the myth of meaning; 2) the myth of subjectivity. The myth of meaning establishes the self-evident structures of 'common knowledge' that are assumed to be obvious within a given society, and, if this meaning is in doubt, rhetoric furnishes the 'proofs' necessary to restate the existing hierarchy. The myth of subjectivity supplies an ideology of interiority (e.g., Skinner's indwelling agents and Pêcheux's Munchausen effect) whereby individuality has an extra-social 'internal' origin. "All the philosophies of consciousness and of the subject ... find here their ideological function ... which is to repress into the subject ... the command" (Herbert, 1966). Myths exhibit a dual structure, on one hand, they satisfy an apparent demand for social order, and on the other, they command belief via persuasion (e.g., Plato's noble lie). Furthermore, myths enable individuals to be 'characterized' – in the literary sense of a story character – what the myth 'means' depends on how a character's 'subjective'

---

7   While the university apparatus may appear to support the open and impartial advancement of knowledge, in practice, this ideal is not always achieved. Indeed, the education system often prescribes (commands) what will be known to the students (e.g., curricula, syllabi &c.).

qualities relate to the plot (*muthos*). As a result, mythological beliefs may provide important epistemic clues to explain the ideology of agency and personhood (i.e., 'subjectivity'). Paul Hirst examines aspects of such a theory in the article "Ideology, Culture and Personality" (1983) where he suggests that the person is an ideological construct borne of certain social practices.

> The capacities for humans for self-representation and self-reflection depend on definite forms of discourse and definite activities in which they are trained and implicated as agents. These capacities vary. The concept of 'person' is intelligible only with reference to a definite substratum of categories, practices and activities which together give the agent its complex and differentiated form.
>
> HIRST, 1983: 120

A person does not pre-exist the practices which 'embody' its agency, rather, the person is the effect of such individuating structures (i.e., the person effect).[8] A subject's agency is determined by the particular institutional practices which enable 'subjective' acts to be realized socially.

> Thus it is important to stress that subjects or social agents are the differentiated terminals of the varied capacities and practices in which they engage. The subject as social agent does not have a unitary form, even if it is *represented* as a unity in various discourses or before various institutions (confession, the courts, etc.).
>
> ibid.

The person – as pre-established unity – is really a myth due to the *subjective* basis of identity. Hirst explains that 'a number of French authors' including Althusser, Barthes and others have challenged the metaphysical status of the 'person' (ibid.: 121–122).

> This challenge consists first and foremost in demonstrating that the 'person' is a metaphysical concept and not a simple reality. Challenged is the notion of the person as a given entity, the author of its acts and centred in a unitary, reflexive and directive consciousness.
>
> ibid.: 121

---

8 As soon as the subject – as a person – is symbolically represented it may be subjected to certain ideologies via forms of discursive practice. "Thus the ideological subject *in person* forms part of ideological discourse, *is present in person* in it, since it is itself a determinate signifier of this discourse" (Althusser, 2003: 49).

Barthes contends that myth is a type of language, and, under certain circumstances, myth informs political practice. Moreover, the mythical beliefs
associated with signifying structures (i.e., semiotic systems) appear to produce
imaginary representations of 'reality'.

> We must here recall that the materials of mythical speech (the language
> itself, photography, painting, posters, rituals, objects, etc.), however dif-
> ferent at the start, are reduced to a pure signifying function as soon as
> they are caught by myth.
>
> BARTHES, 1972: 113

A pre-eminent political myth is that a person is 'free' and this *belief* appears in
various ideological apparatuses that support mythologies of freedom (strictly
speaking – for an object to be free it must be supernatural). The myths of
person-ality associated with political ideologies require the perpetuation of
certain imaginary constructs, e.g., 'free will', 'free choice', &c.

> Politics and the metaphysical status of the 'person' are closely entwined
> ... The notion that persons are 'free agents', directed by a sovereign and
> integral consciousness, is a metaphysical 'fiction'... It is implicated to a
> greater or lesser degree in our legal system, in our conceptions of con-
> tract and the wage-labour relationship, in many of our assumptions
> about education, and so on.
>
> HIRST, 1983: 121–122

Under the rubric 'person' there lies an immense mythology which explains
everything from the origin of speech acts, and volition, through to what
Pêcheux calls the 'Munchausen effect' (the subject as a cause of itself).[9]
What is typically absent from the metaphysics of the person is an account of
the social structures which legitimate such beliefs (i.e., the social genesis of
'personality').

> Social organisation and conduct do not, and cannot, correspond to
> the suppositions of personalist metaphysics. In certain circumstances

---

9   Such myths are prescribed by existing representations of 'subjectivity', however, according
    Pêcheux, Althusser, Skinner, and Hirst, these 'characterizations' of the 'self' are no more than
    explanatory fictions and while storytelling may be convenient for purposes of social control
    it does not, in fact, represent how a signifying structure may be 'attached' to a human body
    vis-à-vis institutional systems (e.g., the state apparatus).

individuals are held to be 'free agents', in others they cannot be. Social organisation and social relations cannot be reduced to the 'fiction' of a domain of interacting and consenting 'free agents'.

ibid.: 122

The everyday myth of the 'free' subject is a metaphysical guarantee for social organization that appeals to 'personal liberty': in Pêcheux's terms such freedom is a demand/command which 'keeps everything in place'.[10] Hirst also holds this view:

The metaphysics of the 'person' gives rise to fantasies in which social organisation is made consistent with the needs of the 'free agent'... Personalist metaphysics is not merely a product of the systems of philosophers; rather, those philosophers construct systems on the basis of the categories in popular patterns of belief.

ibid.

These popular patterns of belief are evidence of, what I am calling here, the rhetoric of freedom. The rhetoric of freedom supports the metaphysical assumptions of free agency in socially prescribed situations. Aristotle's *Rhetoric* outlines various methods of persuasion for ensuring that the required 'proofs' correspond with what is to be believed and this – *compelling* – practice may be applied to the metaphysics of the person.

Hence the three kinds of rhetoric are: 1) deliberative; 2) forensic; 3) epideictic ... The business of the deliberative kind is to exhort or dissuade ... of the forensic to accuse or defend ... of the epideictic praise or blame ....

ARISTOTLE, 1926: XXXIII

Although deliberative and epideictic rhetoric may be used to convince individuals of their culpability forensic rhetoric provides an exceptionally clear

---

10   The metaphysics of free will supports what Foucault calls the 'sovereignty of consciousness' where the subject is assumed to represent 'itself' via 'its own' discourse. Yet, this myth cannot explain how a given subject is prescribed by existing discursive formations that define what it 'knows' about itself and the world. "Statements should no longer be situated in relation to a sovereign subjectivity but recognize in the different forms of the speaking subjectivity effects proper to the enunciative field" (Foucault, 1972: 122). The enunciative field defines the 'archives' (existing forms of discourse) in terms of which the 'free' subject may compose a statement.

example of persuasive techniques concerning personal freedom vis-à-vis legality. According to Aristotle:

> Forensic oratory, which deals with accusation and defence, requires the consideration of 1) the motives of wrongdoing; 2) the frame of mind of the wrongdoer; 3) the kind of people to whom he does wrong. Wrongdoing is defined as voluntarily inflicting injury contrary to the law ... Its motives arise from human actions generally, which are *voluntary* or *involuntary*.
>
> ibid.: xxxv

In forensic oratory the 'person' is the object of rhetorical persuasion in terms of the voluntary or involuntary actions which led to the wrongdoing.[11] By such techniques the accused is made answerable as to whether or not the incident was 'freely' committed. According to Hirst there is an obvious connection between the personalist metaphysics and legal norms:

> The categories which organise an inescapable social practice like law – such as contract, obligation, responsibility, fault and guilt – involve definite suppositions and beliefs about persons.
>
> HIRST, 1983: 122–123

Pêcheux finds that the subject is 'pinned down' by its enunciations despite the fact that it does not freely choose the language it 'uses'. The subject-form of discourse is preconstructed by the ideological state apparatus (Pêcheux, 1982). According to Hirst: "Lawyers and judges use categories which suppose that, except in certain specified cases of incapacity, actions arise from the consciously determined purposes of individuals" (Hirst, 1983: 123). Describing the mechanisms of 'meaning' that pin down the responsible subject Pêcheux refers to effects of 'imaginary identification' (Pêcheux, 1983: 125). The subject's 'freedom' is, in practice, sustained by certain imaginary beliefs. Social myths and other types of rhetoric serve to reinforce the accepted fictions of meaning, self, and freedom so that coherent reality may be imagined to validate 'personality'.[12] The person as a 'free agent' is one example of such metaphysical rhetoric.

---

11   Thomas Wardlaw Taylor declares: "The consciousness of wrongdoing is the essential element in responsibility under the law" (Taylor, 1898: 285).

12   Indeed, the invisible interiority of 'consciousness' may function to perpetuate certain ideologies of agency that serve to mis-represent the institutional sources of 'personality'. "Personality is, for the law, conscious being in relation to a certain environment. Consciousness and position are both necessary to it, indeed the relation between them is personality" (Taylor, 1898: 285). Taylor, however, does not objectively establish how this 'conscious being' is aware of its personality. Thus, he does not broach the problem of legal ideology.

Hirst cites the anthropological research of E.E. Evans-Pritchard (1902–1973) to suggest that even 'advanced' cultures may employ prescientific beliefs associated with magic and witchcraft. According to Hirst 'we' (members of 'developed' society) believe that conscious acts of choice exist in much the same way that the Zande people of Central Africa were documented followers of the occult (i.e., as superstitious devotees).

> Evans-Pritchard was provoked to say: 'Witches, as the Azande conceive them, clearly cannot exist'. All of us believe this. But can we say, examining our own beliefs with as much scepticism as we can muster, that conscious acts of 'choice' exist. We 'believe' in them as much as the Azande believe in witchcraft.
>
> HIRST, 1983: 123

Pêcheux, Lacan, Skinner, and Hirst all seem to arrive at the same conclusion – albeit using different concepts – the 'free' subject is a myth. This myth survives because ideologies of agency – supporting 'personality' dogma (i.e., subjective evidence) – appear so essential to everyday *beliefs* about social reality. Hirst writes:

> The human psyche is therefore inconceivable as an integral 'subject' coincident with consciousness ... Theories of the social agent cannot conceive individuals as necessarily unitary subjects centred in a determinative consciousness. This point is evident if the results of ethnography and cultural analysis (which reveal *other* modes of conceiving and specifying social agents) and of psychoanalysis (which challenges the view of the subject as self-possessed by consciousness) are taken into account.
>
> ibid.: 124–125

Hirst's reference to Evans-Pritchard regarding the 'witchcraft' of free agency is an important observation which concerns the myths of subjectivity encountered in so-called advanced societies. The state apparatus supports certain beliefs associated with the person as 'cause of itself', however, as Pêcheux maintains such ideological activity depends on imaginary forms of discourse (Pêcheux, 1982). According to Barthes grammar and writing determine certain forms of ideological representation that are conveyed linguistically by the 'persons' of grammar.

> It is understood that this first person is *imaginary* ... Writing is precisely
> that space in which the persons of grammar and the origins of discourse
> mingle, combine, and lose each other until they are unidentifiable: writ-
> ing is the truth not of the person (of the author), but of language.
>
> BARTHES, 1988: 8

Myth functions in contemporary society via rhetorical practices of conviction-
persuasion and the origin of rhetoric as an 'art', according to Barthes, is derived
from certain juridical matters (i.e., the ideological superstructure). "Rhetoric
(as a metalanguage) was born in the legal actions concerning property"
(ibid.: 16). The practice of rhetoric allowed dominant groups in society to control particular forms of speech activity: "Rhetoric is that privileged technique
(since one must pay in order to acquire it) which permits the ruling classes to
gain *ownership of speech*". (ibid.: 13–14). Various rhetorical devices (including
myths, polemic, oratory 'arguments' &c.) could then be used, by those who
were suitably trained, to establish and maintain political power.[13] Hence, the
value of rhetoric as the 'art of persuasion' which constitutes a set of strategies
to *convince* the audience/reader of a text that it is 'true'. The chimerical stories
that circulate in society as myths persuade free subjects to voluntarily accept
certain forms of social subjugation (e.g., structures of stratification). Barthes
suggests narrative systems function to bind form (i.e., syntax/grammar) and
meaning (i.e. semantics) via everyday language.[14] Individuals are then situated
syntactically in relation to the mythical narratives which supposedly represent
reality in forms of imaginary meaning.

> Language proper can be defined by the concurrence of two fundamental
> processes: articulation, or segmentation, which produces units (this what
> Benveniste calls form) and integration, which collects these units of a
> higher rank (this is meaning). This double process is recognizable in the
> language of narrative, which also knows an articulation and an integra-
> tion, a form and a meaning.
>
> BARTHES, 1988: 128[15]

---

13   As forms of ideology social myths produce a fictional (imaginary) 'depiction' of lived
      experience and because they appear 'correct' these beliefs are typically unquestioned
      and, as such, 'perceived-accepted suffered' (cf. Althusser, 2005; Pêcheux, 1982).

14   Barthes' system of narration appears to exemplify the structural duplicity that Herbert/
      Pêcheux outlines in terms of syntactic and semantic ideologies (see chapter one).

15   See chapter fifteen for further information regarding the linguistic research of Émile
      Benveniste.

While his theory of narration may appear convincing, Barthes assumes grammar and meaning are 'self-evident' structures of language without objectively explaining how they function causally. He does make some attempt to attempt to address this issue, however, his account is limited to a *rhetorical* description of 'meaningful' narratives.

> Narration can actually receive its meaning only from the world which makes use of it: beyond the narrational level begins the world, i.e., other systems (social, economic, ideological), whose terms are no longer only the narratives, but elements of another substance (historical phenomena, determinations, behaviors, etc.).
>
> ibid.: 127

Meaning, is apparently tied to a given 'situation' via Barthes 'pragmatic' account of narration which relies on certain principles of rhetoric (and relatedly social myths) to establish *accepted* beliefs.

> Linguistics knows this kind of frontier ... under the name of situation ... In the same way we can say that every narrative is dependent on a 'narrative situation,' a group of protocols according to which the narrative is 'consumed'.
>
> ibid.: 127

When an individual has been persuaded a myth is successfully 'consumed' as a legitimate belief (and this includes Barthes' 'narrative' mythology). By means of a particular speech act the subject is rhetorically ensnared – by a meaning – expressed in a mythological language. Hence Pêcheux's 'Munchausen effect', Skinner's 'indwelling agents', and the everyday occult of 'free' will that Hirst observes, are myths that are often 'automatically' adopted in matters of popular opinion.[16]

---

16   The Saussurian break separates linguistic ideologies (myths, rhetoric, and meaning) from linguistic science by demonstrating how graphic (e.g., alpabetic scripts) and phonic structures (e.g., auditory recognition of speech sounds) are ideologically associated in certain forms of psycho-social practice (cf. Pêcheux, 1983; Saussure, 1959).

Ludwig Wittgenstein (1889–1951)

The names of Ludwig Wittgenstein, and Bertrand Russell, and Gottlob Frege, appear in *Language, Semantics, and Ideology* with regard to the social implications of sense and reference, however, of these three logicians, Frege's work receives the most extensive commentary by Pêcheux. Yet, I find that Pêcheux's persistent questioning of philosophical 'knowledge' is much more closely paralleled in Wittgenstein's research than in Frege's – although Pêcheux does not propose this in either, *Language, Semantics, and Ideology* or *Automatic Discourse Analysis*, as far as I can see. Wittgenstein's objections to the practice of philosophy, as found in the *Tractatus Logico-Philosophicus*, *The Blue and Brown Books*, and *Philosophical Investigations*, suggest that much of what Pêcheux labels 'ideology' Wittgenstein calls *philosophy*. Despite the fact that Wittgenstein identifies 'grave mistakes' in the *Tractatus Logico-Philosophicus* it still contains a range of analytic criteria for linguistic phenomena that he continues to develop in later works, and foremost among these, apply to the epistemic status of 'meaning' (Wittgenstein, 1963). In this respect Wittgenstein's research 'method' is not radically different from Pêcheux's in so far as they both seek to explain how 'meaning' functions *without* recourse to ideological presuppositions, i.e., philosophies of meaning. Near the end of the *Tractatus Logico-Philosophicus* Wittgenstein writes:

> The correct method in philosophy would really be the following: to say nothing except what can be said, i.e., propositions of natural science – i.e., something that has nothing to do with philosophy – and then, whenever someone wanted to say something metaphysical, to demonstrate to him that he had failed to give a meaning to certain signs in his propositions.
>
> WITTGENSTEIN, 1974: 73–74

Philosophy is, then, 'meaningless', because only the propositions of natural science exhibit the form of a real language. Thus conceived a *philosophical* idea can serve to indicate when someone is framing an event metaphysically, vis-à-vis ideology, rather than engaging in scientific practice (i.e., philosophy – in many cases – is a sign for nonsense).[1] In the preface to the *Tractatus*

---

1 According to Althusser: "The primary function of philosophy is to draw a line of demarcation between the ideological of the ideologies on the one hand, and the scientific of the sciences on the other" (Althusser, 1990: 83).

Logico-Philosophicus Wittgenstein asserts that the work is not a textbook, yet, its aim is evidently directed towards the *correction of thought*. "The book deals with the problems of philosophy, and shows, I believe, that the reason why these problems are posed is that *the logic of our language is misunderstood*" (ibid.: 3; emphasis added). Philosophical problems are basically – according to Wittgenstein – instances of linguistic misuse, and furthermore, by their correct apprehension such problems *practically* disappear, i.e., metaphysics is replaced by the propositions of natural science. "It will therefore only be in language that the limit can be drawn, and what lies on the other side of the limit will simply be nonsense" (ibid.). Wittgenstein's linguistic analysis of philosophy is informed by the logical works of Frege and Russell to whom he attributes significant importance for the development of his own research. "... I am indebted to Frege's great works and to the writings of my friend Mr Bertrand Russell for much of the stimulation of my thoughts" (ibid.).

Wittgenstein's 'philosophical method' provides various solutions to problems that are articulated by Pêcheux in *Language, Semantics, and Ideology*. Indeed, the *Tractatus Logico-Philosophicus* presents many of the same notions that Pêcheux discusses in terms of ideology, e.g., signs, meaning, names, 'everyday language', syntax, sense, free will, and subjectivity, however, these notions are not represented by Wittgenstein metaphysically, he instead, subjects such ideas to analysis via *propositional* logic. Wittgenstein's research addresses what can be linguistically *proposed* for a given 'state of affairs' to occur *factually*. Anything outside of this 'logical space' cannot be proposed because it is not a 'fact' of such space. The propositions of logic structure the world necessarily and this is a matter of *fact*.

> The world is all that is the case ... The facts in logical space are the world ... *The world divides into facts ... In logic nothing is accidental: if a thing can occur in a state of affairs, the possibility of the state of affairs must be written into the thing itself.*
>
> ibid.: 5; emphasis added

To dispense with philosophical errors Wittgenstein suggests that propositions should be limited to what can be said in the language of natural science.[2] If sufficient attention is paid to what can be said, then, metaphysical 'accidents' will naturally be avoided.

---

2   Hence ideological propositions are forms of non-science which attempt to present unproven assumptions regarding a given 'state of affairs' as veridical knowledge.

> The method of projection is to think of the sense of the proposition ...
> I call the sign with which we express a thought a propositional sign ...
> What constitutes a propositional sign is that it in its elements (the words)
> stand in a determinate relation to one another. A propositional sign is a
> fact.
>
> ibid.: 11–12

Objects that cannot be proposed are, therefore, external to the 'logical space' of facts (and thus outside of *real* consideration). Philosophical mistakes regarding the use of language typically arise when signs do not represent the facts of a given situation (i.e., when the signifier does not represent the signified – in Saussure's terms). According to Wittgenstein language permits numerous 'modes of signification' due the arbitrary nature of signifying structures, i.e., signs may point to – indicate – things that are not facts of propositional logic.[3] "So one and the same sign (written or spoken, etc.) can be common to two different symbols – in which case they will signify in different ways ... *For the sign, of course, is arbitrary*" (ibid.: 15; emphasis added). The arbitrary nature of the sign is a core principle of the Saussurian break found in the *Course in General Linguistics* and although Wittgenstein does not appear to cite Saussure directly in the *Tractatus Logico-Philosophicus* he clearly ascertains that the arbitrary nature of the sign is the source of various philosophical mistakes.[4]

> In everyday language it very frequently happens that the same word has
> different modes of signification – and so belongs to different symbols – or
> that two words that have different modes of signification are employed in
> propositions in what is superficially the same way.
>
> ibid.

The arbitrary nature of the sign (Principle I) together with the linear nature of the signifier (Principle II) are presented in Saussure's *Course in General Linguistics* as fundamental precepts of semiology.

---

3 In consequence, the un/conscious misuse of language may lead to factual errors via inexact propositions which do not represent how a state of affairs really 'works'.

4 Roy Harris notes: "Although some people in Wittgenstein's circle of acquaintance (C.K. Ogden, for example) were undoubtedly familiar with Sausssure's *Cours de linguistique générale*, there is no indication Wittgenstein had ever read it. If he had, he never referred to it in his writings, and those who knew Wittgenstein do not recall discussing Saussure with him ... There is general agreement, however, on the revolutionary impact of the mature work of both in their respective fields" (Harris, 1990: 1–2).

Principle I: The Arbitrary Nature of the Sign. The bond between signifier and signified is arbitrary. Since I mean by sign the whole that results from the associating of the signifier with the signified, I can simply say: *the linguistic sign is arbitrary*.

SAUSSURE, 1959: 67

Principle II defines the *linearity* of signifiers in 'spatio-temporal' terms:

Principle II: The Linear Nature of the Signifier. The signifier, being audi-tory, is unfolded solely in time from which it gets the following charac-teristics: (a) it represents a span, and (b) the span is measurable in one dimension; it is a line ... Its importance equals that of Principle I; the whole mechanism of language depends upon it ... This feature becomes readily apparent when ... in writing ... the spatial line of graphic marks is substituted for succession in time.

ibid.: 70

Both Saussure and Wittgenstein posit that linguistic signs do not exist in a state of strict necessity with what they represent, i.e., symbolic structures are – to a certain extent – arbitrarily determined. To understand what something 'means', according to Wittgenstein, one should identify how it (i.e., the pro-posed meaning) is used symbolically in a given situation, or, in other words, designate what the meaning is *for*. "In order to recognize a symbol by its sign we must observe how it is used with a sense ... If a sign is useless, it is meaningless" (Wittgenstein, 1974: 16). Wittgenstein, in the *Tractatus Logico-Philosophicus*, then outlines a broadly pragmatic theory of language based on *certain prop-ositions* which define logic of language. "A propositional sign, applied and thought out, is a thought. A thought is a proposition with a sense. The totality of propositions is language" (ibid.: 19). As I stated above Wittgenstein appears to discern that language is often ideologically mis/recognized in day-to-day use given that its real mechanisms often escape cognition.[5]

Man possesses the ability to construct languages capable of expressing every sense, *without having any idea how each word has meaning or what its meaning is – just as people speak without knowing how the individual*

---

5   Meaning effects may appear 'self-evident', yet, how a given meaning is generated is not typi-cally revealed by the verbal system that is assumed to convey significant implications in use (e.g., the structure of 'ordinary language'). Thus, meaning seems to function by certain un/ conscious presuppositions which are adopted in various forms of ideological practice.

> *sounds are produced.* Everyday language is part of the human organism
> and is no less complicated than it.
>
> ibid.; emphasis added

Such misunderstandings result in an abundance of 'meaningless' or, as
Wittgenstein calls it, 'useless' language where sense and reference are not
thought via *propositional* logic. Moreover, Wittgenstein suggests this lack of
'sense' may be due to various epistemic problems concerning the adequacy of
a given language to represent a state of affairs without any kind of implicit or
explicit bias from existing linguistic structures (e.g., preconceived ideas).

> *Language disguises thought.* So much so, that from the outward form of
> the clothing it is impossible to infer the form of the thought beneath it,
> beneath it, because the outward form of the clothing is not designed to
> reveal the form of the body, but for entirely different purposes. *The tacit
> conventions on which the understanding of everyday language depends are
> enormously complicated.*
>
> ibid.; emphasis added

A useless proposition may be tacitly accepted and, for Wittgenstein, this is
clearly evinced by the practice of 'philosophy'.

> Most of the propositions and questions to be found in philosophical
> works are not false but nonsensical. Consequently we cannot give any
> answer to questions of this kind, but can only point out that they are non-
> sensical. Most of the propositions and questions of philosophers arise
> from out of failure to understand the logic of our language ... And it is
> not surprising that the deepest problems are in fact not problems at all.
>
> ibid.

In this sense philosophy mis/represents what can be thought by voicing
accepted 'nonsense'. Evidently philosophy is, then, a form of ideological practice which is quite distinct from natural science.

> The totality of true propositions is the whole of natural science (or the
> whole corpus of the natural sciences). *Philosophy is not one of the natural
> sciences.* (The word 'philosophy' must mean something whose place is
> above or below the natural sciences, not beside them.).
>
> ibid.: 25; emphasis added

For philosophy to be 'above' science that would make it supernatural – and if it is below – prescientific. By either definition philosophy has the characteristics of an ideological practice. Despite the fact that philosophy is not a science, according to Wittgenstein, it continues to serve a critical function for certain epistemological reasons:

> Philosophy aims at the logical clarification of thoughts ... Philosophy sets limits to the much disputed sphere of natural science. It must set limits to what can be thought; and, in doing so, to what cannot be thought. It must set limits to what cannot be thought by working outwards through what can be thought.
>
> ibid.

By setting limits to what can be thought, philosophy, in Wittgenstein's approach, is deconstructed vis-à-vis natural science, however, by the same criteria – this suggests that everyday language is nonsense.[6] *"The limits of my language* mean the limits of my world ... We cannot think what we cannot think; so what we cannot think we cannot *say* either" (ibid.: 56–57). If one's speech and thought are circumscribed by vernacular forms of language it follows that the 'worldview' presented by this system of 'meaning' will be – in various ways – ideological. Moreover, Wittgenstein maintains, as does Pechêux, that the 'subject' is a fiction. "There is no such thing as the subject that thinks or entertains ideas" (ibid.: 57). Wittgenstein's 'propositional logic' appears to follow a mechanical schema whereby what is proposed functions logically as an interconnected system of axiomatic statements.[7] Hence Wittgenstein's research appears – in principle – to agree with the non-subjective theory of language that Pêcheux outlines in *Language, Semantics and Ideology*. According to Wittgenstein:

> Mechanics determines one form of description of the world by saying that all propositions used in the description of the world must be obtained in a given way from a given set of propositions – the axioms of mechanics.
>
> ibid.: 68

---

6 Ordinary language – following Wittgenstein – is ineffective because it leads to equivocation, misunderstandings, and other spurious forms of linguistic practice. Consequently, such activity invariably causes various attributional 'accidents' via various forms of nonsense.

7 Wittgenstein's notion of 'useless' propositions appears to typify those descriptive systems which do not, in fact, represent what they supposedly denote, i.e., a symbolic structure is being misused to represent something that cannot be represented by the form of language employed. For example, a physical problem cannot be solved in the language of metaphysics.

Wittgenstein thus advances an account of language that is broadly *mechanical* in nature:

> If I know an object I also know all its possible occurrences in states of affairs (Every one of these possibilities must be part of the nature of the object.)... Every statement about complexes can be resolved into a statement about their constituents and into the propositions that describe the complexes completely.
>
> ibid.: 6–7

In the abstract to "Wittgenstein's Aeronautical Investigation" Ian Lemco writes:

> After a rigorous German education in the physical sciences, young Ludwig Wittgenstein entered Manchester University as an aeronautical engineering research student. There he devised and patented a novel aero-engine employing an airscrew propeller driven by blade tip-jets.
>
> LEMCO, 2006: 39

Furthermore, "Hertz's rigorous approach to science argued for in his book *The Principles of Mechanics* much impressed Wittgenstein" (ibid.).[8] Wittgenstein's 'philosophy' was then – to a certain extent – anti-philosophical:

> Wittgenstein retained throughout his life an interest in the logic of machines. Engineering is not absent from his later philosophical writings, for example when using metaphors to get over his linguistic ideas.
>
> ibid.: 49

The *Tractatus Logico-Philosophicus* contains a number of references to physics, mechanics, and mathematics and these scientific systems clearly inform Wittgenstein's purportedly philosophical work.

> Mathematics is a method of logic ... Mechanics is an attempt to construct according to a single plan all the true propositions that we need for the description of the world ... One might say, using Hertz's terminology, that only connexions that are *subject to law are thinkable*.
>
> WITTGENSTEIN, 1974: 66–69

---

8   Heinrich Rudolp Hertz (1857–1894) – the author of *The Principles of Mechanics* – was Professor of Physics and Director of the Physics Institute in Bonn, Germany. The SI unit for frequency 'hertz' – Hz – (the number of times a repeated event occurs per second) honours his research.

Given that Wittgenstein's non-philosophical attitude towards philosophy exhibits a mechanical basis his apparent rejection of incorporeal subjectivity seems to be consistent with his early scientific training. According to Wittgenstein:

> If I wrote a book called *The World as I found it*, I should have to include a report on my body, and should have to say which parts were subordinate to my will, and which were not, etc., this being a method of isolating the subject or rather of showing that in an important sense there is no subject; for it alone could not be mentioned in that book.
>
> ibid.: 57

Applying Wittgenstein's mechanical protocols to philosophical questions seems to demonstrate that in many cases the subject is a kind of 'nonsense' in so far as it is a metaphysical belief and, therefore, logically outside the domain of scientific investigation (e.g., the subject as cause of itself).[9] In Wittgenstein's terms the subject appears to denote a 'useless' concept. "(In philosophy, 'What do we actually *use* this word or this proposition for?' repeatedly leads to valuable insights.)" (ibid.: 65; emphasis added). When the word 'subject' is used what is being done with this word? What is being proposed logically in terms of 'subjectivity'? Typically, nothing that would lead to formulation in scientific language. "When the answer cannot be put into words, neither can the question be put into words. *The riddle* does not exist. If a question can be framed at all, it is also possible to answer it" (ibid.: 73). The 'problems' of philosophy, are not, in fact real problems but rather misunderstandings that persist as abstruse speculations.

> The solution of philosophical problems can be compared with a gift in a fairy tale: in the magic castle it appears enchanted and if you look at it outside in daylight it is nothing but an ordinary bit of iron (or something of the sort).
>
> WITTGENSTEIN, 1978: 11e

---

9   Questions regarding the subject and forms of subjectivity (e.g., the ethical subject, the subject of history, the transcendental subject &c.) are perennial philosophical concerns, yet, they are not matters that admit of scientific solutions. Hence the discipline of philosophy is furnished with its own lexicon which is not a scientific language. "Traditional philosophy can provide answers to its own *questions*, it does not provide answers to scientific, or other, *problems* – in the sense which scientists solve their problems" (Althusser, 1990: 81).

If philosophical questions appear 'timeless' this is, Wittgenstein suggests, due to a lack of real – as opposed to figmental – linguistic problem-solving.[10]

> People say again and again that philosophy doesn't really progress, that we are still occupied with the same philosophical problems as were the Greeks. But the people who say this don't understand why it has to be so. It is because our language has remained the same and keeps seducing us into asking the same questions.
>
> ibid.: 15e

For Wittgenstein, the problems of philosophy are inseparable from – redundant – forms of grammar and 'literary' devices such as metaphor.

> As long as there continues to be a verb 'to be' that looks as if it functions in the same way as 'to eat' and 'to drink', as long as we still continue to talk of a river of time, of an expanse of space, etc., etc., people will keep stumbling over the same puzzling difficulties and find themselves staring at something which no explanation seems capable of clearing up.
>
> ibid.

Pêcheux/Herbert suggests that ideology functions in terms of syntactic and semantic beliefs which function as 'guarantees' of reality (see chapter one). Much Wittgenstein's work also follows this critical approach in so far he finds that the 'meaning' of ordinary language is frequently misunderstood due to 'ordinary' conventions.

> *Language sets everyone the same traps*; it is an immense network of easily accessible wrong turnings ... What I have to do then is erect signposts at all the junctions where there are wrong turnings so as to help people past the danger points.
>
> WITTGENSTEIN, 1978: 18e; emphasis added

Linguistic 'traps' are none other than examples of misuse or mis/recognition regarding given practices of everyday language e.g., what Wittgenstein calls

---

10 In this sense philosophy is an index of problems without *real* solutions because philosophical discourse cannot *represent* the structure of a science.

philosophical 'nonsense'.[11] Moreover, Wittgenstein's account of 'dogma' provides a description of how ideology functions that parallels some of Pêcheux's work on unconscious subjection.

> People will live under an absolute, palpable tyranny, though without being able to say they are not free ... For dogma is expressed in the form of an assertion, and is unshakeable, but at the same time any practical opinion can be made to harmonize with it ... It is not a *wall* setting limits to be what can be believed, but more like a *brake* which, however, practically serves the same purpose; it's almost as though someone were to attach a weight to your foot to restrict your freedom of movement. This is how dogma becomes irrefutable and beyond the reach of attack.
>
> ibid.: 28e

In *Language, Semantics, and Ideology* Pêcheux writes:

> Let me simply point out that the common feature of these two structures called respectively ideology and the unconscious is the fact that they conceal their own existence within their operation by producing a web of 'subjective' evident truths, 'subjective' here meaning not 'affecting the subject' but in which the subject is constituted.
>
> PÊCHEUX, 1982: 104

As noted above Wittgenstein's 'philosophy' is informed by his understanding of mechanical principles to the degree that he dismisses most philosophical questions as nonsensical. Paul Henry maintains that Pêcheux also found the discipline of philosophy sorely lacking in objectivity:

> Pêcheux was a philosopher by training, but for reasons which were deeply rooted in his personal history and family background, he was a philosopher who was fascinated by machines, instruments and technologies ... *He was a philosopher who was convinced that the classical practice*

---

11 Following the work of Saussure, Pêcheux, Skinner and Austin, philosophical non-sense is the basis of 'ordinary language'. For example, the normative conventions of grammar convey metaphysical assumptions that are performatively realized in speech acts. Vernacular forms of communication auto-construct certain ideological conditions by way of simple incantations which realize associations of sound and 'meaning'. Semantic structures then appear to 'work by themselves'.

of philosophy was meaningless, or at best a failure, especially where the sciences were concerned.

HENRY, 1995: 25; emphasis added

Both Wittgenstein and Pêcheux attempted to revise the philosophy of language so that its 'problems' (i.e., ideological constructs) would be correctly perceived as verbal nonsense. Pêcheux's application of Saussure's theory leads to an analysis of 'meaning' as a normative practice through which certain ideological effects are realized (e.g., the meaning of 'everyday language').[12] Wittgenstein outlines a similar view in the *The Blue and Brown Books*:

> What is the meaning of a word ... Studying the grammar of the expression 'explanation of meaning' will teach you something about the grammar of the word 'meaning' and will cure you of the temptation to look about you for some object which you might call 'the meaning'.
>
> WITTGENSTEIN, 1969: 1

Wittgenstein maintains that a given meaning is always *realized in use*, that is, meaning is an effect of how a given language is used within certain circumstances. In 'normal' conditions, however, meaning appears self-evident, yet this is because individuals rely on words (with assumed meanings) that occult the process of semantic production.

> It seems that there are *certain definite* mental processes bound up with the working of language, processes through which language alone can function. I mean the process of understanding and meaning ... These latter activities seem to take place in a queer kind of medium, the mind; and the mechanism of the mind, the nature of which, it seems, we don't quite understand, can bring about effects which no material mechanism could.
>
> ibid.: 3

Meaning does not exist 'in the mind', for Wittgenstein, it may seem that way superficially, however, that is not how signifiers signify. According to Wittgenstein:

---

12   Saussure's epistemological break in the field of linguistics establishes a conceptual system for differentiating *langue* from *parole* which thus permits a structural analysis of social norms vis-à-vis the formal properties of linguistic structures (e.g., syntax, semantics, and pragmatics).

> Without a sense, or without the thought, a proposition would be an utterly dead and trivial thing ... But if we had to name anything which is the life of the sign, we should have to say that it was its *use*. ... The sign (the sentence) gets its significance from the system of signs, from the language to which it belongs. Roughly: understanding a sentence means understanding a language.
>
> ibid.: 4–5

What is 'meant' by a sentence (i.e., its significance) is a result of how it is used vis-à-vis socially accepted signs.[13]

> *It is misleading then to talk of thinking as of a 'mental activity'. We may say that thinking is essentially the activity of operating with signs.* This activity is performed by the hand, when we think by writing; by the mouth and larynx, when we think by speaking; and if we think by imagining signs or pictures, I can give you no agent that thinks.
>
> ibid.: 6; emphasis added

The 'mental' ('a queer kind of medium') is an occult domain for Wittgenstein in so far it mystifies a real process, i.e., the operation of signs.

> If then you say that in such cases the mind thinks, I would only draw your attention to the fact that you are using a metaphor, that here the mind is an agent in a different sense from that in which the hand can be said to be the agent in writing.
>
> ibid.: 6–7

Here Wittgenstein does not want to fall into the linguistic trap of attributing the source of thought to an ideal subject. Skinner ('indwelling agents'), Pêcheux ('subject as cause of itself'), and Hirst ('metaphysics of the person') also advance similar descriptions of mystified 'mental activity'. For Wittgenstein, use of the word 'mind' is evidence of an individual who is trained to express metaphysical ideas, i.e., they have been taught to use signs *philosophically*. In the *Blue Book* he outlines how one may have learnt the meaning of 'yellow'. 'Yellow' is basically an effect of repeated association or the application of a rule.

---

13   The principal effect of ideology is to represent signifying structures as always-already-accepted. The un/conscious adoption of accepted signs determines the full spectrum of semantic traps that occur within ordinary language (see chapter six).

> If we are taught the meaning of the 'yellow'... this teaching can be looked
> at in two different ways ... A. The teaching is a drill ... The drill of teaching
> could in this case said to have built up a psychical mechanism. ... B. The
> teaching may have supplied us a with a rule which is itself involved in a
> process of understanding, obeying, etc.
>
> ibid.: 12

The 'mind', by the same means, would designate the source of 'mental activity', however, this word does not represent how thinking really functions,
which, according to Wittgenstein is 'operating with signs'. The notion of
'mental' health is therefore, in this Wittgensteinian sense, misleading in so far
as it designates a 'queer kind of medium' which is typically misunderstood.
Furthermore, Wittgenstein's research suggests that if the actual language of
thinking were clearly known such ideological problems regarding 'mental'
phenomena would cease to exist.[14]

> I want you to remember that words have those meanings which we have
> given them; and we give them meanings by explanations. I may have
> given a definition of a word and used the word accordingly, or those who
> taught me the use the word may have given me the explanation.
>
> ibid.: 27

Evidently meaning is a result of practical human activity, yet, what something
means can, upon closer inspection, provide a less than adequate explanation of a particular state of affairs. This is because, according to Wittgenstein,
meaning is constructed and instituted by certain performative practices. In
consequence, a given meaning may be decidedly *unuseful* as in the case of the
word 'mind' when referring to the activity of thinking.

> But let's not forget that a word hasn't got a meaning given to it, as it were,
> by a power independent of us, so that there could be a kind of scientific
> investigation into what the word *really* means. A word has the meaning
> someone has given it.
>
> ibid.: 28

---

14   Quite simply metaphysical 'mental' activity is another example, for Wittgenstein, of lin-
      guistic misuse. Thus individuals may refer to the mind as a source of agency, when, for
      better or worse, they are operating with signs to think.

'Meaning' is structured via *use* and does not pre-exist such fulfilment in a mental domain which is 'always-already-there' (see chapter one).

> Let us sum up: If we scrutinize the usages which we make of such words as 'thinking', 'meaning', 'wishing', etc., going through this process rids us of the temptation to look for a peculiar act of thinking, independent of the act of expressing our thoughts, and stowed away in some particular medium.
>
> ibid.: 43

In *The Brown Book* Wittgenstein suggests that learning a language is very much akin to being trained perform a certain act.

> The child learns this language from the grown-ups by being trained to its use. I am using the word 'trained' in a way strictly analogous to that in which we talk of an animal being trained to do certain things. It is done by means of example, reward, punishment, and such-like.
>
> ibid.: 77

What is called 'meaning' is then a result of practical training in the use of words (i.e., lexical usage) such that an individual's 'individual' thought then manifests such priming.

> We think of the meaning of signs sometimes as states of mind of the man using them, sometimes as the role which these signs are playing in a system of language. The connection between these two ideas is that the mental experiences which accompany the use of a sign undoubtedly are caused by our usage of the sign in a particular system of language.
>
> ibid.: 78

Whatever is defined as 'mental experience', however, cannot pre-exist how one is trained to 'think'. Furthermore, according to Wittgenstein, the symbolic systems a person learns via pedagogy are an example of what he calls 'language games'.

> Children are taught their native tongue by means of such games, and they even have the entertaining character of games. We are not, however, regarding the language games we describe as incomplete parts of language, but as languages complete in themselves, as complete systems of human communication.
>
> ibid.: 80

Meaning is thus a kind of language game where the rules are established by customary usage.[15] More advanced language games, according to Wittgenstein, coincide with more advanced forms of training.

> When the boy or grown-up learns what one might call special techni-
> cal languages, e.g., the use of charts and diagrams, descriptive geometry,
> chemical symbolism, etc., he learns more language games ... The pic-
> ture we have of the grown-up is that of a nebulous mass of language, his
> mother tongue, surrounded by discrete and more or less clear-cut lan-
> guage games, the technical languages.
>
>   ibid.

A rudimentary dialect may be distributed throughout the communicative networks of a given population and, more or less, fully determine what is collectively understood vis-à-vis accepted norms of interaction. "To keep this point of view in mind, it very often is useful to imagine such a simple language to be the entire system of communication of a tribe in a primitive state of society" (ibid.). Without paying careful attention to *how* words function one is liable to become subjected to them ostensibly via 'demonstrated' acts of definition.

> Naming appears as a *queer* connexion of a word with an object. – And
> you really get such a queer connexion when the philosopher tries to bring
> out *the* relation between name and thing by staring at an object in front
> of him and repeating a name or even the word 'this' innumerable times.
> For philosophical problems arise when language *goes on holiday.*
>
>   WITTGENSTEIN, 1963; emphasis added

Although Wittgenstein is often described as a 'philosopher' it is evident he finds the discipline of philosophy to be methodologically problematic. Philosophy does not employ a scientific language. Indeed there are various philosophical terms and particular vocabularies – e.g., 'continental' vs 'analytic' – in use, however, these do not constitute law-governed system. "A philosophical problem has the form: 'I don't know my way about'" (ibid.: 49^e). Philosophy, broadly construed, is simply an exercise in speculation.

---

15   Evidently the meaning of a language may be unconsciously 'used' to communicate a given
     state of affairs, e.g., a set of meanings is performed automatically in so far as what is 'meant'
     is the result of specific forms of training. In such cases 'correct' meaning would represent
     appropriate priming. This outcome is clearly established by the norms of grammar.

> Philosophy simply puts everything before us, and neither explains nor
> deduces anything. Since everything lies open to view there is nothing to
> explain ... One might also give the name 'philosophy' to what is possible
> before all new discoveries and inventions.
>
>   ibid.: 50e

The problem of 'meaning' appears so often in Wittgenstein's work because
everyday language is, like philosophy, unacceptably ambiguous. Meaning, to
paraphrase Wittgenstein, has the form: 'I don't know my way about' in real languages (i.e., meaning is a philosophy). Furthermore, Wittgenstein suggests that
the transmission of meaning may be culturally specific in so far as its acceptance is not strictly necessary and appears to involve the voluntary recognition
of certain 'feelings'. "The familiar physiognomy of a word, the feeling that it
has taken up its meaning into itself, that it is an actual likeness of its meaning – there could be human beings to whom all this was alien" (ibid.: 218e). In
this sense the 'familiarity' of what a word *means* is the result of specific forms
of training. "Wittgenstein holds in *Philosophical Investigations* that the ordinary use of language is a way of behaving, that the various uses of language
represent different kinds of behavior of which assertion is but one" (Brown,
1974: 22). 'Ordinary' meaning is thus a form of linguistic behavior which has
been established via social practice. According to Pêcheux ideology is un/con-
sciously adopted in acts of normative conditioning. Such pre-defined meanings are legitimated by institutional structures.[16] Wittgenstein in the *Blue and
Brown Books* and *Philosophical Investigations* provides a number of examples
where language use is a direct consequence of certain forms of training. This
social conditioning shapes the behavior that individuals exhibit verbally, i.e.,
syntax and semantics are the result of being trained to identify and articulate
objects according to prescribed rules of usage (e.g., *langue* vis-à-vis *parole*).
While Wittgenstein does not appear to refer to the work of Saussure it is evident that Wittgenstein's research expresses a cognate understanding of such
'associated' structures in terms of the accepted 'modes of signification' that are
used to connect meaning and behavior in ordinary language.

---

16   According to Pêcheux the pre-definition of meaning requires certain forms of institu-
     tional support, e.g., ideological state apparatuses, which lead a given individual to *believe*
     in the veracity of ordinary language (Pêcheux, 1982).

CHAPTER 10

Zellig Harris (1909–1992)

The research of Zellig S. Harris was of great significance to Pêcheux for the development of his materialist theory of discourse. "Harris provides the main inspiration for Pêcheux's method of analysis, even if it is somewhat heteroclite" (Gadet, *et al.*, 1995: 52). Pêcheux adapted Harris' distributional theories of language with the aim of producing experimental results via automatic discourse analysis.

> He outlines a theory of meaning as an effect of metaphoric relations (of selection and substitution) which are specific for (the conditions of production of) an utterance or a text ... Precisely because of this exclusion of pre-given meanings, Harris's method of discourse analysis fitted Pêcheux's need of a *formal* instrument.
>
> HELSLOOT & HAK, 1995: 13–14

In "Discourse Analysis" (1952) (published in the journal *Language* by the Linguistic Society of America) Harris suggests that meaning is not subjectively defined: instead 'meaning' is equivalent to the occurrence of morphemes in discourse ('meaning' is thus a numerical relation: a frequency).

> This paper presents a method for the analysis of connected speech (or writing). The method is formal, depending only on the occurrence of morphemes as distinguishable elements; it does not depend on the analyst's knowledge of the particular meaning of each morpheme.
>
> HARRIS, 1952: 1

Harris deliberately avoids the ideological problem of subjective 'expression' by excluding semantic criteria from his analysis.[1] Harris does not assume to apprehend meaning 'in-itself', in his account, meaning is a rate of frequency between linguistic events (e.g., sound and syntax).

---

1   Morphemes are typically assumed to represent the smallest lexical units that convey 'meaning', yet, Harris declines to follow this conventional approach to the study of language by 'bracketing' the problem of what a word *supposedly* means in his attempt to define *how* it may mean something or other. Harris does not suppose that morphemes naturally 'possess' meaning: he posits that 'meaning' is realized when a speech act and a situation 'correspond'.

As a result of this, we discover the particular interrelations of the morphemes of the text as they occur in that one text; and in so doing we
discover something of the structure of the text, of what is being done in
it. We may not know just WHAT a text is saying, but we can discover HOW
it is saying – what are the patterns of recurrence of its chief morphemes.
ibid.

According to Pêcheux in *Automatic Discourse Analysis* certain theoretical
anomalies – such as 'meaning' – appear in the science of language that are
related to existing institutional norms:

But, as is the rule in the history of science, the retreat by which linguistics establishes its scientificity leaves uncovered the territory it has aban-
doned, *the questions which linguistics has to refuse to answer continue to
be asked for both theoretical and practical reasons*: 'What does this text
mean?'; 'What meaning does this text contain?'; 'How does the meaning
of this text differ from that of another text?'.
PÊCHEUX, 1995: 64; emphasis added

'Meaning' persists in institutionally guaranteed discourse and Pêcheux establishes this a direct consequence of misrecognizing the epistemological break
made by Saussure (Pêcheux, 1995). For Pêcheux, meaning remains part of linguistics as a pre-scientific *philosophy* of language (i.e., meaning is a theoretical ideology). Recall Pêcheux/Herbert's dictum "all science – regardless of its
current level of development and its place in the theoretical structure ... is
principally a science of ideology from which it is detached" (see chapter one).
This foundational statement is conceptually parallel to Fichant's version: "A
science detached from its history, such is the condition of a real history of science" (Fichant, 1969). The science of language, in Pêcheux's view, was inaugurated by achieving a rupture with the ideology of meaning. Harris' research
advances this disjunction by attempting to eliminate subjective interpretations of 'meaning' in his discourse analysis.

*The operations make no use of any knowledge concerning the meaning of
the morphemes* or intent or conditions of the author ... Discourse analysis
yields considerable information about the structure of text or a type of
text, and about the role that each element plays in such a structure.
HARRIS.: 1952: 30; emphasis added

Harris, then, does not speculate regarding what the text might 'mean' he assesses how it functions to produce a given structure of discourse.[2]

> Definite patterns may be discovered for particular texts, or for the particular persons, styles, or subject-matters. In some cases, formal conclusions can be drawn from the particular pattern of *morpheme distribution* in a text. And often it is possible to show consistent differences of structure between the discourses of different persons, or in different styles, or about different subject-matters.
>
> ibid.: 1; emphasis added

Discourse analysis, as it is defined by Harris, is an attempt to resolve the theoretical limitations of 'descriptive linguistics':

> The problem. One can approach discourse analysis from two types of problem, which turn out to be related. The first is the problem of continuing beyond the limits of a single sentence at at time. The other is the question of correlating 'culture' and language (i.e. non-linguistic and linguistic behavior)... The first problem arises because descriptive linguistics generally stops at sentence boundaries ... The other problem, that of the connection between behavior (or social situation) and language, has always been considered beyond the scope of linguistics proper.
>
> ibid.: 1–2

Harris uses the concept of 'distribution' to resolve these limitations.[3] Discourse is related to a given social situation in terms of its 'distribution'. A given discourse may be correlated with various social situations in relation to the specific linguistic units that are used as criteria of measurement for such distributions (e.g., phonic, graphic, and syntactic structures).

> Harris' objective was to discover *recurring sequences* as a basis for establishing a classification of categories at the different levels of phonology, morphology and syntax. This involved an empirical analysis of repetition,

---

2 Clearly, structures of speech activity (i.e., written or verbal patterns of lingusitic recurrence) can be studied apart from what they supposedly mean in a given social situation: discourse can be represented objectively. This is the basic *matter* of linguistic science.

3 For Harris the concept of 'distribution' attempts to exhibit possible correlations between structures of discourse and social behavior. Thus his research suggests how a given context may evince patterns of 'meaning' (normative interaction) between persons.

of the referential notions of vocabulary organisation, coupled with objec-
tifying the 'semantic' fields on which they were based. ... To be able to
address the point where these regularisations carry meaning can be the
objective of the hypotheses of the discourse analyst ....

WILLIAMS, 1999: 217–218; emphasis added

Williams draws attention to the fact that Harris sought to identify 'recurring
sequences' of linguistic behavior rather than self-evident manifestations of
'meaning'.[4] In "Transformations in Linguistic Structure" Harris writes:

Since many people have questioned the attitude of formal linguistics to
meaning, I should remark that *the avoidance of defining linguistic relations on the basis of meaning is not because meaning is considered to be
pointless. It is because we are trying, among other things, to discover a formal basis or correlate to meaning rather than to assume meaning as an
undefined linguistic primitive.*

HARRIS, 1964: 420; emphasis added

Pêcheux in *Automatic Discourse Analysis* defines 'discourse theory as a theory
of the historical determination of semantic processes' (Pêcheux, 1995: 123).
A given semantic process is a specific pattern of recurrent lexical distribution
within a given context, however, such distribution does not constitute meaning
in-itself.[5] In Pêcheux's terms semantic processes are historically determined
by discursive formations subject to institutional recognition, and, as such, are
structurally defined by normative social conditions.[6] Harris' groundwork in
"Discourse Analysis" evidently serves as prototype for Pêcheux's research of
discursive formations. Harris states:

The nature of the method. We have raised two problems: that of the distributional relations among sentences, and that of the correlation between
language and social situation. We have proposed that information

---

4   Harris evidently follows empirical principles in his research, but he is not a semantic empir-
    icist, i.e., he does not assume that meaning is a pre-defined reality for linguistic phenomena.
    Thus, Harris is not a linguistic 'idealist'.
5   Meaning 'in-itself' appears in religion, philosophy, and other metaphysical beliefs. The work
    of Saussure, Harris, and Pêcheux attempts to free linguistic analysis from such myths.
6   For example, the ideological apparatus guarantees the 'meaning' of the official language that
    is prescribed by the nation-state.

relevant to both of these can be obtained by a formal analysis of one stretch of discourse at a time.

HARRIS, 1952: 4–5

Broadly considered, Harris' distributional method is a technique for correlating speech activity with particular social situations. In Saussure's research such relations are called 'co-ordinations' (syntagmatic and associative):[7]

> In discourse, on the one hand, words acquire relations based on the linear nature of language because they are chained together ... Combinations supported by linearity are *syntagms* ... We see that the co-ordinations formed outside discourse differ strikingly from those formed inside. Those formed outside discourse are not supported by linearity. Their seat is in the brain; they are part of the inner storehouse that makes up the language of each speaker. They are *associative relations*.
>
> SAUSSURE, 1959: 123

Saussure uses an architectural example to illustrate how such associative and syntagmatic relations are established:

> From the associative and syntagmatic viewpoint a linguistic unit is like a fixed part of a building, e.g. a column. On the one hand, the column has a certain relation to the architrave that it supports; the arrangement of the two units in space suggests the syntagmatic relation. On the other hand, if the column is Doric, it suggests a mental comparison of this style with others (Ionic, Corinthian, etc.) although none of these elements is present in space: the relation is associative.
>
> ibid.: 123–124

Saussure's metaphor is derived from the architecture of 'classical order' found in Ancient Greece.[8] By theoretical expansion the bifurcation of the economic

---

7 Syntagmatic co-ordinations represent graphic and phonic structures of verbal behavior (e.g., writing and speaking) whereas associative co-ordinations are the 'mental' representations of such events.

8 Althusser – following the work of Lacan – posits that the symbolic order of language has 'two stories' or 'tiers'. The first level is phonological (i.e, auditory structures) and above this is the second level of signification (i.e., units of meaning) (Althusser, 1996). To some extent Pêcheux uses the research developed by Harris to explain how such 'levels' of language are combined in discursive formations.

base and the ideological superstructure may be viewed as an 'ordered' schema of syntagmatic and associative relations distributed socially.[9] Darian Wallis states:

> One of the most important, recent theoretical attempts to bridge the gap between ideology and language is the work of the late Michel Pêcheux ... Pêcheux claimed that linguistic meaning is historically determined ... Thus a word or expression does not have a single meaning proper to it, but changes meaning in passing from one discursive formation to another.
>
> WALLIS, 1998 21

Semantic distributions appear to follow associative co-ordinations of syntagma embedded in social interaction (e.g., Chomsky's concept of generative grammar). "The discourse of one individual has no meaning in itself; it must be related to other discourses representative of the same position" (ibid.: 22). In an unpublished manuscript provisionally titled *The Direction of Social Change* Harris states:

> Descriptions and histories of societies suggest that the directly relevant entities for a consideration of social structure are not individuals and interpersonal relations, but certain kinds of (fixed or shifting) groups of individuals ... the participation of the individual is not arbitrary or entirely free, but is with or like others of his subsets in the population (for as long as he is a member of those subsets).
>
> HARRIS (n.d.): 10

Therefore, such groups would therefore share similar syntagmatic and associative relations based on certain forms of speech activity (e.g., lexical distributions in relation to socio-economic differences). Pêcheux notes that the epistemological basis for automatic discourse analysis was derived from four domains: historical materialism, linguistics, and discourse theory, 'traversed and articulated' by 'a theory subjectivity, and that theory is of a psychoanalytic nature' (Pêcheux, 1995: 123). Discursive formations, for Pêcheux, provide ideological functions 'automatically' in so far as discourse structures meaning by superordinate and subordinate associative conditions. According to Pêcheux the 'matrix of meaning' is determined by the discursive formations which

---

9 In this sense the ideological state apparatus determines the 'architecture' of social order (cf. Pêcheux, 1982; Althusser, 2014).

govern the dominant modes of interaction between individuals. Hence the production of meaning is indissociable from the social apparatuses which direct the accepted forms of discourse (ibid.: 128–129). For Harris the structure of society – as a political-economic system – can be viewed as a 'bundle of particular arrangements dealing with particular functions'. Discursive formations, then, convey these social arrangements via certain forms of symbolic interaction:

> The various arrangements are in general intertwined and mutually supporting, but they can change separately under different problems and forces (which is relevant to the development and future of these systems).
>
> HARRIS, (n.d.): 12

For Harris, society is 'arranged' by the following sub-systems: 1) occupational sectors; 2) working and living conditions; 3) decision-making practices for production and consumption; 4) social status; 5) the control of social institutions and public opinion. He suggests that 'occupational groups' are more robust conceptually than 'classes' due to apparent differences amongst occupational group members that are determined linguistically.

> Among the advantages of analyzing in terms occupation rather than of 'class' in general is the ability to recognize that many individuals change their views and social character after changing their relation to production and its decision-making.
>
> ibid.: 11

Society – in a Harrisian sense – could be viewed as a certain distributional form of interaction co-extensive with particular linguistic practices. As he suggests in "Distributional Structure":

> In this sense, language can be structured in respect to various independent features. And whether it is structured ... in respect to say, regular historical change, social interaction, meaning, or distribution – is a matter decidable by investigation.
>
> HARRIS, 1954: 146

Harris then attempts to exclude both meaning and history from his theory of distribution. "Here we will discuss how each language can be described in terms of a distributional structure ... without the intrusion of other features such as history or meaning" (ibid.). Yet, speech acts are distributed amongst individuals by their rate of occurrence. Moreover, each speaker appears to function as the 'bearer' of meanings which are historically defined vis-à-vis social norms.

> Does the structure really exist in the speakers? ... A reasonable expecta-
> tion is that the distribution structure should exist in the speakers in the
> sense of reflecting their speaking habits ... They produce new combina-
> tions of these along the lines of the ones they have heard. The formation
> of new utterances in the language is therefore based on the distributional
> relations – as changeably perceived by the speakers – among parts of the
> previously heard utterances.
>
> ibid.: 149–150

A distributional structure, then, reveals a certain pattern of linguistic acts that is lexically predictable.[10] Based on such predictions, distributional structures would potentially apprehend the morphosemantic assumptions of linguistic behavior. Sound (or text) and 'meaning' may be correlated as an occurrence of linguistic behavior and this suggests that the distribution of lexical units in discourse may be an index of what Pêcheux calls 'meaning-effects'. In the article "On Grammars of Science" Harris posits that different types of language operate according to the realities they are used to represent and are, defini-tively, constrained by the structure specific to each phenomenon (i.e., different objects of representation require distinct forms of language).[11]

> More generally, the differences between science languages, natural lan-
> guage, and mathematics fit the different constraints of reality that are
> involved in the subject-matters of each of these.
>
> HARRIS, 1985: 148

Ideological structures are linked, Pêcheux notes, to the subject-form of dis-course and this imaginary relationship is represented by the meaning of

---

10   Indeed Pêcheux's research attempts establish how ideology may function 'automatically'
      in certain contexts. Thus, an individual may exhibit specific forms of 'automatic dis-
      course' in varied social situations.

11   Althusser also supports this observation: "In other words, the structure of scientific dis-
      course must differ from the structures of ideological discourse, aesthetic discourse, and
      the discourse of the unconscious. It is this difference of structure which allows us to
      characterize (and designate) the different discourses differently; in other words, it is this
      difference which makes it possible to talk about scientific discourse on the one hand and
      ideological discourse on the other, about aesthetic discourse and the discourse of the
      unconscious" (Althusser, 2003: 49).

ideology and, concomitantly, the ideology of meaning. Harris attempts to break with the *idea* of meaning empirically in his research, however, in his distributional analyses this obstacle to linguistic science is still in use. Hence Harris' work is not yet completely detached from certain ideological presuppositions. "Meaning is not a unique property of language, but a general characteristic of human activity" (Harris, 1954: 151). The notion of meaning occasionally re-enters Harris' distributional analysis via certain instances of ideological mis/recognition.[12] Harris establishes that a structure of lexical distribution is not, necessarily, an instance of 'meaning', however, he cannot simply eradicate this 'linguistic primitive' by wishing it away: the problem of subjective meaning appears unresolved because it functions as a theoretical ideology within the discipline linguistics.[13] According to Pêcheux:

> what is peculiar to the knowledges (empirical, descriptive, etc.) *prior to the break* in a given epistemological field is the fact that they *remain inscribed in the subject-form*, i.e., they exist in the form of a *meaning evident* to the subjects who are its historical supports, through the historical transformations that affect that meaning.
>
> PÊCHEUX, 1982: 136

Harris also acknowledges such theoretical issues in his research, yet, he does not present a clear solution to the prevalence of self-evident meaning.[14] "Since there is no independently-known structure of meanings which exactly parallels linguistic structure, we cannot mix distributional investigations with occasional assists from meaning whenever the going is hard" (Harris, 1954: 152). In "The Structure of Science Information" Harris separates colloquial, i.e., everyday, language from scientific language to find that they have different structural conditions of 'realization'.[15] "Consider the differences between the

---

12   This may be due to the fact that Harris is attempting to critically question the notion of meaning while remaining within a ideological system that supports it, i.e., 'natural language'.

13   Harris suggests natural language requires a semantic structure for certain forms of social behavior to 'make sense' subjectively, however, he also cites specialized languages which do not admit of this demand (e.g., scientific languages).

14   Harris does not appear to examine the institutional structures that support forms of pre-given meaning. Pêcheux's work aims to rectify this oversight by establishing how certain discursive formations present the 'always-already-there' of a prescribed society.

15   Ideological realization, in Pêcheux's terms, represents the mis/recognition of the subject as the origin of 'its own' experience. Ordinary language represents an 'actual' experience without an outside, i.e., non-scientific discourse does not establish how it 'means something' objectively.

ordinary use of language (which we will call here, colloquial), and science writing, programming languages, and mathematics" (Harris, 2002: 215). Scientific
languages are restricted in certain ways that systematically define the relations
and results of empirical events. "The restriction of language use in science is a
special case of the form-content correspondence that characterizes all information ... if the structural conditions are altered, the system will no longer
do its work or carry its information" (ibid.). Hence the ideology of 'meaning'
is an unrestricted 'colloquial' language. Ideological language is non-scientific
because meaning functions as a normative guarantee for 'subjective' forms of
explanation.

> It could even be suggested that the way linguistics was constituted as a
> science (in the form of phonology, then morphology and syntax) was pre-
> cisely by a constant discussion of the question of meaning and of the best
> way to banish the question of meaning from its domain.
>
> PÊCHEUX, 1982: 55

The restrictions of scientific language are realized in the 'grammars' of a given
science whereby what is meaningless, irrelevant or non-sensical is deemed
'ungrammatical' (Harris, 1988). The unrestricted structure of ideology reveals
that it does not have an object in so far as a 'form-content' correlation is absent
from ideological discourse, i.e., it does not carry information or 'function'
according to scientific procedures. An epistemological break – in the history of
a science – restricts ideological processes by the demarcation of a new domain
of knowledge which is then verified by experimental activity and other recur-
sive processes. If meaning is a linguistic primitive for linguistics – as Harris
suggests – this is because it eludes functional definition scientifically. Harris'
theory of discourse thus indicates how subjective meaning contributes to the
ideological basis of ordinary language. Moreover, Harris' research programme
lays the theoretical groundwork for Pêcheux's non-subjective theory of subjectivity in so far an individual's speech activity is the product of pre-determined
forms of lexical distribution. According to Wallis:

> For Pêcheux it is not the mind, personality, or cognitive structures of
> the individual that determine the words or expressions he or she uses.
> Rather, it is economic, institutional, and ideological factors tied to a posi-
> tion occupied by the individual in a social structure. Such factors make
> up the conditions of production of the individual's discourses and condi-
> tions of interpretation of those he/she receives.
>
> WALLIS, 1998: 21–22

Harris references the work of Benjamin Lee Whorf and Edward Sapir in "Distributional Structure" and he suggests the Sapir-Whorf hypothesis is doubtful with regard to empirical verification.

> Here we have discussed whether the distributional structure exists in the speakers as a parallel system of habits of speaking and of productivity. This is quite different from the dubious suggestion made at various times that the categories of language determine the speakers' categories of perception ... which is not seriously testable as long as we have so little knowledge about people's categories of perception.
>
> HARRIS, 1954: 151

Despite his critical reception of this 'dubious suggestion' a re-statement of the Sapir-Whorf hypothesis is clearly articulated by Harris to illustrate how distributional structures function:

> The perennial man in the street believes that he speaks freely he puts together whatever elements have the meaning he intends; but he does so only by choosing members of those classes that regularly occur together, and in the order in which these classes occur.
>
> ibid.: 146

Harris is, therefore, stating that 'intended meaning' is, in fact, relative to lexical distribution within a given speech act.[16] This observation would also imply that what one 'thinks' is also subject to the same processes in so far as 'meaning' is intentional thought. "The Sapir-Whorf hypothesis, also known as the linguistic relativity hypothesis, refers to the proposal that the particular language one speaks influences the way one thinks about reality" (Lucy, 2001: 903). Lucy notes that the linguistic relativity hypothesis connects language to thought via certain associations (e.g., patterns of linguistic behavior).

> For example, claims about linguistic relativity depend on understanding the general psychological mechanisms linking language to thinking, and on understanding the diverse uses of speech in discourse to accomplish acts of descriptive reference. Hence, the relation of particular linguistic

---

16   The man in the street does not, in fact, express 'his own' meaning. His lexicon represents the patterns of association that are realized in forms of linguistic practice which constitute the basis of this supposedly 'subjective' behavior.

structures to patterns of thinking forms only part of the broader array of
questions of about the significance of language for thought.

> ibid.

In "Discourse Analysis" Harris declares that the distributional analysis of discourse can exhibit correlations within particular forms of situated behavior
(e.g., social contexts):

> distributional analysis within one discourse at a time yields information
> about certain correlations of language with other behavior. The reason
> is that each connected discourse occurs within a particular situation –
> whether of a person speaking, or of a conversation ... The concurrence
> between situation and discourse only makes it understandable, or possi-
> ble, that such formal correlations should exist.
>
> HARRIS, 1952: 3

The perennial man in the street – according to Harris – *believes* he speaks freely
when, in fact, his speech is the product of particular distributive conditions.[17]
Edward Sapir posits that what is called 'meaning' in linguistics is, in fact, an
instance of association (i.e., a psycho-semantic habit).

> This 'element' of experience is the content or 'meaning' of the linguistic
> unit; the associated auditory, motor, and other cerebral processes ... are
> merely a complicated symbol of or signal for these 'meanings'... for habit
> soon makes this association nearly as automatic as any and more rapid
> than most.
>
> SAPIR, 1921: 9–11

Here Sapir suggests that meaning is a certain habituated performance whereby
the man (or woman) in the street articulates an intended 'message' in a more
or less automatic fashion. Pêcheux's research in *Automatic Discourse Analysis*
refers to the possibility of analyzing discursive structures automatically in
terms of algorithmic systems (via a computer programme), however, this
objective is only possible in so far a subject's discourse is 'automated' or at least
tendentially so. In a discussion of potential applications for ADA (automatic
discourse analysis) Pêcheux notes that:

---

17   Patterns of ordinary language therefore define the distributional structure of speech
      activity for the 'man in the street'.

the sociologist has been left with the task of providing a detailed definition of the specific features which characterize conditions of discursive
production in terms of the *situation* and *position* of the protagonists of
discourse in a given social structure ... it has been left to the mathemati-
cian to define a *minimal sequence of algorithms* capable of carrying out
the analysis.

PÊCHEUX, 1995: 117

For Harris a given social situation and its associated discursive behavior can be
considered correlates of distributional structures. Pêcheux also supports this
theory, however, he adds that the distribution of discourse depends on effects
determined by the imaginary. Certain imagined projections seem to determine
subject positions and situations within forms of discourse:

If this is the case, rules for projection must exist within the mechanisms
of any social formation, and they must establish both *situations* (which
can be defined objectively) and *positions* (representations of situations).

PÊCHEUX, 1995: 85

Harris describes his theory of discourse analysis as the interconnection of
social situation and language 'beyond the limits of a single sentence at a time'
(Harris, 1952). Recurrent sequences of discourse are structured according to
correlative conditions of sentential seriality. In Pêcheux's account of discourse
analysis such correlations involve particular *anticipations* of meaning whereby
a subject's speech activity is preconstructed vis-à-vis institutional conditions
(Pêcheux, 1995). Harris finds that discursive structures, in certain circumstances, assume regularity of meaning in transformation, i.e., some forms of
discourse appear to share corresponding semantic content across different
syntactic occurrences.[18]

To what extent, and in what sense, transformations hold meaning constant is a matter for investigation; but enough is known to make transformations a possible tool for reducing the complexity of sentences under
semantically controlled conditions.

HARRIS, 1957: 340

---

18   In such cases meaning is anticipated by the performative relations associated with a given
      speech act.

The correlation of language and situation via distributional structures is, then, dependent on transformational instances of sentence recurrence.[19] Transformation theory studies how one sentence may be transformed into another.[20] For Pêcheux it is evident that inter-discursive transformations are related to imaginary systems of mis/recognition (e.g. subject positions).[21] "Thus the space of reformulation-paraphrase that characterizes a given discursive formation becomes the site of the constitution of what I have called the *linguistic imaginary* (verbal body)" (Pêcheux, 1982: 126). Edward Sapir also comments on the imaginary nature of 'natural' speech:

> Speech is so familiar a feature of daily life that we rarely pause to define it ... Yet it needs but a moment's reflection to convince us that this *naturalness of speech is but an illusory feeling* ... Eliminate society and there is every reason to believe that ... he [man] will never learn to talk, that is, to communicate ideas according to the traditional system of a particular society.
>
> SAPIR, 1921: 1–2; emphasis added

Harris suggests that transformational analysis may be able explain how 'meaning' is sustained by certain discursive regularities (e.g., syntactic forms of distribution). Hence the importance of transformation theory to explain distributive conditions of discourse.

> The consideration of meaning ... is relevant because some major element of meaning seems to be held constant under transformation ... The determination and explication of this meaning relation is no simple matter ... But it points to one of the major utilities of transformational analysis.
>
> HARRIS, 1957: 290

Pêcheux's notion of the linguistic imaginary appears to offer a solution to the problem of transformation in discursive structures, however, it implies that

---

19   For example, the same sentence repeated is assumed to convey the same meaning in each case. Yet the transformation that occurs from speech sound or graphic representation to meaning is a normative condition and not a necessary one.

20   See Chomsky's research on transformational grammar in *Aspects of the Theory* of Syntax where he posits that 'deep structures' are responsible for the continuity of meaning in ordinary language.

21   According to Harris transformations 'normalize' discourse, yet, he appears to overlook how this process is, typically, unconscious to the subjects who 'use' such discursive formations (cf. Harris, 1957; Pêcheux, 1995).

the associative structures of natural language constitute an ideology of 'meaningful' speech activity.

> To this linguistic imaginary should no doubt also be attached the 'evident' lexical facts inscribed in the structure of the *langue* ... This marks, I believe, the ascendancy of ideological-discursive processes over the system of the *langue* and the historically variable limit of the autonomy of that system.
>
> PÊCHEUX, 1982: 126

Discourse analysis – in Pêcheux's terms – attempts to demonstrate that the subject-form is 'always-already-there' as an ideological effect of ordinary language.[22]

> It is these relationships, within which *the thinkable* is constituted ... in the form of a materialist theoretical approach to *the operation of representations and 'thought' in discursive processes* ... this presupposes an examination of the relationships between the subject and what represents him, i.e., a theory of identification and of the material effectivity of the imaginary.
>
> ibid.: 84

Meaning pre-constructs certain 'points of view' which individuals mis/recognize as their own 'perception' of a given situation. The symbolic domination of meaning induces subjects to believe that the discourse they articulate is 'their own'. Harris finds that discourse follows definite patterns of articulation which exhibit associative relations from a given social situation to particular linguistic forms and vice versa, i.e., recurrent lexical distributions carry meanings associated with certain social conditions.[23] The significance of distributional structures for discourse analysis is evident when considering probabilities of correlation between what is stated (an enunciation) and what Pêcheux calls its 'meaning effects' (e.g., forms of social practice). In a footnote from *Structural Linguistics* Harris writes:

---

22   In this sense speech acts appear to derive from the depths of subjectivity when, in fact, they are the effect of discursive preconstruction. Distributions of 'meaning', then, constitute the ideological background of everyday forms of linguistic interaction.

23   Skinner's S-O-R (stimulus-organism-response) model is applicable to Harris' work given that lexical distributions are probabilities of linguistic response in relation to contextual conditions.

It should be noted that even when meaning is taken into consideration *there is no need for a detailed and involved statement of the meaning of the element, much less of what it was that the speaker speaker meant when he said it. All that is required is that we find a regular difference between two sets of situations* (those in which s occurs and those in which it does not).

HARRIS, 1951: 187; emphasis added

In this sense meaning is 'realized' when a certain linguistic distribution has occurred together with a given set of circumstances. "This is the meaning of utterances, or, in the last analysis, the correlation of utterances with the social situation in which they occur" (ibid.). Pêcheux, then, attempts to further Harris' problematic by establishing how particular meanings are produced by discursive formations which 'represent' ideological conditions of existence.

CHAPTER 11

Roman Jakobson (1896–1982)

Pêcheux appears to cite Roman Jakobson only once in *Language, Semantics, and Ideology* whereas in *Automatic Discourse Analysis* his references to Jakobson are more numerous. In the former Pêcheux associates Jakobson's research with a particular theoretical direction in linguistics "called the 'linguistics of *parole*' (of 'enunciation', of 'performance', of the 'message', the 'text', of 'discourse', etc.); in this tendency certain preoccupations of rhetoric and poetics, are reintroduced, via a critique of the linguistic primacy of communication" (Pêcheux, 1982: 6). In addition to Jakobson, Émile Benveniste, Oswald Ducrot, Roland Barthes, Algirdas Julien Greimas and Julia Kristeva are also included as adherents of this doctrine. The first page of Jakobson's *Six Lectures on Sound and Meaning* (henceforth *Six Lectures*) evinces one example of the ideological preoccupations noted by Pêcheux.[1] Jakobson writes:

> I am sure you are familiar with Edgar Allan Poe's famous poem *The Raven*, and with its melancholy refrain, 'Nevermore'... This vocable, which amounts to no more than a few sounds, is none the less *rich in semantic content*.
>
> JAKOBSON, 1978: 1; emphasis added

This poetic reference illustrates Jakobson's general thesis for the *Six Lectures*: 'semantic content' exists, or, in other words, meaning is a 'property' of language. While Pêcheux proposes to advance Saussure's epistemological break between sound and meaning Jakobson advocates the opposite, i.e., a pre-Saussurian regression in which sound and meaning are one.

> The utterance of Poe's refrain involves only a very small number of articulatory motions ... In short, only minimal phonic means are required in order to express and communicate the wealth of conceptual, emotive and aesthetic content. Here we are directly confronted with the mystery of the idea embodied in phonic matter, the mystery of the word, of the Logos, a mystery which requires elucidation.
>
> ibid.: 2

---

1 Jakobson seems – in principle – unwilling to further the Saussurian break between sound and meaning, instead, he attempts to represent the study of language rhetorically: he endeavours to *persuade* the reader that ordinary language is 'full of meaning'.

Jakobson's purpose is to convince the reader that sound and meaning are inextricably connected via sign systems to support his theoretical ideology.

> *Of course, we have known for a long time that a word, like any verbal sign, is a unity of two components.* The sign has two sides: the sound, or the material side on the one hand, and meaning, or the intelligible side on the other ... Every word, and more generally every verbal sign, is a combination of sound and meaning ... But while the fact that there is such a combination is perfectly clear, its structure has remained very little understood.
>
>   ibid.: 2–3; emphasis added

Jakobson, then, proceeds throughout the *Six Lectures* to promote and defend the metaphysics of meaning.[2] As I noted in chapter one Pêcheux discusses the theological implications of hermeneutic analyses in an interview for the book *La Langue Introuvable.*

> The more everyday, secularized forms of this theological lecture ... were inscribed within the spontaneous sender/receiver figures which were becoming prominent within the human and social sciences under the many forms of 'content analysis' of communication.
>
>   PÊCHEUX, 1983: 25

Recall that Poe's refrain 'Nevermore', according to Jakobson, is 'rich in semantic content'.[3] Jakobson's *Six Lectures* thus attempts to reinterpret Saussure's research in terms of self-evident meaning (i.e., semantic theology).

> It is said that every word, and more generally every linguistic sign, is an entity with two sides. Every linguistic sign is a unity of sound and meaning, or in other words, of signifier [*significant*, Latin *signans*], and signified [*signifié*, Latin *signatum*].
>
>   JAKOBSON, 1978: 23

---

2 Jakobson supports the mystical union of sound and meaning while Pêcheux, Harris, Skinner, and Wittgenstein generally work towards the opposite, i.e., they aim to demonstrate that 'meaning' has no place in scientific practice.

3 Jakobson thus suggests that meaning is a form of communicative 'content', yet this assertion simply conveys his *belief* that meaning-in-itself is part of the structure of ordinary language.

Although Jakobson clearly makes use of certain elements of Saussure's research he does so with the aim of returning Saussure's work to an earlier stage of theoretical development, i.e., one that is less empirical and more 'meaningful'.

> ... the *Course in General Linguistics* contains serious contradictions in its manner of understanding and describing the phonic resources of language. These contradictions are indicative of the intermediate position of Saussure's teaching between two successive currents of thought in linguistics, those of naive empiricism on the one hand and of the structuralist tendency in modern science on the other.
>
> ibid.: 46

While Jakobson describes the physical features of language in some detail he is reluctant to separate sound and meaning, rather, for him, they belong together as the object of semantics.

> In the second half of the nineteenth century linguistics became dominated by the most naive form of sensualist empiricism, focusing directly and exclusively on *sensations*. As one would expect the intelligible aspect of language, its signifying aspect, the world of meanings, was lost sight of was obscured by its sensuous, perceptible aspect, by the substantial, material aspect of sound. Semantics, or the study of meaning, remained undeveloped ... while phonetics made rapid progress and even came to occupy the central place in the scientific study of language.
>
> ibid.: 4

While Jakobson believes sound and meaning are, in fact, united, he does indicate that such a connection is problematic because phonemes (i.e., sound units) are apparently 'devoid of meaning' (ibid.: 69).[4] Thus, any definite connection between a morpheme (minimal unit of meaning) and a phoneme (minimal speech sound) is – paradoxically – impossible in so far as phonemes are not bearers of meaning.

> Only the phoneme is a purely differential and contentless sign ... A phoneme signifies something different from another phoneme in the same position; this is its sole value ... This phoneme language is the most

---

4 Jakobson's research cannot, therefore, avoid the transformation problem raised by Harris and Chomsky, i.e., how sound (a physical wave) becomes meaning (a subjective belief).

important of the various sign systems ... which simultaneously signify and yet are devoid of all meaning.

ibid.: 66–67

Despite the fundamental importance of the phonetic function for differentiating various objects within a given language this theory presents a dilemma vis-à-vis consistent intelligibility, i.e., semantic continuity. "We have arrived ... at the view that phonemes, phonic elements by means of which words are differentiated ... have no positive and fixed meaning of their own" (ibid.: 69). Yet, Jakobson's apparent awareness of the physical basis of phonemes does not prevent him from resurrecting the ideology of 'meaning' when his defence of the notion requires it.[5]

In order to be in a position to describe the phonological system of a given language, in other words *the system of phonic means which serve to distinguish words of different meanings,* we must first identify and classify all the system's elements ... any attempt to describe and classify the sounds of a language without taking account of their relation to meaning, is inevitably doomed to failure.

ibid.: 89; emphasis added

Speech sounds are integral to what is usually called 'meaning' yet Jakobson does not explain, definitively, *how* phonemes 'cause' semantic effects.[6]

The task is to investigate speech sounds in relation to the meanings with which they are invested, i.e., sounds viewed as signifiers, and above all to throw light on the structure of the relation between sounds and meaning ... The phoneme, although it is an element at the service of meaning, is itself devoid of meaning.

ibid.: 109

---

5 Jakobson seems to be aware that he cannot objectively demonstrate that 'meaning' exists, however, this does not stop him from repeatedly trying to persuade the reader that 'semantic content' is real.

6 Speech sounds are both meaningful and meaningless, according to Jakobson, yet he does not detail how such changes of state, in fact, occur. What Jakobson appears to lack is an theory of *structural causality* in terms of institutionally determined 'meaning-effects' (cf. Pêcheux, 1995; Jakobson, 1978).

Phonemes are apparently 'devoid of meaning' however, the differences between these speech sounds somehow produce it as the 'substance' of meaning. According to Jakobson:

> Saussure taught that the important thing about a word is not the sound in itself, but those phonic differences which allow this word to be distinguished from all others, for it is these which are the bearers of meaning.
>
> ibid.: 41

Claude Lévi-Strauss in his preface to Jakobson's *Six Lectures* remarks upon this issue in the following statement: "The only linguistic entity without conceptual content, the phoneme, which does not itself have a meaning, is a tool which serves to discriminate between meanings" (Lévi-Strauss, 1978: xv). This claim appears to be indicative of certain ideological assumptions whereby sound (vibratory movement) becomes meaningful by way of spontaneous assumptions, i.e., phonic differences that are 'realized' as semantic structures, e.g., words, sentences, and so on. The plurality of human languages suggests that meaning arises in social practice (i.e., pragmatically) due to the variety of empirical speech sounds exhibited throughout the history of oral languages. If sound is 'devoid of meaning' (i.e., as physical waves of matter) the process by which it becomes meaningful should be relatively simple to disclose, however, this is not the case in Jakobson's research. He appears, in my view, to assert contradictorily, that in one sense meaning exists, and in another, it does not. *Six Lectures* is a problematic presentation of how meaning is generated and sustained in so far as it superficially adopts Saussure's research without resolving the double structure that pertains to auditory and semantic phenomena. As I indicated above, for Jakobson, phonemes are devoid of meaning yet, on other occasions, he finds that phonetic difference is the basic principle for the designation of meaning. Jakobson's troubled bifurcation suggests that there are conceptual limits to whatever ideological guarantees are afforded by 'self-evident' meaning. Furthermore, Pêcheux's demarcation between type A (Technical/Empiricist) and type B (Political/Speculative) ideologies appears to explain how the 'always-already-there' is represented via associations of sound and 'meaning' (see chapter one). Pêcheux maintains that language is the material site of meaning effects and Jakobson's *Six Lectures* provides an excellent example of some of the theoretical problems that are generated by ideologies of meaning:

it was Saussure himself who, in his *Course*, correctly defended the view that the meanings of words themselves vary from one language to another ... There is no meaning in and by itself; meaning always belongs to something which we use as a sign; for example, we interpret the meaning of a linguistic sign, the meaning of a word.

> ibid.: 111

Paradoxically Jakobson, then states:

> *Contrary to Saussure's thesis, the connection between signifier and signified, or in other words between the sequence of phonemes and meaning, is a necessary one* ... but the only necessary relation between the two aspects is here an association based on contiguity ... whereas association based on resemblance ... is only occasional.
>
> ibid.: 112; emphasis added[7]

Sound and meaning ostensibly correspond due to certain conditions of association in which these objects are related by acts of repetition (e.g., pedagogical practices). Semantic contiguity is thus a kind of trained recognition in which certain associations between sound and meaning are made – and through consistent practice – structure the 'always-already-there' as a pre-defined reality.[8] In *Automatic Discourse Analysis* Pêcheux maintains that Jakobson's research is ideologically related to the Munchausen effect (i.e., the subject as a cause of itself).

> Current difficulties in theories of enunciation stem from the fact that those theories usually reflect a necessary illusion that constitutes the subject; in other words, they are content to *reproduce the illusion of the subject at a theoretical level* by following the tradition of Bally, Jakobson and Benveniste and by adopting the idea that the enunciating subject is endowed with choices, intentions and decisions (and here we come close to the notion of speech).
>
> PÊCHEUX, 1995: 137

---

7   I note that one meaning may *resemble* another syntactically by associations based on contiguity. Hence Jakobson's distinction between contiguity and resemblance appears represent a speculative ideology (see chapter one).

8   The term 'contiguity' is used in psychology to denote recurring relationship between stimulus and response, i.e., contiguity is a structure of reinforced conditioning.

Despite such ideological presuppositions Pêcheux does use other elements of Jakobson's work to further his materialist theory of discourse. Pêcheux imports Jakobson's 'information schema' to articulate how discourse can be modelled with reference to meaning effects:

> ... it will be noted that information theory ... leads Jakobson to describe the information that is transmitted as a *message* ... I prefer to use the term *discourse*, which implies that we are not *necessarily* dealing with information transmitted from A to B but, more generally, with a 'meaning-effect' that occurs between points A and B.
>
> ibid.: 84

In *Selected Writings II – Word and Language* Jakobson outlines an information model with reference to code recognition between addresser and addressee.

> A message sent by its addresser must be adequately perceived by its receiver. Any message is encoded by its sender and is to be decoded by its addressee. The more closely the addressee approximates the code used by the addresser, the higher is the amount of information obtained.
>
> JAKOBSON, 1971: 130

Codes and messages exhibit a double structure in which sender and receiver are syntactically connected via the transmission of a given linguistic performance.[9]

> Both the message (M) and the underlying code (C) are vehicles of linguistic communication, but both of them function in duplex manner; they may at once be utilized and refer to the code or to another message, and on the other hand, the general meaning of a code unit may imply a reference (*renvoi*) to the code or to the message.
>
> ibid.

These coded informational structures are a more technical expression of Saussure's familiar signifier/signified distinction in which a syntactic object represents a designatum. For example, 'I' represents the first person (the speaking subject) who 'encodes' a certain message that conveys an 'agency effect'.

---

9   Syntax appears to support semantic contiguity given that it permits associations to be formed on the basis of existing lexical norms. Thus, the sender/receiver model of communication implies the use of shared grammatical conventions.

According to Jakobson the 'I' which is used to designate this agentic message functions as a 'shifter'.[10]

> *I* means the person uttering *I* ... The peculiarity of the personal pronoun and other shifters was often believed to consist in the lack of a single, constant, general meaning ... In fact, shifters are distinguished from all other constituents of the linguistic code solely by their compulsory reference to the given message.
>
> ibid.: 132

Shifters, then, appear to 'realize' certain meaning-effects in so far as a given message is 'connected' to a personal pronoun. Moreover, shifters are used in narratives where speech acts are defined by means of 'verbal categories'.

> In order to classify the verbal categories two basic distinctions are to be observed: 1) speech itself (^{S}), and its topic, the narrated matter (^{n}); 2) the event itself (E), and any of its participants (P), whether 'performer' or 'undergoer'... Person characterizes the participants of the narrated event with reference to the participants of the speech event. Thus first person signals the identity of a participant of the narrated event with the performer of the speech event, and the second person, the identity with the actual or potential undergoer of the speech event.
>
> ibid.: 133–134

Jakobson situates person-ality (i.e., the linguistic properties of a 'person') within a system of verbal categories which structure the transmission of meaning effects.[11] "In language and in the use of language, duplicity plays a cardinal role. In particular, the classification of grammatical, and especially verbal, categories requires a consistent discrimination of shifters" (ibid.: 133). Pêcheux maintains a given meaning is enacted via the subject-form as an ideological construct and, moreover, this 'associative' process is revealed by Saussure's

---

10   Shifters facilitate the transmission of agency in context: addressee and addresser are related via deictic acts of reference conveyed in 'subjective' forms of grammar (I, you, she, we, they, me &c.).

11   Agency is a product of particular 'genres' of narration in which the agent actively defines – or is passively defined by – certain verbal acts. Consequently agency 'shifts' according to how shifters are represented by the discourses that determine such speech acts. In this sense the subject is a product of those discursive formations which 'encode' various forms of 'subjective' experience (e.g, psychology, law, literature, journalism &c.).

epistemological break.[12] Shifters – designating subject positions – are, according to Pêcheux in *Automatic Discourse Analysis*, embedded within 'imaginary formations' (Pêcheux, 1995: 85). These imaginary formations 'reflect' the perception of individual speech acts vis-à-vis prescribed 'meaning effects'.[13] Pêcheux, then, appears to adapt Jakobson's sender/receiver model and apply it to the study of ideological interlocution:

> we have already noted ... that any discursive process presupposes that the sender *anticipates the receiver's representation*, and that the strategy of his discourse is based upon his expectations. ... We can see that in each case A's expectations of what B will say depend upon the 'distance' A imagines there to between A and B ....
>
> ibid.: 87

The imaginary representations that are articulated between the interlocutors are encoded transmissions that convey social positions. According Jakobson, citing the work of Otto Jespersen, shifters are a decisive part of a given 'linguistic code'. "Any linguistic code contains a particular class of grammatical units which Jespersen labelled SHIFTERS: the general meaning of a shifter cannot be defined without a reference to the message" (Jakobson, 1971: 131). Pêcheux further develops his account of imaginary formations in "A Method of Discourse Analysis Applied to Recall of Utterances" which appears to include certain elements of Jakobson's addresser/addressee model in terms of a 'discourse structure' comprised of the following: 'L = linguistic system; D_x = discursive string; A = the addresser; B = the addressee; and R = the referent or subject-matter of the discourse' (Pêcheux, 1971: 67). A discourse structure, according to Pêcheux, is defined by certain 'production conditions'. The primary conditions include: (1) the representation that A has of himself in the discourse; (2) the representation that A has of B in the discourse and (3) the representation that A has of R in the discourse (ibid.). These representations that determine a given speech act are, in Pêcheux's view, typically unconscious in colloquial

---

12 The Saussurian break indicates that sound and meaning are associated under conditions of 'constant conjunction'. In Pêcheux's reading of Saussure's work this apparent coincidence of sound and meaning is the result of certain institutional structures which pre-define the forms of enunciation available to a 'free' subject.

13 The subject as cause of itself is an imaginary representation of the real conditions of linguistic activity. On this account – following the work of Pêcheux and Skinner – the subject is a literary fiction.

forms of discourse.[14] Jakobson, too, finds that linguistic research must engage with 'unconscious' phenomena:

> in our habitual use of language the deepest foundations of verbal struc-
> ture remain inaccessible to the linguistic consciousness; the inner rela-
> tions of the whole system of categories – indisputably function, but
> they function without being brought to the rational awareness by the
> participants in verbal communication and only the intervention of expe-
> rienced linguistic thought, equipped with a rigorous scientific method-
> ology, is able to approach the innermost workings of linguistic structure
> consciously.
>
> JAKOBSON, 1980: 128

Pêcheux appears to relate Jakobson's linguistic code theory to particular semantic effects which are *unconsciously* adopted as prescribed meanings in certain discursive structures. "I propose to use the term *process of production* to designate all those formal mechanisms which produce a discourse of a given type in given 'circumstances'" (Pêcheux, 1995: 77). According to Pêcheux the socio-historical factors which determine the production conditions for discur-sive structures are not typically recognized by the subjects who 'spontaneously' articulate speech acts and this is due to imaginary identifications that appear within the symbolic order: "this identification, which founds the (imaginary) unity of the subject, depends on the fact that the elements of interdiscourse ... are re-inscribed in the discourse of the subject himself" (Pêcheux, 1982: 114).

The subject – as a shifter – in Jakobson's sense – is thus verbally instantiated by utterances involving personal pronouns, however, such utterances are not 'freely' chosen vis-à-vis the linguistic systems which enable acts of 'communi-cation'. Jakobson and Halle explain the limits of 'free speech' in *Fundamentals of Language*:

> Speech implies a selection of certain linguistic entities and their com-
> bination into linguistic units of a higher degree of complexity ... *But the*
> *speaker is by no means a completely free agent in his choice of words*: his
> selection (except for the rare case of neology) must be made from the
> lexical storehouse which he and his addressee possess in common.
>
> JAKOBSON & HALLE, 1956: 58; emphasis added

---

14   According to Pêcheux, meaning-effects are 'attached' to forms of automatic discourse in
      which subjects un/consciously re-present their own subjection to practical ideologies via
      the apparent legitimacy of ordinary language.

The 'free' selection of linguistic units is an ideological notion in so far as meaning is generated by a process of discursive production via certain institutions.[15] Jakobson and Halle are still willing, however, to assert that 'meaning' is a property of language even though 'the speaker is by no means a completely free agent in his choice of words'.

> Linguistic analysis gradually breaks down complex speech units into morphemes as the ultimate constituents endowed with proper meaning and dissolves these minutest semantic vehicles into their ultimate components, capable of differentiating morphemes from each other.
>
> ibid.: 3–4

Following Pêcheux, the 'connection' between a given meaning and a subject (shifter) appears to rely on certain imaginary relations between the interlocutors who are involved in a discursive process (e.g., a speech act). Such ideological conditions determine the image each subject has of the other *dramatis personae*. Pêcheux's colleague Paul Henry cites Jakobson's research on 'intersubjective' communication in the article "On Processing of Message Referents in Contexts" in regard to such considerations:

> according to Jakobson (1960), any communication process involves at least six elements: a speaker, an addressee (or receiver), a linguistic code, a communication channel, a message, and referent of the message ... we will suggest a conception of referent which may be useful to the study of some aspects of communication processes, in particular to the study of ideological processes.
>
> HENRY, 1971: 77

Shifters – within a given discourse – are referents used to denote the subject-form, however, subjective distributions of word 'choice' prescribe certain meaning effects as a result of particular social conditions.[16] According to Pêcheux the preconstructed discourse of the always-already-there 'supplies-imposes' the verbal reality which determines 'the domination of the subject-form' (Pêcheux, 1982: 115). Hence, the subject of discourse is semantically controlled

---

15   Harris suggests each individual in a given society will exhibit a particular 'distribution' of language which generally conforms to their social situation.

16   Thus, superordinate and subordinate forms of communication are performatively enacted via systems of ideological mis/recognition which precipitate the expected speech acts associated with prescribed subject positions.

by the discursive processes associated with the always-already-there. This pre-constructed ideology of social relations represents the 'obviousness' of meaning conveyed in ordinary language.[17]

> The study of discursive processes, of discourses functioning in connection with other discourses, implies that we work with a corpus of messages and that we take into account the loci of speakers and addressees.
>
> HENRY, 1971: 84

Henry notes discourse is determined in relation to the 'loci' and 'positions' of subjects which structure the transmission of and reception of speech acts situationally.

> Conditions of production are tied to a locus determined by economic, institutional, and ideological factors ... In messages or discourses, people take positions according to the state of their conditions of production ... What we call referent is considered to be constructed in discourses which are tied to specific conditions of production.
>
> ibid.: 83; emphasis in original

As noted above Henry adapts some of Jakobson's concepts to further his studies of messages in context. According to Jakobson: "Any elucidating interpretation of words and sentences – whether intralingual (circumlocutions, synonyms) or interlingual (translation) – is a message referring to the code" (Jakobson, 1971: 131). Pêcheux follows a similar distinction in terms of interdiscourse and intradiscourse, however, these modes of communicative behavior (codes) may also induce certain forms of self-subjection.[18] Interdiscourse establishes the 'coincidence' of meaning that is generated between subjects within a given discursive formation. Such semantic continuity is established by the 'spontaneous' acceptance of social speech patterns (Pêcheux, 1982: 117–118). Intradiscourse structures a subject's speech activity by the apparent correspondence of discursive structures with particular imaginary positions connected to certain

---

17   Evidently shifters are prescribed by the forms of enunciation that are found in socially 'accepted' forms of linguistic behavior, yet, this does not imply that the speaking subject is aware of the imaginary structures that governs these forms of interaction (cf. Pêcheux, 1982; Jakobson, 1971).

18   Shifters encode 'intersubjective' messages, however, in ordinary language pronominal designations are ideologically incorporated within preconstructed discursive environments. Pêcheux's research, then, suggests that forms of subjection may occur simply by following the conventions of grammar.

social loci (i.e., received meaning-effects). According to Pêcheux the 'intra-discourse effect' is a basic mechanism of imaginary identification (ibid.: 190). Henry and Jakobson both maintain that message interpretation involves the encoding and decoding of verbal material. Furthermore, Henry also suggests, as does Pêcheux, that such interpretation occurs via socially determined systems, i.e., 'conditions of production' (Henry, 1971: 93). According to Jakobson:

> Roughly, the encoding process goes from meaning to sound and from the lexicogrammatical to the phonological level, whereas the decoding process displays the opposite direction – from sound to meaning and from features to symbols.
>
> JAKOBSON, 1971: 575

'Interpretation' seems to be an act in which meaning and sound are transformed via general processes of encoding and decoding. As Henry notes in his analysis of contextual message transmission:

> it is possible to analyse real, assumed, or imagined events, states of affairs, etc., in many different ways ... *Thus, it is necessary to differentiate between the empirical object which can be associated to a message and the way it is presented in the message.* The difference becomes very important when political, ideological or scientific positions are involved.
>
> HENRY, 1971: 90; emphasis added

In Pêcheux's analysis meaning functions as an ideology via the assumptions it generates regarding the self-evidence of ordinary language (Pêcheux, 1982). Meaning becomes part of an agent's 'consciousness' despite the fact that the 'content' of meaning is derived from pre-scientific forms of discourse (myths, literature, &c.). Consequently, the 'interiority' of subjective experience is literally constituted by forms of communication that fictionalize the real genesis of such imaginary effects. According to Jakobson:

> When we say that language or any other sign system serves as a medium of communication ... it was often overlooked that besides the more palpable, interpersonal face of communication, its intrapersonal aspect is equally important. Thus, for instance inner speech ... as an 'internal dialogue' is a cardinal factor in the network of language and serves as a connection with the self's past and future.
>
> JAKOBSON, 1971: 662–663

Pêcheux's account of this linguistic relation (interpersonal/intrapersonal) is defined in terms of interdiscourse and intradiscourse. While Jakobson finds that intrapersonal communication 'serves a connection with the self's past and future' Pêcheux maintains the subject of discourse is an ideological construct. Pêcheux, therefore, seeks to explain how such discursive effects are sustained as imaginary formations (Pêcheux, 1995: 85–90). Thus any 'connection' that exists between a subject's past and future is mediated by ordinary language which directly represents preconstructed forms of the 'always-already-there', for example, shifters vis-à-vis subject positions (cf. Herbert, 1966; Jakobson, 1971). Hence the the ideology of meaning generates particular forms of literal subjection which are conveyed via particular discursive formations.[19]

Juan Carlos Rodríguez in his book *Theory and History of Ideological Production* maintains that the emergence of literature was directly related to the emergence of the 'free' subject. The free subject is an *imaginary* creation that has its roots in certain literary practices. This subjective fiction is an essential part of what Rodríguez calls the 'ideological unconscious'.

> The ideological unconscious in question is configured around the image of the *free subject* ... beginning with the figure of the poetic 'I' that henceforth will be considered the unequivocal basis or *given* of any kind of Western discursivity. Hence the importance that we attach to the appearance of the *free subject*.
>
> RODRÍGUEZ, 2002: 12–13

Pêcheux in *Language, Semantics, and Ideology* and *Automatic Discourse Analysis* connects the ideology of free speech to the ideology of free labour and Rodriguez identifies the same imaginary relationship in the *Theory and History of Ideological Production*.

> To reiterate, literary discourses, including philosophy (considered as literary genre in itself), are radically historical, in the sense that literature can only be said to have been born with the appearance of the image of the free subject, who possesses a soul that is both free and beautiful, and who considers himself to the private owner of his language, ideas and feelings ... Within the context of capitalist freedom, it is presumed that

---

19   The ideological state apparatus appears to determine the conditions of production for 'acceptable' speech acts in so far as its institutionality materiality defines ordinary language. Moreover, the received definitions of such discourse may constitute the imaginary basis of this structure-in-dominance.

the free 'I' is innate, that it is not inscribed by anyone, that it is something given by oneself to oneself.

RODRÍGUEZ, 2002: 14

This magical image of freedom is a result of the literary discourse which represents the illusion of free subjectivity (ibid.: 14). As noted above, Jakobson suggests that the encoding and decoding of language involves the transformation of meaning to sound and vice versa, i.e., phonetic and semantic 'metamorphosis'. Thus, under ideological conditions sound or text would appear to be 'magically' invested with meaning.[20] The 'magic' of meaning is indissociable from the literary (phantasmatic) character of the humanities and social sciences where such ideologies substitute belief for empirical evidence.

---

20   Without determining precisely how meaning 'represents' particular acts of subjective intent ordinary language does appear to function as a literary fiction (i.e., a product of the imagination). Indeed, such beliefs do not have recourse to scientific validity, yet, literary allusions (illusions) still constitute an *accepted* form of 'everyday' communication.

CHAPTER 12

Jacques Derrida (1930–2004)

Pêcheux refers to Jacques Derrida (together with Gilles Deleuze and Michel Foucault) in the article "La Langue Introuvable" with regard to 'ideological struggles of movement' (Pêcheux, 1983: 27). There are no direct references to Derrida's work in *Language, Semantics, and Ideology*, however, in the bibliography of *Automatic Discourse Analysis* there are two entries for 'Derrida'. The first is to 'Structure, sign and play in the discourses of the human sciences' from *The Structuralist Controversy: The Languages of Criticism and the Sciences of Man* and the second is to 'Levi-Strauss dans le dix-huitième siècle' (co-authored by J. Mosconi) from the journal *Cahiers pour l'analyse*.[1] This use of Derrida's work by Pêcheux evinces the incorporation of Derridean 'deconstruction' within the field of discourse analysis. In consonance with Pêcheux's research programme Derrida questions the obviousness of meaning:

> What is 'meaning', what are its historical relationships to what is purportedly identified under the rubric 'voice' as a value of presence, presence of the object, presence of meaning to consciousness, self-presence in so-called living speech and in self-consciousness?
>
> DERRIDA, 1981: 5

Here Derrida conveys the focal point of the Saussurian break: the problem of how sound (phonetics) and meaning (semantics) are linguistically 'connected'. He appears to suggest that 'meaning' is related to the *idea* of 'self-consciousness'. In *Language, Semantics, and Ideology* Pêcheux discusses such phantasmatic associations via the 'subject-form of discourse': 'Of course I am myself' (Pêcheux, 1982: 110).[2] In this sense the ideological subject is supposed to accept certain practices of socialisation in which its discourse is prescribed

---

1 *Cahiers pour l'Analyse* also published "For a General Theory of Ideologies" (Herbert, 1968) and "Reflections on the Theoretical Situation of Social Science, and Especially, of Social Psychology" (Herbert, 1966). Both of these articles address certain problems in relation to the ideology of meaning.

2 Pêcheux attempts to deconstruct the 'meaning' of self-consciousness with his materialist theory of discourse. His challenges idealist conceptions of personal identity by demonstrating how 'consciousness of self' is linguistically mediated by discursive formations (Pêcheux, 1982).

by existing linguistic norms (e.g., 'natural' language). "Henceforth I shall call a *discursive formation* that which ... determines *'what can and should be said'* (articulated in the form of a speech, a sermon, a pamphlet, a report, a programme, etc.)" (Haroche, Henry, and Pêcheux, 1971 cited in Pêcheux, 1982: 111). Subjects are thus literalized by the discursive formations which establish customary forms of communication (e.g., what can and should be said regarding the conditions of their subjection). Moreover, these subject positions are 'realized' via certain literary practices which describe 'meaningful' contexts for such illusory forms of control (i.e., semantic structures are supported by the ideological state apparatus). Hence, the 'meaning' of literature represents the imaginary basis of particular linguistic norms:

> The discourses to which today we apply the term 'literary' constitute a historical reality that has been able to emerge only with the advent of a particular, unique set of conditions, namely those we associate with the ideological level characteristic of 'modern' or 'bourgeois' social formations understood in the general sense.
>
> RODRÍGUEZ, 2002: 17

According to Derrida the 'obvious' union of sound and meaning is an *a priori* condition for metaphysical thought:

> All the metaphysical determinations of truth ... are more or less immediately inseparable from the instance of the logos ... Within this logos, the original and essential link to the *phonè* has never been broken ... As has been more or less implicitly determined, the essence of the *phonè* would be immediately proximate to that which within 'thought' as logos relates to 'meaning', produces it, receives it, speaks it, 'composes' it.
>
> DERRIDA, 1997: 10–11

Thus, 'meaning', for Derrida, is an 'accepted' pretence.[3] Metaphysics is, by definition, 'higher/beyond', physics, and concerns speculative – i.e., *philosophical* – accounts of ultimate reality. Ideology – in Pêcheux's terms – appears to designate the *imaginary systems of meaning* that are distributed throughout the symbolic structures of a given society (e.g., philosophy, religion, myths, literature &c.).

---

3   In natural language words are assumed to convey meaning, yet, such ideological beliefs do not establish *how* a given speech act is, 'in fact', meaningful. The metaphysics of meaning – as Derrida suggests – is a *philosophical* problem.

I shall say that it is proper to every discursive formation to conceal, in the transparency of meaning formed in it, the contradictory material objectivity of interdiscourse ... I shall close on this point by saying that the operation of Ideology in general ... supplies 'each subject' with his 'reality' as a system of evident truths and significations perceived-accepted-suffered.

> PÊCHEUX, 1982: 113

Moreover, according to Pêcheux, ideology appears legitimate due to the *belief* that each subject's discourse is 'its own':[4]

> the ego, i.e., the imaginary in the subject (the place in which is constituted for the subject his imaginary relationship to reality), cannot recognize its subordination ... because this subordination-subjection is realised precisely in the subject in *the form of autonomy*.
>
> ibid.: 113–114

The supposedly 'personal' (self-evident) meaning of a given speech situation is, in fact, the product of socially determined linguistic structures. Rodríguez notes:

> Strictly speaking, such a logic (in other words, the image of a 'free', 'autonomous' individual, an origin and end in itself, possessing an 'interior' – a mind, reason, etc. – a sole source of – and solely responsible for – all its ideas, its judgments, its sensations, its tastes, its knowledges and its discourses, etc.) derives directly – and uniquely – from the bourgeois ideological matrix.
>
> RODRÍGUEZ, 2002: 18

Derrida further deconstructs 'meaning' in the essay "Signature Event Context" where he questions the contextual implications of what is called 'communication' (Derrida, 1988).[5] As I noted above Derrida suggests that 'meaning' is

---

4 The subject appears as the cause of itself due to the metaphysical assumptions of 'self-consciousness'. In Derrida's terms the metaphysics of presence 'represents' the purported simultaneity of sound and meaning found in ideological descriptions of subjective experience. In this sense sound and meaning are unified to produce what is immediately 'present' via the imaginary order of grammar (Derrida, 1982).

5 For Pêcheux, 'everyday' (colloquial) communication seems to function as a form of ideology which is tacitly accepted by adhering to the prescribed conventions of natural language (Pêcheux, 1982).

a metaphysical presupposition (i.e., beyond what is known objectively), as a result, this ideology is an article of faith.[6] At what precise point in a given act of communication does sound become meaningful? When does the phonetic become semantic? Although the notion of 'context' broadly attempts to designate the performative conditions required to *enact* meaning, such contextualization may be regarded, according to Derrida, as a form of philosophical activity (i.e., context supports metaphysical assumptions of meaning).[7]

> Is there a rigorous and scientific concept of context? Or does the notion of context not conceal, behind a certain confusion, philosophical presuppositions of a very determinate nature? Stating it in the most summary manner possible, I shall try to demonstrate why a context is never is never absolutely determinable, or rather, why its determination can never be entirely certain or saturated.
>
> DERRIDA, 1988: 3

Moreover, Rodriguez remarks how ideology exhibits a dual structure between its performance (i.e., 'context') and its real conditions of existence.

> For, in effect, the configuration of the ideological level in any social formation is always dual: on the one hand, we have *what it says it is*; on the other, we have *what it really is*. In other words, on the one hand, we have its visible notions, and on the other, how it actually functions.
>
> RODRÍGUEZ, 2002: 22

Pêcheux provides another example of this duplicity in the following statement where the economic base appears to determine the *meaning* of the ideological superstructure:

> It is I who have stressed this reference to the evidentness of *meaning* taken from a commentary on the evidentness of the *subject* ... it makes palpable the superstructural link – determined by the economic infrastructure – between the repressive state apparatus ... *and* the ideological

---

6 While ordinary language is assumed to convey meaning the connection between syntactic and 'semantic' phenomena is, according to Pêcheux, mis/represented by certain *beliefs* regarding their *ideal* union (Pêcheux, 1982).

7 Hence it is possible to *speculate* about how a meaning relates to a context because contextual conditions are not verified by scientific procedures.

state apparatuses, i.e., the link between the 'subject in law'... *and* the ideological subject (he who says of himself: 'It's me!')

PÊCHEUX, 1982: 105

In *Of Grammatology* Derrida (interpreting Aristotle) attempts to explain
the origin of 'mental' (i.e., ideal/psychological) experience vis-à-vis 'natural'
language:

> Between being and mind, things and feelings, there would be a relation-
> ship of translation or natural signification; between mind and logos, a
> relationship of conventional symbolization ... *This notion remains there-*
> *fore within the heritage of that logocentrism which is also a phonocentrism:*
> *absolute proximity of voice and being, of voice and the meaning of being, of*
> *voice and the ideality of meaning.*
>
> DERRIDA, 1997: 11–12; emphasis added

The act of saying 'It's me!' pronounces the phonocentric discourse of the
always-already-there, i.e., the preconstructed conventions of existing meaning,
in so far as the subject is contextually subjected to 'its own' speech vis-à-vis the
ideological superstructure.[8]

> What is said of sound in general is a fortiori valid for the *phonè* by which,
> by virtue of hearing (understanding) oneself-speak – an indissociable
> system – the subject affects itself and is related to itself in the element
> of ideality.
>
> ibid.: 12

Derrida thus outlines a general schema of logocentric mis/recognition whereby
the subject's identity is pre-defined by the existing 'meaning' of a given discourse. In like manner Pêcheux's research on the Munchausen effect (i.e., subject as a cause of itself) addresses how 'the subject affects itself and is related
to itself in the element of ideality'. According to Pascale Gillot:

> Subject then, understood as the subject of discourse, is not its own origin
> ... One recognizes here the specific mark of the elementary ideological
> effect related to the pseudo-obviousness of being a free spontaneous

---

8 The Saussurian break separates sound from meaning and, therefore, suggests how logocentric linguistic structures 'prescribe' the unconscious psycho-social behaviors that are typically conveyed in the ideology of ordinary language.

subject: the phantasmatic cause of itself, *causa sui*. Pêcheux tried to investigate and analyse this inner contradiction about the subject.

GILLOT, 2014: 100

Rodríguez suggests that 'literature' has been closely related to the ideological experience of interiority in so far as the subject adopts a *literary* interpretation of 'internal' events.[9]

> Could it be that the basic equation between the literary and the pure inti-macy of the subject is the result of a specifically linguistic focus, whereby the image of the literary is identified with the pure intimacy of language ... 'literature' is in general all language that is not verifiable, that is freely imaginative and emotive, etc, that is to say, the most personal, subjective language ... in a word the most 'intimate'.
>
> RODRÍGUEZ, 2002: 26

This intimacy of subjective interiority is another way of describing the 'abso-lute proximity of voice and being ... and the ideality of meaning' that Derrida presents in *Of Grammatology*. Moreover – with reference to the research of Clérambault and Lacan – the imaginary effects of literature may also explain how 'mental automatism' (i.e., the syndrome of passivity) is presented as an ideogenic 'novel'.[10] Pêcheux is critical of 'transparent' meaning, which may be considered 'literally true', because all discourses exhibit certain conditions of production which result in distinct and relatively heterogeneous forms of 'knowledge'.[11] Transparency of meaning suggests *metaphorically* that a mean-ing is 'clear', however, no text can be transparent because it would thus be unreadable (invisible).[12] Pêcheux maintains "[e]*very discursive formation, by the*

---

9   Following the work of Skinner, Harris, and Althusser, the language of science and the language of literature are incommensurable given that the object of science categorically excludes fictive descriptions of reality. By definition science is not imaginary.

10   In Clérambault's terms the *syndrome of passivity* induces automatic forms of behavior. For example, a 'self-directing' monologue may result in a pathological condition if it dis-regards objective reality (e.g., types of psychosis: delusions, hallucinations &c.).

11   Evidently, the 'knowledge' produced by the humanities and social sciences (philosophy, social psychology, linguistics, comparative literature &c.) has not attained the same level of certainty as the natural sciences (e.g., laws of nature). For Pêcheux, Skinner, Althusser and Plon this is because the humanities and social sciences re/produce ideologies of *subjective* experience. Hence, the humanities and social sciences are not completely detached from faith-based practices (e.g., religious convictions).

12   The informational movement from graphic (letters) or phonic (sound) structures to understanding ('meaning') is not either immediate or spontaneous it is the result,

transparency of meaning constituted in it, conceals its dependence on the 'complex whole in dominance' of discursive formations ... imbricated with the complex of ideological formations" (Pêcheux, 1982: 113). Gillot suggests Pêcheux's general ambition is to produce:

> a scientific theory of ideology, inseparable from an anti-idealist understanding of the *subject-effect* and of the *sense-effect (or meaning-effect)*. The recourse to the concept of *discourse*, for this programme, is crucial ... the subject is no longer identified with the individual as the principle of its acts (such as speech acts)... it is rather understood as a produced subject, a *preconstructed* subjective position, always-already taken within a discursive formation.
>
> GILLOT, 2014: 101–102

The *meaning* of a discourse is 'clearly' understood *when the reader identifies with what is written* or *spoken* and 'believes' in a given form of discourse.[13] According to Rodríguez:

> the belief that the text is 'transparent' for the eye of the reader presupposes, in turn, that if the reader and the text can fuse directly together, it is because both possess a common, basic substratum. It is through this literary 'human spirit', common to the reader and the text, that the reader is capable of 'recognizing' himself *transparently* in the text, once the actual lexical or technical obstacles in the latter have been suppressed.
>
> RODRÍGUEZ, 2002: 135

Such *imagined* transparency is, Rodríguez suggests, a belief in magic.[14] "Lurking behind the alleged 'transparency' of the text is the magicist/romantic presupposition that incarnated in a 'language'... is the 'essential truth'..." (ibid.: 135). Derrida's analysis of 'context' and 'writing' conveys that what is called communication is never a 'transparent' process. Morphologically the prefix *con-* (with/

---

according to Wittgenstein, Skinner and, Pêcheux, of specific forms of training (e.g., learning to read and listen).

13   Scientific practice does not require personal *belief* to produce results objectively – the evidence of science determines what is real *in fact* – whereas ideological discourse appears *self-evident* when really it is not (Althusser, 2003).

14   Hence the 'meaning' of text may take the form of an incantation, sermon, or 'lecture' used to deliver an (occult) 'message' which is imaginary. Ordinary language (i.e., self-evident meaning) would thus – in this sense – 'direct' supernatural beliefs.

thoroughly, e.g., con-centric) appears prior to *text* when the word context is read left to right. What, then, is accompanied or connected *with* the text that a context provides? Derrida suggests that a context 'represents' how a given text is 'subjectively' interpreted in certain speech situations, and furthermore, such interpretation is a form of *philosophical* activity. "I would even go so far as to say that it is the interpretation of writing that is peculiar and proper to philosophy" (Derrida, 1988: 3). The speculative 'content' of a context may include not only written texts but also oral and gestural communication which functions as a vehicle for 'generalized writing', i.e., the social inscription of 'meaning' by voice, signal, or graphic notation. Derrida and Pêcheux both utilize the Saussurian break to convey certain observations regarding the metaphysical assumptions of 'meaning in context':

> The question of the origin of writing and the question of the origin of language are difficult to separate ... does one not find efficaciously at work, in the very movement by which linguistics is instituted as a science, a metaphysical presupposition about the relationship between speech and writing?... To develop this question, I should like to approach, as a privileged example, the project and texts of Ferdinand de Saussure.
>
> DERRIDA, 1997: 28–29

Prior to Derrida's grammatological research ('grammatology' – defined as the science of writing) he studied – in considerable detail – the phenomenology of Husserl. This is evinced in *The Problem of Genesis in Husserl's Philosophy* and *Voice and Phenomenon* (Introduction to the Problem of the Sign in Husserl's Phenomenology). Interpreting Husserl's philosophy of 'meaningful signs' in the chapter entitled "Meaning as Soliloquy" from *Voice and Phenomenon* Derrida writes:

> Expression as a meaningful sign *<signe voulant-dire>*... is therefore a double exiting of sense (*Sinn*) outside of itself in itself, in consciousness, in the with-itself and the nearby-itself that Husserl begins by determining as the 'solitary life of the soul'.
>
> DERRIDA, 2011: 27

A soliloquy is 'self-talk' in which particular monological acts direct the imaginary interlocution of 'talking to oneself'. The 'solitary life of the soul' appears to portray another example of what Rodríguez calls the intimacy of subjective experience as a specific 'literary effect' within philosophy.[15]

> Again, what we are dealing with here is the unfolding of a central idea regarding the identity between literature and the intimacy of the subject ... In sum, the ways in which the dominant theoretical ideology characterizes literary discourse ... amount to nothing more than the unfolding of the primary 'subject'/'intimacy' relation ... specific and unique to literature, indeed to the 'aesthetic' in general.
>
> RODRÍGUEZ, 2002: 26

According to Derrida (commenting on Husserl's phenomenological literature): "The 'I' alone achieves its meaning in solitary discourse and functions outside of discourse as 'universally operative indexical'" (Derrida, 2011: 60). Furthermore, in *Of Grammatology* Derrida outlines a concept of 'linearization' (following the research of André Leroi-Gourhan) whereby symbolic linearity (such as the text *you* are now reading) functions as a – typically forgotten – precondition for the history of thought (including 'philosophy').

> The enigmatic model of the *line* is thus the very thing that philosophy could not see when it had its eye open on the interior of its own history ... In fact for a long time its possibility has been structurally bound up with that of economy, of technics, and of ideology.
>
> DERRIDA, 1997: 86

In *Voice and Phenomena* Derrida notes that phenomenology (the philosophy of 'consciousness') *surveils* speech:[16]

> We will be less astonished confronting the effort of phenomenology – an effort that is laborious and oblique, even tenacious – *to keep watch over speech, in order to assert an essential link between the logos and the phonē,*

---

15   In certain respects, Husserl's phenomenological research – while attempting to produce a 'the science of the essence of consciousness' – regresses into an ideology of subjectivity via 'spiritual' (metaphysical) narratives. This ideological aspect of Husserl's work suggests that – in Pêcheux's terms – 'the subject is the cause of itself' by 'its own' self-evident meaning.

16   According to Althusser philosophical ideologies serve to 'guarantee' certain forms of non-scientific self-knowledge (i.e., ideologies of subjectivity). Philosophy 'observes-monitors-prohibits-commands' what subject may know about itself using certain *literary* effects. Know thyself!

since the privilege of consciousness ... is only the possibility of the living voice. Since self-consciousness appears only in its relation to an object whose presence it can keep watch over and repeat, self-consciousness is never perfectly foreign or prior to the possibility of language.

DERRIDA, 2011: 13; emphasis added

Word (*logos*) and sound/speech (*phonē*) are unified in certain scripts, i.e., forms of phonetic writing, and thus any understanding of 'internal' or 'external' discourse presupposes an ideology of meaning that is pre-scribed in everyday language. The notion of 'linear phonography' (e.g., lines used to represent sounds: consonants, vowels, and so on) is defined by Derrida to explain the linearization of sound in textual structures (e.g., orthography).

The system of speech, of hearing-oneself-speak ... could only represent itself as order and predominance of a temporal linearity by *seeing* itself or rather *handling* itself, within its own self-reading. *It is not enough to say that eye or hands speak. Already, within its own representation, the voice is seen and maintained* ... This form of successivity is in return imposed upon the *phonè*, upon consciousness and upon preconsciousness from a certain determined space of its inscription.

DERRIDA, 1997: 289

Consider 'hand-writing' – or 'typing' (typography) – which is another technically mediated instance of 'hand-writing' – this inscription process demonstrates the apparent 'link' between the *logos* and the *phone*, however, such linear phonography is not typically de-scribed in acts of communication.[17] According to Derrida linear graphism (writing) has always been the logical (logos = word) precondition for organised religion, the transmission of knowledge, the advancement of technology, and law:

access to the written sign assures the sacred power of keeping existence operative within the trace and of knowing the general structure of the universe ... all clergies, exercising political power or not, were constituted the same time as writing and by the disposition of graphic power

---

17   Within everyday communication the social positions of the interlocutors are typically 'written into' the speech acts which are 'communicated'. Therefore, simply by making a statement (e.g., articulatory phonation/graphic notation) the subject reproduces its position within the structure-in-dominance 'using' ordinary language (i.e., self-evident meaning).

... strategy, ballistics, diplomacy, agriculture, fiscality, and penal law are linked in their history and their structure to the constitution of writing ... the very sense of power and effectiveness in general ... which could appear as such, as meaning and mastery (by idealization), only with so-called 'symbolic' power, was always linked with the disposition of writing ... The constitution of a science or a philosophy of writing is a necessary and difficult task.

> ibid.: 93

The historical movement of writing – whether actual or virtual (ideal) – then *represents* the veritable inscription of the world by the *alignment* of sound and meaning. Pêcheux's theory of discourse – as found in *Language, Semantics, and Ideology* and *Automatic Discourse Analysis* – seeks to demonstrate how such linguistic structures function via forms of unconscious discourse. According to Gillot:

The insertion of Freudian-Lacanian categories ... inside discourse analysis in general, reveals the theoretical originality, the richness, of the attempt made by Pêcheux to link theory of ideology and theory of the unconscious in the fields of Marxism, philosophy, and linguistics.

> GILLOT, 2014: 106

Gillot highlights the imaginary interplay of intradiscourse and interdiscourse in processes of unconscious subjection (this double structure may also be presented in Husserlian terms of consciousness/living voice or Derridean terms of inscription/transcription).[18]

If we may allude to Pêcheux's discourse analysis ... the subject as subject of discourse is nothing but a paradoxical *causa sui* (the supposed prior subject) produced in reality as a *result*, an effect. It is the result of the interdiscourse dissimulated within an intradiscourse ... At the same time, it conceals itself and its own causal effectiveness in the very production of its effects, which defines the typical causal structure of the unconscious and of ideology.

> ibid.: 97

---

18   Individual and 'interpersonal' forms of ideological subjection are defined within the contextual conditions of ordinary language by Pêcheux. In consequence, the un/conscious recognition of apparently context-appropriate verbal behavior may reproduce certain pre-scientific beliefs (e.g., myths, theoretical ideologies, and other fictions).

Derrida presents a comparable theory of 'unconscious discourse' in "Freud and the Scene of Writing" found in *Writing and Difference* where he describes the possibility of 'psychographic' inscription.

> From Plato and Aristotle on, scriptural images have regularly been used to *illustrate* the relationship between reason and experience, perception and memory ... The gesture sketched out by Freud ... opens up a new kind of question ... It will eventually invade the entirety of the psyche. Psychical content will be *represented* by a text whose essence is irreducibly graphic. The *structure* of the psychical *apparatus* will be *represented* by a writing machine ... what is a text, and what must the psyche be if it can be represented by a text?
>
> DERRIDA, 1978: 250; emphasis added

Derrida's commentary in "Freud and the Scene of Writing" includes references to the following works by Freud: "Note on the Mystic Writing Pad", *Project for a Scientific Psychology*, "The Unconscious" and "The Dream-Work", "Letters to Fliess" and *Beyond the Pleasure Principle*. Derrida's general aim is to explain the theoretical limits of psychographism vis-à-vis memory traces (i.e., neuronal plasticity). "Memory, thus, is not a psychical property among others; it is the very essence of the psyche: resistance, and precisely, thereby, an opening to the effraction of the trace" (ibid.: 252). A 'mystic writing pad' is the image presented by Freud to *characterize* 'psychical writing' and Derrida questions how effective this metaphor is for Freud's psychological research. The word psychology suggests the connection that Freud further describes in terms of mental inscription (i.e., the *logos* (word/writing) of the psyche), yet, Derrida's point of difference is to challenge the metaphysics of the *phonē* – as 'self-consciousness' – via Freud's psychoneurology of 'traces'. "If the Freudian break-through has an historical originality, this is not due to its peaceful coexistence or theoretical complicity with linguistics, at least in its congenital phonologism" (ibid.: 249). Derrida does not appear to dispute the existence of unconscious psychological structures, rather, he is initiating an analysis of how the *logos* (as a phonological form) could determine the psyche without implicit recourse forms of imaginary mis/recognition.[19] *"We thus already know that psychic life is neither*

---

19   The 'connection' between sound and meaning, according to Saussure, is determined by forms of psychological association. Derrida, then, questions how un/conscious structures may be inscribed by such 'psychic writing' when neuronal traces are subject to various contingencies (e.g., ordinary language, formal education, 'personal' experience, cultural differences &c.).

the transparency of meaning nor the opacity of force but the difference within the
exertion of forces" (ibid.: 253; emphasis added). Psycho-logical experience is, in
Derrida's reading, subject to linguistic *différance*, i.e., the syntactic, semantic,
and pragmatic differences that constitute a given discourse. Derrida outlines
Freud's theory of 'contact barriers' and 'breaching' (i.e., neuronal pathbreak-
ing) to explain the formation of memory traces in 'psychic life'.

> Breaching, the tracing of a trail, opens up a conducting path. Which pre-
> supposes a certain violence and a certain resistance to effraction. The
> path is broken, cracked, *fracta,* breached ... It is the difference between
> breaches which is the true origin of memory, and thus of the psyche.
>
> ibid.: 252

The concept of 'breaching' challenges the sovereignty of the subject (i.e., subject as cause of itself) given that the *logos* of the psyche is structured (i.e.,
traced/inscribed) by a system of linguistic differences.[20]

> If there were only perception, pure permeability to breaching, there
> would be no breaches ... nothing would be recorded; no writing would
> be produced, retained, repeated as legibility ... But pure perception does
> not exist: we are written only as we write, by the agency within us which
> always keeps watch over perception, be it internal or external. The 'sub-
> ject' of writing does not exist if we mean by that some sovereign soli-
> tude of the author. The subject of writing is a *system* of relations between
> strata: the Mystic Pad, *the psyche, society, the world.* Within that scene, on
> that stage, the punctual simplicity of the classical subject is not be found.
>
> ibid.: 285; emphasis added

Ideology may, then, be linked to certain forms of un/conscious repression (e.g.,
the Munchausen effect).[21] "Repression, as Freud says, neither repels, nor flees,
nor excludes an exterior force; it contains an interior representation, laying out

---

20   According to Althusser: "The differential nature of the subject-effect, and the place (posi-
      tion) that the subject which it characteristically 'produces' as an effect occupies with
      respect to a given discourse, must be correlated with assignable *differences of structure* in
      the structures of that discourse. In other words, the structure of scientific discourse must
      differ from the structures of ideological discourse, aesthetic discourse, and the discourse
      of the unconscious" (Althusser, 2003: 49).

21   According to Freud: "Words provoke affects and are in general the means of mutual influ-
      ence among men" (Freud, 1961: 17).

within itself a space of repression" (ibid.: 246). Such an 'interior representation' would be the result of certain breaches in which memory traces are inscribed vis-à-vis discursive formations.[22]

> Writing is unthinkable without repression ... It is no accident that the metaphor of censorship should come from the area of politics concerned with the deletions, blanks, and disguises of writing ... The apparent exteriority of political censorship refers to an essential censorship which binds the writer to his own writing.
>
> ibid.: 285[23]

Philosophical discourse, according to Derrida, effaces and represses the materiality of writing as a signifying practice by means of logocentric dissimulation (i.e., the truth of the *logos* and its 'meaning').[24]

> Philosophy is, within writing, nothing but the movement of writing as effacement of the signifier ... The evolution and properly philosophic economy of writing go therefore in the direction of the effacing of the signifier, whether it take the form of forgetting or repression ... The concept of repression is thus, at least as much as that of forgetting, the product of a philosophy (of meaning).
>
> DERRIDA, 1997: 286

The subject-form, for Pêcheux, is a syntactic belief used to denote the ideological structure of subjectivity that may constitute psycho-social repression via certain forms discourse.[25] According to Gillot:

---

22   For both Pêcheux and Althusser it appears that the constitution of 'subjective' memory traces is a function of ideological state apparatuses which impose socially dominant forms of psychological association via prescribed forms of discourse.

23   For example, the Munchausen effect makes the subject 'responsible' for its speech acts despite the fact that it is not the author of the official language it is expected to use 'freely' (cf. Pêcheux, 1982; Derrida, 1978).

24   For further discussion of this problem in terms of speculative and empirical ideologies see chapter one.

25   Pêcheux suggests that individuals usually fail to recognize that 'their own' discourse is constituted by pre-existing systems of 'meaning'. Although subjects appear to speak 'spontaneously' such speech acts are principally the result of socio-historical linguistic structures (Pêcheux, 1982).

In Pêcheux's theory of discourse, the subject-form is, of course, obtained through a process of forgetting as regards the antecedence of the unasserted – the interdiscourse – with respect to the intradiscourse itself ... This double forgetting is compared by Pêcheux to the Freudian theory of repression, in so far as it can be considered a twofold repression: a repression dependent on the Unconscious system, and a repression dependent on the Preconscious system.

GILLOT, 2014: 104–105

This dual structure of inscribed repression between interdiscourse and intradiscourse is censored-forgotten via 'meaning' (and its philosophical truth) to produce the ideological guarantee of semantic continuity.[26] "The system of language associated with phonetic-alphabetic writing is that within which logocentric metaphysics, determining the sense of being as presence has been produced" (Derrida, 1997: 43). Logocentric discourse (i.e., self-evident meaning and the always-already-there) is thus forgotten/repressed by unconscious imaginary structures (i.e., ideological associations of sound and meaning) which subsequently obfuscate the real production of a subject's discourse (e.g., primary socialization).

Pêcheux isolates, in his theory of the subject form of discourse ... the general dissimulation of the exteriority of interdiscourse within the discursive formation in which the subject is inscribed ... This necessity of obliteration or 'forgetting' ultimately refers then to the specific and paradoxical effectiveness or *causality of Ideology* in so far as it may be compared, and identified, with the *causality of the Unconscious*.

GILLOT, 2014: 104

Pêcheux's research programme, as outlined in *Language, Semantics and Ideology*, and *Automatic Discourse Analysis*, can be translated into Derrida's grammatological vocabulary given that the history of metaphysics is an ideological practice dissimulated by the 'spontaneous' apprehension of imaginary

---

26   While the discipline of philosophy may appear to support 'open' forms of theoretical enquiry it does not produce positive knowledge. The 'truth' of self-evident 'meaning' takes the place of scientific practice. Karl Marx and Fredrich Engels address this matter in *The German Ideology*. "Where speculation ends, where real life starts, there consequently begins real, positive science, the expounding of the practical activity, of the practical process of development of men. Empty phrases about consciousness end, and real knowledge has to take their place. When the reality is described, a self-sufficient philosophy ... loses its medium of existence" (Marx and Engels, 1976: 37).

associations found in certain discursive structures (e.g., myths of subjectivity). Glyndwr Williams in *French Discourse Analysis* makes a series of remarks concerning interdiscourse, meaning, and the forgetting of intradiscourse in relation to the illusory conditions of subjective experience that – in principle – support this view.

> Interdiscourse also has a relationship to the issue of ambiguity of meaning ... the interdiscourse is the space where the objects which link to their intra-discourse, with the illusion of expressing 'thoughts' and of expressing things of an external world, are constituted and articulated – and, in doing so, forgetting that this involves the 'preconstructed' character of these elements.
>
> WILLIAMS, 1999: 190–191

Derrida's project of 'deconstruction' endeavours to disassociate the grammatological elements of language from various metaphysical accounts of self-evident meaning to demonstrate the logocentrism of phantasmatic 'self-presence'.[27] "Consciousness is the experience of pure auto-affection ... From Descartes to Hegel. ... God's infinite understanding is the other name for the logos as self-presence" (Derrida, 1997: 98).[28] The experience of 'hearing-oneself-speak' as self/consciousness implies the use of certain linguistic norms, however, these conventions are not typically cognized in daily life; in fact, for Derrida, vernacular forms of communication are distinctly ideological.[29]

> Now, 'everyday language' is not innocent or neutral. It is the language of Western metaphysics, and it carries with it not only a considerable number of presuppositions of all types, but also presuppositions inseparable

---

27   Every ideology is thus logocentric in so far as its 'meaning' generates the 'always-already-there' in the form of self-evident assumptions of everyday experience. Yet, natural language is not usually considered to be an ideology because it is, in effect, the vehicle of metaphysical mis/recognition. In Derrida's terms natural language 'has no outside' (Derrida, 1997).

28   'Self-presence' and 'auto-affection' appear to represent the same problem that Pêcheux addresses in terms of the Munchausen effect, i.e., how a subject supposedly affects itself via received forms of speech.

29   The ideology of 'hearing-oneself-speak' and God's infinite understanding also appear in Chomksy's research – via the grammar of the Port-Royal School – as 'deep structure'. The metaphysical 'connection' between the two beliefs – God and self – solves the transformation problem in linguistics (i.e., sound becomes meaning spiritually).

from metaphysics, which, although, little attended to, are knotted into a
system.

DERRIDA, 1981: 19

The association of sound and meaning are preconstructed in everyday language thus suggesting that social communication is an effect of particular
forms of discursive pre-scription.[30]

> There is much to say about the fact that the native unity of the voice
> and writing is *prescriptive*. Arche-speech is writing because it is a law. The
> beginning word is understood, in the intimacy of self-presence, as the
> voice of the other and as commandment.
>
> DERRIDA, 1997: 17

Discursive prescription may constitute an effaced 'space of repression' via
mythic sources of authority (e.g., epistemological obstacles – according to
Gaston Bachelard). For Williams the 'effacement' of discursive prescription is
the result of imaginary forms of agency:

> Thus all formulations [of interdiscourse] are found in an intersection
> involving two axes, the vertical of the preconstructed, involving the
> domain of memory; and the horizontal, involving the linearity of dis-
> course, which occults the first axis since the subject enonciateur, in an
> illusory manner, is produced as interiorized in the preconstructed that
> imposes its discursive formation on all formations.
>
> WILLIAMS, 1999: 191

Memory and preconstructed discourse interpose an ideological experience
of interiorized meaning through which the subject *believes* it is the cause of
its own speech (Pêcheux, 1982). Derrida describes his concept of *différance*
in terms that imply a general framework of interdiscursive supplementarity
whereby phonic and graphic structures intersect referentially to form the
pluri-temporal structures of textual experience (i.e., the grammatological conditions of interdiscourse):

---

30   Arche-speech is established psychoanalytically by the 'name of the father' as a primary
      source of *authority*. Arche-speech appears to *mark* the beginning of human culture.
      According to Lacan: "It is in the *name of the father* that we must recognize the basis of the
      symbolic function, which since the dawn of time, has identified his person with the figure
      of the law" (Lacan, 2006: 230).

This concept can be called *gram* or *différance* ... Whether in the order of spoken or written discourse, no element can function as a sign without referring to another element which itself is not simply present. This interweaving results in each 'element' – phoneme or grapheme – being constituted on the basis of the trace within it of the other elements of the chain or system. This interweaving, this textile, is text produced only in the transformation of another text.

DERRIDA, 1981: 26

Signifying structures, according to Derrida, are constantly deferred, effaced, and re-presented, by the 'interweaving' of différance throughout the linguistic structures which appear as interposed forms of discourse.[31] "The system of the sign has no outside" (Derrida, 1997: 234). Williams explains a homologous process via the notion of 'intertextuality'.

Intertextuality involves how texts contain elements of other texts. Such an organization involves a chain of textual elements which can be added to, the new elements responding to prior texts, while also having the capacity to modify prior texts, that is, to transform the past ... Furthermore, as has already been implied in our reference to intertextuality, the inter-discourse consists of a process of incessant reconfiguration in which a discursive formation is led to incorporate the preconstructed elements produced outside itself.

WILLIAMS, 1999: 191

Intertextuality, interdiscourse and *différance* are 'supplementary' systems in which 'presence' is apparently determined by the heterogeneity of repeated inscriptions. "Originary difference is supplementarity as *structure*" (Derrida, 1997: 167).

If supplementarity is a necessarily indefinite process, writing is the supplement par excellence since it marks the point where the supplement proposes itself as supplement of supplement, sign of sign, *taking the*

---

31   Derrida's notion of *différance* appears to have descended directly from Saussure's research in the *Course in General Linguistics*. Saussure writes: "Everything that has been said up to this point boils down to this: *in language there are only differences* ... Whether we take the signified or the signifier, language has neither ideas nor sounds that existed before the lingusitic system, but only conceptual and phonic differences that have issued from the system" (Saussure, 1959: 120; emphasis added). Derrida critically discusses Saussure's theory of linguistics in *Of Grammatology, Margins of Philosophy* and *Positions*.

place of a speech already significant ... It marks the place of the initial doubling.

DERRIDA, 1997: 281

Derrida's answer to the problem posed by the Saussurian break, i.e., the double structure of language, is the logic of the supplement.[32]

---

32   While Derrida's *philosophy* of language suggests that supplementarity repeatedly renews the 'meaning' of natural language by the logic of the supplement (i.e., semantic surplus) he does not appear to demonstrate how scientific systems function *without* ideological presuppositions (e.g., the exact sciences do not make any appeal to meaning as a real process). In other words, science doesn't support untestable hypotheses (e.g., speculative ideologies).

CHAPTER 13

Mikhail Bakhtin (1895–1975)

Mikhail Bakhtin's name does not appear in the bibliography of *Language, Semantics, and Ideology* or *Automatic Discourse Analysis*, however, a number of the main topics associated with the works of 'Bakhtin' are present in the aforementioned works by Michel Pêcheux. Moreover, Bakhtin's writings are evidently the object of polemic regarding matters of recognized authorship (and *authority*). Commenting on these issues Pam Morris notes in the introduction to *The Bakhtin Reader*:

> It is an irony ... that the body of texts, represented in this Reader, articulating some of the most influential thinking about questions of authoring and meaning in language, are themselves the subject of scholarly and political dispute.
>
> MORRIS, 1994: 1

I do not find these *beliefs* ironic: they are an expected consequence of *interpreting* the ideological function of an 'author'.[1] Michel Foucault outlines this practice in "What is an Author?":[2]

> The author's name manifests the appearance of a certain discursive set and indicates the status of this discourse within a society and a culture ... The author function is therefore characteristic of the mode of existence, circulation, and functioning of certain discourses within a society.
>
> FOUCAULT, 1984: 107–108

Pêcheux (1982) and Rodríguez (2002) also consider certain implications for the assumed authority of the subject-form[3]. For purposes of citation, I use the name

---

1 To be the author of such-and-such an event is typically understood to denote the person responsible for a particular act (whether figuratively or literally). The author/originator may be blamed, praised or otherwise identified within certain parameters of agency, however, in ordinary language this individual-agent is the result of certain linguistic practices (e.g., the norms of grammar). Thus, 'authority' may be disputed because the notion is *subjective*.

2 I also direct the reader to Terry Eagleton's notion of 'authorial ideology' described in *Criticism and Ideology* (Eagleton, 1976: 58–60).

3 For a concise theoretical description of ideological agency see the article "Remark on the Category: 'Process without a Subject or Goal(s)'" from *Essays in Self-Criticism* (1976) by

'Bakhtin' to refer to those writings included within the *Bakhtin Reader*, however, as Morris suggests some of these texts, may, actually, have been written by other authors (e.g., Pavel Nikolaevich Medvedev and Valentin Nikolaevich Voloshinov). Saussure, Freud, and Marx, figure as key theorists in Pêcheux's research and the same may be said for a number of studies connected with Bakhtin's name. Pêcheux's conceptual apparatus generally corresponds to Bakhtin's field of research (i.e., semiotics): for example, meaning, ideology, social conditions of dialogue, and the philosophy of language, are addressed by both theoreticians. Pêcheux's 'subject-form of discourse' finds parallel expression in Bakhtin's writing as 'individualistic subjectivism'.[4] Individualistic subjectivism: "considers the basis of language ... to be the individual creative act of speech. The source of language is the individual psyche" (Bakhtin, 1994: 26). This psychological genesis of language implies – as Pêcheux maintains in *Language, Semantics and Ideology* – a circular explanation of linguistic origination (i.e., an individual's language is apparently acquired from itself). In Pêcheux's account of linguistic acquisition 'meaning' originates not internally (i.e., subjectively) but externally (i.e., via conditions of discursive production) in the history of discursive formations.[5] According to Montgomery and Allan:

> Pêcheux's integration of an Althusserian position on ideology with a fresh approach to discourse analysis creates the conceptual space necessary to begin the work of *explicating the constitution and potentialities of the forces governing subjectivity, and furthermore, the conditions for an oppositional politics of meaning production.*
>
> MONTGOMERY & ALLAN, 1992

For Pêcheux such 'forces of subjectivity' are *imaginary* in so far as they are the product of unconscious linguistic structures which establish the dissimulation

---

Althusser. Both Pêcheux and Rodríguez adapt elements from Althusser's œuvre to advance their individual theories of ideological subjection.

4 According to Pêcheux the subject-form of discourse determines the non-sense of the production of the subject as the cause of itself via the 'spontaneous' self-evidence of ideology. See the chapter "The Subject-Form of Discourse" in *Language, Semantics, and Ideology* (1982).

5 Individualistic subjectivism, then, dehistoricizes the production of discourse so that each subject seems to articulate 'its own' speech acts. The real history of language is thus dissimulated by self-evident meaning which appears to legitimate dominant forms of discursive interaction. Following Derrida 'there is nothing outside the text' because the history of textuality is effaced as it is written by the metaphysical assumptions of ordinary language (Derrida, 1997).

of the subject as the cause of itself.[6] Correlatively, Bakhtin's research suggests that speech activity is constrained by normative conditions which strictly limit how 'free' any individual is with regard to its language use and acquisition.

> Language stands before the individual as an invoilable [sic], incontestable norm which the individual, for his part, can only accept ... The individual acquires the system of language from his speech community completely ready-made. Any change within that system lies beyond the range of his individual consciousness. The individual act of articulating sounds becomes a linguistic act only by measure of its compliance with the fixed (at any given moment in time) and incontestable (for the individual) system of language.
>
> BAKHTIN 1994: 27

Hence, this normative inculcation theoretically limits explanations of 'individualistic subjectivism' vis-à-vis the production and dissemination of 'self-evident' meaning. Pêcheux addresses this disjunction in terms of 'spontaneous' and 'preconstructed' linguistic forms. The performative assumptions of 'spontaneous' discourse indicate that the speaking subject must comply with generally established standards of usage, i.e., it is unaware that discursive formations *preconstruct* possible socio-linguistic norms (Pêcheux, 1982). Pêcheux's intradiscourse/interdiscourse distinction *re-presents* how spontaneous 'interpretation' implies the use of preconstructed symbolic systems. As Montgomery and Allan state:

> Any enunciation within intradiscourse opens up implicational spaces either for the operation of the preconstructed or for the sustaining effect. These spaces (inferential gaps) require completion by the subject to secure the intelligibility of whatever has been enunciated. The subject supplies the sense of the enunciation by recourse to transverse discourse ... Crucially, of course, this may occur outside the level of conscious awareness.
>
> MONTGOMERY & ALLAN, 1992

---

6 Bahktin's notion of 'individual subjectivism' refers to the same illusion of autonomy that Pêcheux outlines in terms of the Munchausen effect. The subject forgets that ordinary language presents a certain – *prescribed* – view of 'reality' and, subsequently, speaks under the illusion of apparent autonomy. The subject speaks from an inside – without an outside – that is always-already defined.

Transverse-discourse conveys the spontaneous apprehension of 'new meaning' vis-à-vis the preconstructed effects of existing discursive formations.[7]
According to Pêcheux metonymy is an instance of transverse-discourse (i.e.,
a 'transformational grammar'). "Note that the operation of the 'transverse-
discourse' belongs to what is classically called *metonymy* as a relationship of
part to whole, cause to effect, symptom to what it designates, etc" (Pêcheux,
1982: 116). In 'Notes for a General Theory of Ideologies' Pêcheux/Herbert
remarks how semantic ideology is a speculative discourse exemplified by
instances of *metonymic* subjection in established forms of social interaction
(e.g., grammatological repression).

> We will advance the term metonymy ... to designate the effect by which
> the 'subjects' are taken in the signifying syntactic organization, which
> gives them the status of subject ... as a support for rights and duties in
> which the identification takes place.
>
> HERBERT, 1968

Pêcheux/Herbert specifies certain theoretical differences between the effects
of discursive dominance in empirical and speculative modes of ideological
preconstruction. On one hand, such effects are attributed to 'semantic metaphorical dominance' and, on the other, 'syntactic metonymic dominance'
(ibid.). 'Metaphor' derives from Greek *metaphora/metapherein* 'a transfer'; 'to
carry, or bear' e.g., from one word to another. '*Meta*' (after/beyond) + '*pherein*'
(change; alter), i.e., 'after the change'. 'Metonymy' refers to the Greek word
metōnymia 'change of name'.[8] Pêcheux's research suggests that metaphoric
and metonymic ideologies function by 'repositioning' meaning and nomination (naming) *ex post facto*.[9]

> The metaphorical effect consists of a displacement of meanings ...
> assigns to the agent of production his position in the process ... *repressed*

---

7   The notion of transverse-discourse attempts to address the problem of linguistic transfor-
    mations (cf. Pêcheux, 1982; Chomsky, 1965). For example, sound must be transformed into
    meaning and one meaning must be 'transformed' into another. In Derrida's terms meton-
    ymy and metaphor designate logocentric 'presence', i.e., metaphysical linguistic norms
    (Derrida, 1997).
8   In Bakhtin's terms the ready-made appearance of language appears to support certain
    forms of ideological interaction via established social norms. Hence, Pêcheux's notion of
    transverse-discourse may explain how individual subjectivism is related to certain literary
    techniques within customary forms of speech activity.
9   The word nomination owes its etymology to Latin *nominatio* 'act of mentioning by name'; 'a
    naming, designation'.

and disguised as other signifying chains which have the effect of simultaneously signifying this position to the subject-agent of production, without being able to escape it, and to conceal from him that this position is
assigned. In other words, the metaphorical effect produces meanings by
moving them.

HERBERT, 1968

Semantic metaphorical dominance then proceeds via the 'translation' of
meanings within given discursive formations that 'repress and disguise' (i.e.,
dissimulate) the conditions of production that generate such imaginary
effects; whereas syntactic metonymic dominance appears as a rational (i.e.,
'self-evident') structure which enables the subject to freely 'accept' its discursive subjection.[10]

The metonymic effect, as a horizontal articulation of the ideological
elements according to a syntactic structure produces a rationalization-
empowerment at each structural level considered, which therefore
appears with 'internal consistency'. This is how the subject's identification with political and ideological structures which constitute *subjectivity*
as the origin of what the subject says and does ... conceals from the agent
his position in the structure.

ibid.

If the subject refuses or otherwise fails to 'voluntarily' adopt the norms of
dominant discursive structures it may be labelled 'bad' – i.e., censured – for
not 'receiving' a self-evident meaning (e.g., an identificatory obviousness).[11]
According to Montgomery and Allan:

The discourse of what then becomes a *bad* subject 'turns against' the
dominant identification, primarily by *taking up a position* that consists
in initiating a separation, challenge or revolt ... That is, Pêcheux argues,

---

10   Syntactic ideology is articulated in the grammar of ordinary language such that the
     'always-already-there' is established via the obviousness of self-evident lexical systems ('I
     know what I read').

11   In Althusserian terms the ideology of ordinary language appears to function as an 'absent
     cause' which governs what subjects 'mean' *a priori*. The speaking subject is subordinated
     to the structure-in-dominance by the invisible order of semantic 'necessity'. This meta-
     physical system prescribes the necessary illusions to support the *idea* of linguistic self-
     direction. Hence, subjects define their own subjection – 'autonomously' – via the mean-
     ing of the always-already-there which stipulates what is 'accepted' within a given speech
     situation.

the 'trouble-making' subject does not recognize those meanings lived by
the good subjects as being 'obvious' or 'natural', but rather as achieved
contradictorily, and therefore the identity on offer is refused.

> MONTGOMERY & ALLAN, 1992

Bakhtin presents a theory of official/unofficial ideology that parallels some
aspects of Pêcheux's identification/disidentification duality[12]. Official and
unofficial ideology designate particular forms of 'meaning' realized in linguistic behavior (e.g., speech acts).

> Let us call that inner and outward speech that permeates our behavior in
> all its aspects 'behavioral ideology'... In the depths of behavioral ideology
> accumulate those contradictions which, once having reached a certain
> threshold, ultimately burst asunder the system of official ideology ... The
> content of composition of the unofficial levels of behavioral ideology (in
> Freudian terms, the content and compositions of the unconscious) are
> conditioned by historical time and class to the same degree as are its lev-
> els 'under censorship' and its systems of formulated ideology (morality,
> law, world outlook).

> BAKHTIN, 1994: 45–46

Behavioral ideology – according to Bakhtin – is a product of social conditioning in which verbal interaction is structured by established forms un/con-
scious discourse.

> The social environment is what has given a person words and what *has
> joined words with specific meanings and value judgments*; the same envi-
> ronment continues ceaselessly to determine and control a person's ver-
> bal reactions throughout his entire life

> ibid.: 44; emphasis added

In Pêcheux's account of this phenomena each subject's intradiscourse is the
product of certain preconstructed *interdiscursive* forms of speech (Pêcheux,

---

12   According to Pêcheux 'disidentification' denotes a 'non-subjective position' epistemologi-
      cally. In this sense science necessitates the disidentification of the subject from the object
      of scientific practice. Whereas 'official ideology' typically seeks to retain the ideology of
      the subject (e.g., legal personality, ordinary language &c.) as a means to demonstrate the
      meaning of unofficial ideology (e.g., subjects in need of discipline-correction-reform) (cf.
      Pêcheux, 1982; Bakhtin 1994).

1995). Semantic and syntactic dominance appear, then, to be instances of official ideology in Bakhtin's sense, and the rejection of such discourse would, therefore, indicate a non-compliant attitude toward such norms (i.e., an 'unofficial' subject position).

> I propose to call this 'complex whole in dominance' of discursive formations 'interdiscourse', with the qualification that it too is subject to the law of unevenness-contradiction-subordination which I have described as characterising the complex of ideological formations ... Thus we are led to examine the discursive properties of the subject-form, of the 'imaginary ego' as 'subject of discourse'.
>
> PÊCHEUX, 1982: 113–114

According to Bakhtin behavioral ideology is a consequence of socially determined conditions which – to use Pêcheux's terminology – structure the subject positions articulated in transverse-discourse.

> *The verbal component of behavior is determined in all the fundamentals and essentials of its contents by objective-social factors* ... Therefore, nothing verbal in human behavior (inner and outward speech equally) can under any circumstances be reckoned to the account of the individual subject; the verbal is not his property but the property of his social group (his social milieu).
>
> BAKHTIN, 1994: 44

Neither Pêcheux/Herbert, nor Bakhtin, support the view that the speaking subject is the cause of itself *in situ*.[13]

> From the objective point of view, both sets of motives, those of the unofficial as well as of the official conscious, are given completely alike in outward speech and both alike are not a cause of behavior but a component, an integral part of it.
>
> ibid.: 44

---

13   Both Bakhtin and Pêcheux appear to follow Saussure's research in the *Course in General Linguistics* with respect to the *social basis* of language. "The concrete object of linguistic science is the social product deposited in the brain of each individual, i.e., language" (Saussure, 1959: 23).

Without understanding the objective pre-conditions of given forms of speech activity the *illusion of subjectivity* is perpetuated in semantic and syntactic forms of subjection.[14]

> Let us say ... that this *subjective illusion* contains within it the essential recognition-misunderstanding function of the ideological process ... We can therefore state that any subject empirically encountered in a social formation supports the ideological effects of which it is the träger [agent; carrier] ... namely: 1. the semantic group of *stated and practiced norms* ... defining the form its behavioral structures (gestures and words) ... 2. the syntactic group of *ideological phraseology* and *institutional structures* in which his words and gestures take place as part of statements.
>
> HERBERT, 1968

Bakhtin's research suggests that speech acts – official and unofficial – may be differentiated socio-historically according to the enunciative zones or assumed contexts which support particular forms of discursive interaction.[15]

> Officially the palaces, churches, institutions, and private homes were dominated by hierarchy and etiquette, but in the marketplace a special kind of speech was heard, almost a language of its own, quite unlike the language of the Church, palace, courts, and institutions ... The festive marketplace combined many genres and forms, all filled with the same unofficial spirit.
>
> BAKHTIN, 1994: 213

Pêcheux's colleague, Paul Henry, explains such context effects in terms of the discursive formations which determine a subject's 'locus' within a given social structure (Henry, 1971). In fact, the speaking subject may be *unaware* that its intradiscourse is an effect of this träger [support]-function.[16]

---

14   In ordinary language *self-evident* meaning is 'represented' by the norms of grammar, however, for Pêcheux, Skinner, and Wittgenstein linguistic 'subjectivity' is a prescientific belief.

15   In Pêcheux's terms 'what can and should be said' in a given conversation will 'reflect' the imaginary positions which are assumed by a social context. Typically, each interlocutor will position ('perceive') the other in terms of what each person 'expects' from the speech situation (Pêcheux, 1995).

16   For example, a subject may un/consciously agree to its own subjection simply by using forms of preconstructed language that recreate the existing relations of production via certain speech acts.

Freud has clearly shown, and other investigators in the same area confirm, that what we do and what we say, even the words we use, are highly dependent upon factors which are out of our conscious control. And in a given situation, at a given moment, there are utterances and discourses that a person cannot produce even if he has the required competence.

HENRY, 1971: 81

The double structure of the Saussurian break – that Pêcheux takes as his object for the study of semantics – is also identified by Bakhtin: "Let us underscore Saussure's main thesis: *language stands in opposition to utterance in the same way as does that which is social to that which is individual*" (Bakhtin, 1994: 31). This bifurcation is also found in many other discursive predicates: e.g., interior/ exterior, sound/meaning, spontaneous/preconstructed, conscious/unconscious, base/superstructure, semantic/syntactic, monologue/dialogue and so on. According to Bakhtin, language – as a system of *socially situated* 'speech performances' (comprised of linguistic units, e.g., words, sentences, phrases) – is the primary mechanism for the realization of ideology.

The problem of the interrelationship of the basis and superstructures ... can be elucidated to a significant degree through the material of the word ... The word is implicated in literally each and every act or contact between people ... In turn, from the conditions, forms, and types of verbal communication derive not only the forms but also the themes of speech performances ... All these forms of speech interchange operate in extremely close connection with the conditions of the social situation in which they occur and exhibit an extraordinary sensitivity to all fluctuations in the social atmosphere.

ibid.: 53–54

Bakhtin posits that social psychology represents an inter-mediate relation linking a given socio-political order and its prevailing ideology.

Production relations and the sociopolitical order shaped by those relations determine the full range of verbal contacts between people, all forms and means of verbal communication ... Social psychology exists primarily in a wide variety of forms of the 'utterance'... All these speech performances, are, of course, joined with other types of semiotic manifestation and interchange – with miming, gesturing, acting out, and the like.

ibid.: 54

Furthermore, Henry's theory regarding the correspondence of social loci and 'referents' (i.e., objects of discourse) finds a comparable definition in Bakhtin's account of 'speech genres':

> Each period and each social group has had and has its own repertoire of speech forms for ideological communication in human behavior. Each set of cognate forms, i.e., each behavioral speech genre, has its own corresponding set of themes.
>
> ibid.: 55

A referent represents the object of a given speech act, and Henry maintains such 'parts of speech' are institutionally embedded via conditions of discursive production:

> What we will call *referent is considered to be constructed in discourses which are tied to specific conditions of production* ... More precisely, the referents are constructed in discourses corresponding to a state of the conditions of production in which the relevant elements are associated with the institution in which they occur.
>
> HENRY, 1971: 83

Bakhtin's research suggests 'speech genres' may represent various 'levels' of discursive dominance within a given social order[17].

> Were we to apply a more detailed analysis, we would see what enormous significance belongs to *the hierarchical factor* in the processes of verbal interchange and what a powerful influence is exerted on forms of utterances by the hierarchical organization of communication.
>
> BAKHTIN, 1994: 55

Such superordinate and subordinate discursive structures are also outlined in Pêcheux's theory of ideological mis/recognition in so far as such 'messages' are conveyed via certain speech performances. According to Montgomery and Allan:

---

17   A speakers 'authority' is contextually determined by certain speech situations. The ability to present one's 'point of view' or issue a command is regulated by certain social positions within the structure-in-dominance. Consequently, social order is maintained by the administration of *what is said* according to different 'speech genres' (cf. Bakhtin, 1994; Pêcheux, 1982).

Intradiscourse, then, is always the 'discourse of a subject', while interdiscourse is embedded in previous statements: the word, symbol or concept, to be recognizable as such, must be linked with a pre-existent 'given'... within the complex whole in dominance of discursive formations ... When then the intelligibility of an intradiscourse leans for support on its intersection with pre-established discursive material from interdiscourse, Pêcheux chooses to call this phenomenon *transverse discourse*.

MONTGOMERY & ALLAN, 1992

Social hierarchies appear to correlate with superordinate and subordinate speech performances whereby a subject's intradiscourse is determined vis-à-vis particular interdiscursive meaning effects located in structures of transverse-discourse (e.g., Plato's noble lie).[18]

Every sign, as we know, is a construct between socially organized persons in the process of their interaction. *Therefore, the forms of signs are conditioned above all by the social organization of the participants involved and also by the immediate conditions of their interaction.*

BAKHTIN, 1994: 55

Furthermore, 'communication' is not a neutral (non-partisan) form of linguistic interaction, instead, the ideology of the subject-form 'reveals' the various modalities of interdiscursive dominance (e.g., coercion, 'jokes', repression, 'pressure', banter &c.) that are conveyed in ordinary language.[19]

The point is that we have to understand how the agents of the system spontaneously recognize their place without being formally ordered to adopt a place within a system of production ... In order to understand this process, which simultaneously 'places' individuals and conceals the way they are 'placed'... we have to abandon the communication view of language.

HENRY, 1995: 31-32

---

18   According to Pêcheux meaning effects 'spell out' the imaginary positions of subjectivity that are conveyed in ordinary language. The function of ideology – in this sense – it to make the imaginary appear real. In practice 'meaning' is a *literary* effect (cf. Pêcheux, 1982; Rodríguez, 2002; Skinner, 1957).

19   The subject-form of discourse – as an ideological belief – is supported by the normative assumptions that 'specify' the *mythical* self-evidence (i.e., meaning) found in pre-scientific forms of language. Thus, ordinary language is a vehicle for the various forms of psycho-social subjection found in spontaneous ideologies of agency.

The subject of discourse (individual-agent) receives and conveys speech performances within a dual structure of addressivity and answerability.[20] Such linguistic interaction facilitates the connection of addresser and addressee via certain forms of 'correspondence'.[21]

> An essential (constitutive) marker of the utterance is its quality of being directed to someone, its *addressivity* ... Both the composition and, particularly, the style of the utterance depend on those to who the utterance is addressed, how the speaker (or writer) senses and imagines his addresses, and the force of their effect on the utterance.
>
> BAKHTIN, 1994: 87

Addresser and addressee are reciprocally engaged, according to Bakhtin, in dialogical interaction. Yet dialogue is also determined by ideological (i.e., semantically preconstructed) conditions:

> The living utterance, having taken meaning and shape at a particular historical moment in a social specific environment ... woven by socio-ideological consciousness around the object of an utterance ... cannot fail to become an active participant in social dialogue.
>
> ibid.: 76

The dialogical basis of social interaction, then, instantiates certain monological experiences ('soliloquys') of 'self-experience' wherein existing linguistic norms are intersubjectively accepted which may – following Henry's injunction above – explain how individuals 'spontaneously' identify with their own intradiscursive subjection.[22] What Pêcheux calls the 'complex whole in dominance' of a given social formation determines forms of discourse which function as the superordinate and subordinate 'communicative' practices of

---

20   The double structure of addressivity and answerability is another example of the various types of linguistic duality outlined by Saussure in the *Course in General Linguistics*: interior/exterior, phonic/graphic, spontaneous/restricted, syntactic/semantic, &c.

21   Primitive linguistic correspondence between persons is provided by 'natural' language, however, the acquisition of this syntax is not necessarily a conscious process. Indeed – as Saussure suggests – sound and meaning are associated by *unconscious* psycho-social mechanisms (Saussure, 1959).

22   Individuals 'believe' in their own experience of subjectivity because they are 'using' a linguistic system that does not – in Derrida's terms – have an outside, i.e., natural language. Metaphysical self-subjection is then 'represented' by non-scientific forms of language which *prescribe* the ideology of everyday speech acts.

structural addressivity.[23] These *indexical* designations of 'subjectivity' – found in certain speech performances – are *confirmed* by the intradiscursive assumptions of the extant ideological apparatus. According to Bakhtin:

> Only by ascertaining the forms of whole utterances and, especially, the forms of dialogic speech, can light be shed on the forms of inner speech ... and on the peculiar logic of their concatenation in the stream of inner speech ... *The ideological sign is made viable by its psychic implementation just as much as psychic implementation is made viable by its ideological impletion.*
>
> BAKHTIN, 1994: 57

Furthermore, an 'obvious' (self-evident) connection frequently occurs between acceptability and addressivity, i.e., the linguistic criteria which permit 'acceptable' speech acts are established by existing discursive formations (see chapter ten). The meaning of a speech performance, in this sense, will always be relative to the social positions of the interlocutors, i.e., meaning effects are the result of *preconstructed* interaction. The relative autonomy of meaning effects are thus – in Pêcheux's account of 'the complex whole in dominance' – articulated via the discursive formation/s in which they are authorized-foretold.

> Pêcheux demonstrates in a convincing manner the advantages of theorizing meaning as a function, not of particular words or wordings, but rather of the discursive formation in which such expressions occur ... More precisely, any instance of enunciated discourse has its intelligibility ensured, at least in part, by the operation of rules of inclusion and exclusion or *interdiscourse*.
>
> MONTGOMERY & ALLAN, 1992

Pêcheux/Herbert suggests in "Reflections on the Theoretical Situation of the Social Sciences, and Especially of Social Psychology" that the discursive practices of these disciplines (i.e., social science/psychology) are, in fact, theoretical ideologies that function to legitimate certain forms of social order (Herbert, 1966). The 'social sciences' are, Pêcheux contends, technical practices for ideological *control* over socio-political conditions of existence.

---

23 Structural addressivity defines who and/or what is addressed by a given speech act according to the subject positions supported by the structure-in-dominance. Hence, social interaction may be preconstructed by certain forms of linguistic behavior defined in relation to the state apparatus.

Ideological contents exist ... with technical and political practices ... in their reciprocal relations. Indeed, the discoveries we will make by questioning technical practices and policy, will serve as intermediate results to address the problem of the status of the social sciences, which is at the center of of our concerns.

ibid.

In Bakhtin's terminology the social sciences, then, appear to support the discourses that define the legitimacy of 'official consciousness' and theoretically reject (repressively censure) 'unofficial consciousness'.[24] According to Pêcheux/Herbert ideological practice generates self-consciousness (i.e., the subject as cause of itself) 'by means of a reflexion of consciousness on itself' (ibid.).[25] Henry explains Pêcheux's critical project in the following way:

We can see, then, that in Pêcheux's view the 'social sciences' are primarily techniques which are closely bound up with political practice and with the ideologies which have developed alongside that practice, and that their instrument is discourse.

HENRY, 1995: 30

Furthermore, there is little question that the social sciences (and the 'humanities') are the institutional precondition for a number of what Bakhtin calls 'speech genres':

the category of speech genres should include short rejoinders of daily dialogue ... everyday narration, writing (in all its various forms), the brief standard of military command ... the fairly variegated repertoire of business documents ... and the diverse world of commentary (in the broad sense of the word: social, political). And we must also include here the diverse forms of scientific statements and all the literary genres (from the proverb to the multivolume novel).

BAKHTIN, 1994: 81–82

---

24   According to Pêcheux/Herbert social science is a repressive ideology that literally 'co-ordinates' syntactic and semantic forms of subjection-repression. The always-already-there is prescribed by certain modes of textuality which define official and unofficial forms of linguistic interaction within the structure-in-dominance. Indeed, state power prescribes the 'official language' for its territory which is then used to define the social order.

25   For example, the subject is 'taught' to recognize certain forms of speech activity as 'its own', however, one purpose of 'self-reflection' is to administer the official language of a given society (i.e., as automatic discourse).

Social science, then, produces and disseminates certain 'speech genres' using those discursive practices that articulate the 'always-already-there' of the existing social order (e.g., the subject as cause of itself).

> The 'social sciences' developed in societies in which the aim political practice is primarily, according to Pêcheux, to transform social relations in such a way that the overall structure of social practice remains unchanged. The 'social sciences' are a direct extension of ideologies developed in relation to political practice ... the instrument of political practice is *discourse* or, to be more accurate ... the function of political practice is to transform social relations by re-formulating social demands through discourse.
>
> HENRY, 1995: 30

The discursive formations of the social sciences and humanities – in this sense – determine the preconstructed imposition-concealment of official ideology via mechanisms of generalized writing that are transmitted as 'speech genres'. Both Pêcheux and Bakhtin challenge the notion of self-evident meaning and the ideological subject who is supposedly its agent (i.e., the preconstructed effects of the träger-function).[26]

> 'Meaning' and 'consciousness' are the two basic terms of all bourgeois theories and philosophies of culture. Idealist philosophy ... posits a 'transcendental consciousness' or 'general consciousness'... between the individual consciousness and meaning, the role of which is to preserve the integrity and purity of abstract ideas from disturbance and dissolution in the living generation of material reality.
>
> BAKHTIN, 1994: 126

Pêcheux defines the aforementioned theoretical ideologies with reference to 'meaning effects' and the 'subject as cause of itself' (i.e., the preconstruction of

---

26 The träger-function (support-function) is an Althusserian concept that is outlined in "Three Notes on the Theory of Discourses". Each individual within a given social structure supports the mode of production according to the specific ideological role/s they are expected to follow. Consequently, these individuals exhibit the 'reasons-of-a-subject' ('consciousness') appropriate to their position within such social formations. According to Althusser: "These reasons-of-a-subject appear explicitly in its ideological discourse that relates the subject to which it is addressed, and therefore necessarily includes the subject as a signifier of this discourse; that is why the subject must appear in person among the signifiers of ideological discourse" (Althusser, 2003: 52).

meaning by 'social science' depends on the ideology of subjectivity). As Gillot notes these socio-political forms of discourse are principally derived from variations of the Munchausen effect [ME].

> The ME characterizes ... subjectivism: that is, the repetition, in the field of theory itself, of the typical illusions produced by ideology – the *illusions of meaning and of subject*, the common illusions of a priority and 'obviousness' of meaning (*'le sens'*) and of subject ... that would lead to the absurdity of asserting endlessly a subject at the origin of the subject, or a meaning at the origin of meaning.
>
>   GILLOT, 2014: 96

Similarly, Bakhtin maintains that illusions of subjective interiority and self-evident meaning are, in fact, the result of certain forms of social practice:

> Every ideological product and all its 'ideal meaning' is not in the soul, not in the inner world, and not in the detached world of ideas and pure thoughts ... Social intercourse is the medium in which the ideological phenomenon first acquires its specific existence, its ideological meaning, its semiotic nature.
>
>   BAKHTIN, 1994: 126–127

According to Bakhtin 'literature' inscribes the ideological reproduction of social structures in so far it defines an 'interpretive' schema for various forms of discourse that define subject positions vis-à-vis certain economic conditions (e.g., individual subjectivism).

> The literary structure, like every ideological structure, refracts the generating socioeconomic reality, and does so in its own way. But, at same time, in its 'content', literature reflects and refracts the reflections and refractions of other ideological spheres (ethics, epistemology, political doctrines, religion, etc.). That is, in its 'content' literature reflects the whole of the ideological horizon of which it is itself a part.
>
>   ibid.: 128–129

The literature of the humanities and the social sciences, according to Pêcheux/Herbert, represents and instils certain forms of socially prescribed ideology. Semantic metaphorical dominance conceals from the agents of social practice the preconstructed origins of speech via the hermeneutics of *interdiscourse*, and syntactic metonymic dominance rationalizes the subjective illusion of 'self-evident' *intradiscourse*. Furthermore, such interdiscursive and

intradiscursive effects are elicited by the implementation-solicitation of transverse discourse.[27] Bakhtin maintains that literature (i.e., generalized writing)
is coextensive with other forms of ideological discourse (e.g., religion, metaphysics, morality).[28] "Literature always represents man, his life and fate, his
'inner world', in the ideological purview ... The ideological environment is the
only atmosphere in which life can be the subject of literary representation"
(ibid.: 129). What separates ideology from science, according to Pêcheux, is the
formalization of an experimental practice and an epistemological break with
the subject-form of discourse (i.e., the Munchausen effect [ME]). According to
Helsloot and Hak:

> In his very first publication (Herbert 1966), Pêcheux applies Bachelardian
> and Althusserian concepts to the social sciences, in particular to social
> psychology. His diagnosis is that these sciences have not established
> themselves as proper sciences, because they have not established their
> own theoretical object. In other words, they have not accomplished the
> necessary epistemological break with ideology. These 'sciences', there-
> fore, do not produce scientific knowledge but reproduce the ideology of
> the social system.
>
> HELSLOOT & HAK, 1995: 8–9

The pre-scientific status of the humanities and 'social sciences' is thus indicative of their imaginary character, i.e., as theoretical ideologies which support
what Pêcheux calls 'the complex whole in dominance'.[29] In Bakhtin's account
of literature as an ideological form he distinguishes between two distinct
mechanisms of 'realization': 1) literary 'representations' of discursive practice
and 2) the conditions for the possibility of ideology in general.

> Therefore, when speaking of the refraction of reality in literature, these
> two types of reflection should be strictly separated: 1) the reflection of the

---

27 Transverse-discourse represents the imaginary connection of sound and meaning that is
    typically prescribed by interdiscourse and intradiscourse in given speech performances.
    Subject positions are solicited-implemented by appeals to the self-evident meaning of
    ideology that correspond to preconstructed forms of social interaction.

28 According to Rodríguez and Skinner the myth of 'inner man' is perpetuated by literary
    descriptions of the subject. The phenomena of subjectivity is thus a genre of fiction used
    to actualize ideological forms of intradiscourse via prescientific interdiscursive condi-
    tions (cf. Rodríguez, 2002; Skinner, 1957).

29 Ideological state apparatuses define the linguistic superstructure insofar as speech acts
    conform to the norms of the educational apparatus.

ideological environment in the content of literature; 2) the reflection of the economic base that is common to all ideologies.

BAKHTIN, 1994: 130

The material foundation of speech activity is, then, effaced by the always-already-there of historical ideologies via forms of 'common knowledge' (e.g., the received 'meaning' conveyed by ordinary language). If the humanities and social sciences can be defined as ideological constructs this is due to their broadly metaphysical presuppositions and associated – 'literary' – interpretations of social reality.[30] Saussure's break initiates the scientific analysis of literature vis-à-vis morphology, syntax, and semantics – according to Pêcheux – this rupture must be advanced by the development of testable hypotheses (i.e., experimental practice) for the study of discursive formations. According to Helsloot and Hak:

> Discourse analysis is aimed at a description of the functioning of ideologies in general, and of how this functioning is an obstacle for the establishment of a real social science in particular ... he [Pêcheux] wanted to establish a *social scientific* theory of 'discourse', and he emphasized the need for developing an instrument for creating experimental (vs. experiential) results.
>
> HELSLOOT and HAK, 1995: 10–11

In their present state the social sciences and humanities appear restricted – theoretically and practically – by various forms of philosophical hermeneutics (i.e., interpretive *beliefs*), and therefore, do not attain the status of real sciences because of the ideological practices associated with existing forms of social interaction (e.g., semantic metaphorical dominance and syntactic metonymic dominance). Thus, an epistemological break within the domain of social science is required to separate the ideological history of this field from its *actual* material basis.

Whereas the current practice of the 'social sciences' consists of transforming (ideological) discourse into other (ideological discourse), social

---

30   The social sciences and humanities literalize society via the discursive formations that support the linguistic structure-in-dominance. According to Pêcheux philosophy, psychology, and the humanities more generally, provide the ideological screen to disguise the self-evident subjection of individuals to state apparatuses.

science proper would transform that discourse into something else, which would be expressed in terms of a new theory.

> ibid.: 9

Such a theory, I suggest, would begin the severance of philosophical fictions from real scientific practice, i.e., the separation of preconstructed narratives from the discovery of objective social relations.

CHAPTER 14

Jürgen Habermas (1929–)

The writings of Jürgen Habermas notionally intersect with Pêcheux's œuvre along the axes of metaphysics, communication, ideology, and Marxism. Despite their theoretical proximity no bibliographic entries for Habermas are found in either *Language, Semantics, and Ideology* or *Automatic Discourse Analysis*. Yet – for the purposes of developing Pêcheux's theories of 'meaning' – vis-à-vis discourse analysis – Habermas' research is of certain importance. In the first chapter from *Communication and the Evolution of Society* entitled "What is Universal Pragmatics?" Habermas states: 'The task of universal pragmatics is to identify and reconstruct universal conditions of possible understanding [*Verständigung*]' (Habermas, 1979: 1). Pragmatics – in linguistic theory – is typically defined as the process by which a particular social situation or 'context' affects a given speech act. The title "What is Universal Pragmatics?" could thus be rephrased "What is Universal Context?". This paraphrastic meaning effect suggests the paradoxical result of Habermas' research question. Pragmatic conditions are *particular* ('pertaining to or affecting a single thing or person; pertaining to some and not to all') – rather than universal – 'causes' of discursive behavior which are supposed to influence semantic and syntactic 'choices' in a given speech situation. The situated (i.e., particular) nature of discursive interaction is the principal requirement for pragmatic action *per se,* therefore, 'universal' pragmatics (i.e., universal context) appears to contradict the very idea of pragmatics in linguistic theory. Habermas' intention is to categorically define how understanding can be 'reached' in speech situations. Habermas appears to discern the Saussurian break (*langue/parole*) and its implications for contextual (pragmatic) comprehension, however, Habermas insists that his project to 'identify and reconstruct universal conditions of understanding' remains valid.[1]

> The abstraction of *language* from the use of language in *speech* (*langue* versus *parole*) ... is meaningful. Nonetheless, this methodological step is not sufficient reason for the view that the pragmatic dimension of

---

1 Saussure's epistemological break demonstrates that sound and meaning are 'associated' by certain forms of social practice. As a result, 'understanding' is open to the effects of ideology in so far as context is a philosophical notion. For further discussion regarding the possibility of *contextual* communication see "Signature Event Context" in *Limited Inc* (Derrida, 1988).

language from which one abstracts is beyond formal analysis ... The separation of the two analytic levels, language and speech, should not be made in such a way that the pragmatic dimension of language is left exclusively to empirical analysis – that is, to empirical sciences such as psycholinguistics and sociolinguistics.

    ibid.: 6

In other words, context (i.e., a given speech situation) can be analyzed via 'universal pragmatics' but this should not be achieved by strict empirical methods, rather, the physical properties of language and the ideological conditions of speech ought to remain together methodologically.[2] The material/mental (i.e., empiricist vs. idealist) distinction finds expression in Habermas' 'universal pragmatics' in terms of 'observation' (sensory experience) and 'communicative experience' (understanding).[3]

Observation is directed to perceptible things and events (or states); understanding is directed to the meaning of utterances ... I shall not here analyze the complex relationship between observation and understanding ... but I would like to direct attention to one aspect – the difference in level between perceptible reality and the understandable meaning of a symbolic formation.

    ibid.: 9

In consequence, 'communicative experience' (i.e., the meaning of utterances) interposes a particular (not universal) interpretation of events via certain pragmatic conditions.[4] The apprehension of 'understanding', according to Habermas, is a result of recognizing the apparent meaning of a given context.[5]

---

2 Habermas attempts to delineate the difference between 'perceptible reality' and 'understandable meaning', however, he does not appear to resolve how empirical reality is subject to interpretation.

3 Colloquially the statement 'I see what you mean' may seem obvious, however, on closer inspection it is not so clear. This is because one cannot see directly *how* an observation is understood in so far as comprehension is the result of preconstructed semantic and syntactic associations which occur 'in' language (cf. Pêcheux, 1982; Saussure, 1959).

4 Habermas seems to overlook the fact that observation is mediated by concepts which determine what is observed. Consequently, observation and communicative experience are linked via certain discursive formations that proscribe the possibility of naïve empiricism ('direct observation').

5 Meaning effects are thus 'understood' via the apprehension of certain symbolic systems, yet, as Pêcheux suggests, such ideological structures are not self-evident (although they may appear so), they are the result of discursive preconstruction (Pêcheux, 1982). Thus, an

The goal of coming to an understanding [*Verständigung*] is to bring about an agreement [*Einverständnis*] that terminates in the intersubjective mutuality of reciprocal understanding ... and accord with one another ... In everyday life we start from a background consensus pertaining to those interpretations taken for granted among participants. As soon as this consensus is shaken ... the task of mutual interpretation is to achieve a new definition of the situation which all participants can share.

ibid.: 3

Habermas' ideology of 'universal pragmatics' can be translated into Pêcheux's critical theory of subjection in relation to: 1) intersubjective 'guarantees' of meaning 2) preconstructed syntax via 'background consensus' and 3) communicative experience (understanding) as ideological mis/recognition. According to Pêcheux:

... the space in which ... meaning is constituted – is where the unthought (exterior) that determines it is occulted ... this occultation takes place in the reflexive sphere of consciousness and intersubjectivity, i.e., in the borderless and limitless sphere of the subject-form which, like ideology 'has no outside'....

PÊCHEUX, 1982: 127

Moreover, the background consensus – which Habermas notes is taken for granted – is not, in fact, consensually agreed upon, such agreement is *imaginary* in so far as a given meaning pre-exists the subjects who then (after some training) 'understand' it (see chapter five). Habermas suggests that such 'communicative experience' is based on a participatory logic between subjects, yet they only 'share' in this meaning in so far as they use the language according to the *prestructured* 'background consensus' – they do not create the already-existing language.[6] Each subject "who understands meaning is experiencing fundamentally as a participant in communication, on the basis of a symbolically established intersubjective relationship with other individuals even if he is actually alone with a book, a document, or a work of art" (Habermas, 1979: 9). Much of Pêcheux's research in *Language, Semantics, and Ideology*, and *Automatic*

'accepted' meaning suggests that one agrees with an existing order of discourse – which may have been conveyed imperceptibly – via a preconstructed ideology.

6   According to Althusser: 'The child is caught up from birth *in* language' (Althusser, 1996: 71). In consequence, the child enters – in Habermas' terms – a 'symbolically prestructured reality' via the acquistion of language.

Discourse Analysis, aims to demonstrate that 'communicatively mediated access' to meaning is preconstructed by discursive formations which define the parameters of ideological interaction via the accepted norms of ordinary language. Furthermore, Habermas' notion of 'direct access' to reality is conceptually problematic in so far as empirical observations are a product of linguistic systems (i.e., 'facts' mediated by concepts).[7]

> The difference in level between perceptible reality and symbolically pre-structured reality is reflected in the gap between direct access through observation of reality and communicatively mediated access through understanding an utterances referring to events
> ibid.: 10

But Habermas also describes the action of 'superstructural' phenomena (e.g., cultural values, moral representations, and belief systems) thus suggesting that communicative experience is determined by certain socio-linguistic conditions which apparently represent 'perceptible reality' (ibid.: 98).[8] Habermas develops this theory in "Historical Materialism and the Development of Normative Structures":

> The structures of linguistically established intersubjectivity – which can be examined prototypically in connection with elementary speech actions – are conditions of both social and personality systems. Social systems can be viewed as networks of communicative actions; personality systems can be regarded under the aspect of the ability to speak and act. *If one examines social institutions and the action competences of socialized individuals for general characteristics, one encounters the same structures of consciousness.*
> ibid.: 98–99; emphasis added

---

7 The problem of empirical *immediacy* is addressed by Gaston Bachelard in *The Formation of the Scientific Mind* where he demonstrates that epistemological obstacles block the development of scientific knowledge. The first obstacle to scientific knowledge, according to Bachelard, is primary experience (Bachelard, 2002).

8 Evidently, this is another example of Saussure's 'double structure' whereby the linguistic superstructure is conveyed directly in certain forms of 'obvious' syntax, i.e., the *conventional* form of an ideology appears to represent 'direct access' to reality. For further information regarding this idea see 'Nature of the Linguistic Sign' in *Course in General Linguistics* (Saussure, 1959: 65).

Here Habermas approximates a theory of 'behavioral ideology' via the social structures which define individual acts of 'meaningful' experience (see the preceding chapter).

> There are also homologies between the structures of ego identity and of group identity ... No one can construct an identity independently of the identifications that others make of him ... *Thus the basis for the assertion of one's own identity is not really self-identification, but intersubjectively recognized self-identification.*
>
> ibid.: 106–107; emphasis added

In Pêcheux's terms ISAs (Ideological State Apparatuses) inscribe and legitimate certain forms of intersubjective interaction based upon the reproduction of particular social structures (e.g., work, home, and school). Subject positions, then, reproduce the predetermined 'meaning' of existing social practices.

> This theory of ideology entails the conceptual disqualification of a pure, originary subjectivity that would be given before the inscription of human individuals in the institutions, apparatuses, and so on, of social formations.
>
> GILLOT, 2014: 89

According to Pêcheux ISAs administer the dominant ideology that is in/voluntarily 'adopted' in various forms of background consensus, e.g., the ideological kinds of 'agreement' that are interposed between subjects as forms of prescribed social reality.[9] In consequence, Habermas' theory of meaning appears difficult to reconcile with any supposed 'linguistic consensus' in so far as communicatively mediated experience is an effect of ideological state apparatuses.[10] If the social conditions of speech acts are, in the last instance, determined by the substructure then intersubjective consensus seems to function as a theoretical ideology given that the conditions of communicative action are predetermined by existing forms of discourse (e.g., law, social science, and literature). Moreover, Habermas suggests that the arrival of bourgeois society

---

9   For example, Pêcheux's research suggests that the Rule of Law functions as a 'legitimate' form of ideology in so far it supports 'consensual' forms of social domination (Pêcheux, 2014).

10   According to Althusser: "*An Ideological State Apparatus is a system of defined institutions, organizations, and the corresponding practices. Realized in the institutions, organizations, and practices of this system is all or part (generally speaking, a typical combination of certain elements) of the State Ideology*" (Althusser, 2014: 77).

involved the formation of a new collective identity to further the spirit of capitalism.[11] This new theoretical ideology integrated three discursive formations for the development 'free' subjectivity: law, morality and politics. The 'background consensus' required that these subjects view one another as: 1) free and equal subjects of civil law (the citizen as private commodity owner); 2) morally free subjects (the citizen as private person); and 3) politically free subjects (democratic citizens) (Habermas, 1979: 114). Bakhtin explains how shifts in ideology occur via the 'reevaluation' of existing social values in so far as these 'new meanings' are related to the structure of the economy.[12]

> The generative process of signification in language is always associated with the generation of the evaluative purview of a particular social group, and the generation of an evaluative purview – in the sense of the totality of all those things that have meaning and importance for the particular group – is entirely determined by the expansion of the economic basis ....
>
> BAKHTIN, 1994: 37

Base and superstructure are then integrated: theoretical ideologies produce the necessary discursive formations for the reproduction of the relations of production required by the structure-in-dominance.[13]

> Thus the collective identity of bourgeois society developed under the highly abstract viewpoints of legality, morality, and sovereignty; at least it expressed itself in this way in modern natural-law constructions and in formalist ethics.
>
> HABERMAS, 1979: 114

The ideological basis of socially situated speech is revealed, according to Montgomery and Allan, in the meaning effects associated with certain forms of discourse: "discursive formations are particular orders of discourse, each

---

11   Indeed, the transition from feudalism to capitalism appears to have required a coordinated shift from religious predestination to the personalist metaphysics of freedom (cf. Hirst, 1983; Habermas, 1979).

12   If, following the work of Bakhtin and Pêcheux, the ideological superstructure is essentially *linguistic* the economic base would then support this dominant ideology for reasons of legitimation. Thus, the primary function of the ideological state apparatus would be to affirm the linguistic means of subjection via state power.

13   The structure-in-dominance (*structure à dominante*) designates the given forms of authority and subordination evinced throughout ideological history of social formations (*structure toujours-déjà-donnée*) (Althusser, 1970).

imbricated within an ideological formation, *which secure the meaning* of specific words, expressions, and propositions" (Montgomery & Allan, 1992; emphasis added). For a State to demonstrate authority in matters of governance it must, according to Habermas, demonstrate its *legitimacy*, i.e., the State must secure the official power to rule.[14] The language of state power must represent its authority *in words*. Hence the 'background consensus' used to legitimate social order may be based on pre-established forms of semantic domination (i.e., certain preconstructed meanings).

> Legitimacy means that there are good reasons for a political order's claim
> to recognized as right and just; a legitimate order deserves recognition.
> *Legitimacy means a political order's worthiness to be recognized.* This defi-
> nition highlights the fact that legitimacy is a contestable validity claim;
> the stability of the order of domination (also) depends on its (at least) de
> facto recognition.
>
>   HABERMAS, 1979: 178

The operation of ideological subjection – in the writings of the Pêcheux – is inseparable from the functioning of state apparatuses (ISAs). The authority of the State is legitimated via certain conditions of ideological mis/recognition, and moreover, the 'meaning' of its sovereignty is determined by linguistic practices:

> the point is, in the end, to begin to formulate the conceptual conditions
> which will make it possible to analyse scientifically the linguistic support
> for the operation of ideological state apparatuses.
>
>   PÊCHEUX, 1982: 207

According to Nicos Poulantzas:

> The principal role of the state apparatuses is to maintain the unity and
> cohesion of a social formation by concentrating and sanctioning class
> domination, and in this way reproducing social relations, i.e., class rela-
> tions. Political and ideological relations are materialized and embodied,
> as material practices, in the state apparatuses.
>
>   POULANTZAS, 1975: 24–25

---

14   I note here that the State defines the official language that is accepted within its territory.
      Consequently, the subjects of the state are impelled to use the language that re/produces
      the existing socio-political order.

State power, then, maintains its authority in particular ideological 'procedures' facilitated by discursive apparatuses (e.g., educational, political and judicial), however, subjects of the State appear to exhibit *relative autonomy* in respect of this always-already-given structure of legitimacy.

> The state does not itself ... establish the collective identity of the society ... But inasmuch as the state *assumes the guarantee* to prevent social disintegration by way of binding decisions, the exercise of state power is tied to the claim of maintaining society in its normatively determined identity.
>
> HABERMAS, 1979 180; emphasis added

Here Habermas evinces the *contradictory* logic of 'free' societies. Despite the fact the fact subjects are coerced by ideological state apparatuses such coercion cannot appear as a function of legitimacy in so far as this would controvert how a free society is supposed to work *in principle*.

> The political subsystem takes on the task of protecting society from disintegration; but it cannot freely dispose of the capacities of social integration or the definitional power through which the identity of the society is fixed.
>
> ibid.: 180

The modern 'free' society must achieve the effect of *non-coercive coercion* in which its members are *freely* integrated without it appearing that such integration is, in fact, dictated by the State.[15] The State, then, occludes its very functioning in its effects and facilitates the self-identification of 'free subjects' via ideological state apparatuses. The authority of the State is symbolically maintained via the subjective illusion of 'personal' freedom. Hence, ideological mis/recognition of the state apparatus functions to *legitimate* the social order.

> By *legitimacy* I understand the worthiness of a political order to be recognized. The *claim to legitimacy* is related to the social-integrative preservation of a normatively determined social identity. *Legitimations* serve to make good this claim, that is, to show how and why existing (or

---

15   Such non-coercive coercion appears to generally agree with the principles of *laissez-faire* economics whereby the State maintains order and security while leaving individuals 'free' to advance their own interests.

recommended) institutions are fit to employ political power in such a way that the values constitutive for the identity of the society will be realized.

ibid.: 182–183

The modern liberal State proceeds by ideologically 'freeing' its subjects from anything which could impede the functioning of the market between private citizens, i.e., the State institutes a certain superstructure which permits 'free' forms of production and exchange.[16]

> The state organizes the conditions under which the citizens, as competing and strategically acting private persons, carry on the production process ... In other words, the state develops and guarantees bourgeois civil law, the monetary mechanism and certain infrastructures ... Since the state does not itself engage in capitalist enterprise, it has to siphon off the resources for its ordering achievements from private incomes.
>
> ibid.: 189

Ideological state apparatuses are effectively funded by the tax system which reproduces the institutional conditions of 'free' society.

> The modern state is a state based on taxation (Schumpeter). From these determinations there results a constellation of state and civil society which the Marxist theory of the state has been continually concerned to analyze.
>
> ibid.

Divisions of the state apparatus include: police, prisons, the judiciary, civil service, political parties, schools, universities, the military, and social welfare.[17] State apparatuses function on the basis of a 'consensus' which establishes

---

16 According to Foucault: "Liberalism must produce freedom, but this very act entails the establishment of limitations, controls, forms of coercion, and obligations relying on threats, etcetera" (Foucault, 2008: 64).

17 Evgeny Pashukanis writes: "The formal completeness of the concepts 'state territory', 'population', 'state authority' reflects, not only a particular ideology, but also the objective fact of the formation of tightly-centred real sphere of dominance and thus reflects, above all, the creation of an actual administrative, fiscal and military organisation with the corresponding material and human apparatus. The state is nothing without means of communication, without the possibility of transmitting orders and decrees, mobilising the armed forces, and so on" (Pashukanis, 2003: 76).

the procedural legitimacy of the social order funded by taxation, however, in daily life the real basis of the superstructure is mis/recognized as the 'always-already-there'.[18]

State power is *justified* because it appears legitimate, i.e., procedurally correct, yet, the historical genesis of such procedural rationality is typically taken for granted and simply assumed to be lawful.[19]

> Thus, by *levels of justification* I mean formal conditions for the acceptability of grounds or reasons, conditions that lend to legitimations their efficacy, their power to produce consensus and shape motives ... The idea of an agreement that comes to pass among all parties, as free and equal, determines the procedural type of legitimacy of modern times.
>
> ibid.: 184–185

According to Habermas the arrival of the modern state (and its justification) is defined by five fundamental principles: secularization (separation of Church and state), rational law (procedural rationality), abstract right (guaranteed freedom), sovereignty (self-governance), and nation (state territory). Furthermore, faced with challenges to its legitimacy the State must justify its claim to *de jure* recognition. This consequence Habermas calls a 'legitimation problem'.

> The problem consists ... in representing the accomplishments of the capitalist economy as, comparatively speaking, the best possible satisfaction of generalizable interests – or at least insinuating this is so. The state thereby programmatically obligates itself to keep dysfunctional side effects within acceptable limits ... the state provides legitimating support to a social order claiming legitimacy.
>
> ibid.: 196–197

Pêcheux approaches the legitimation problem in terms of dominant and dominated ideologies that are normatively defined by the non-coercive coercion of state power:

---

18   The structure-in-dominance does not typically appear as a system of domination given the *modus operandi* of non-coercive coercion: this is due to the relative autonomy that exists between the various sectors of the mode of production (Althusser, 1970).

19   The modern State defines itself as the *de jure* authority in matters of governance. Hence the rule of law *justifies* the legality of state power. For a brief introduction to the history of this form of legal practice see *The Birth of Biopolitics* (Foucault, 2008: 159–184).

Thus, the dominated ideology cannot be purely and simply the 'ideology of the dominated class'... we must speak of *dominated ideologies in the plural,* and thus of the fact that there cannot be a *single dominant ideology* in a given historical moment; it is precisely for this reason that the question of ideology comes to be placed under the state; the existence of dominated ideologies is indissociable from the contradictions inscribed in the ideological domination of the class in power, which we will mark here in the following thesis: *the dominant ideology never dominates without contradictions*

PÊCHEUX, 2014: 17

The problem of state legitimacy is systemically related to the tacit justification of dominant and dominated ideologies in 'accepted' forms of interdiscourse.[20] Moreover, Pêcheux's research suggests that the relation between state control and everyday life is determined by certain symbolic structures that are realized in 'self-consciousness' (Pêcheux, 1982). In "Self-Reflection as Science: Freud's Psychoanalytic Critique of Meaning" Habermas asserts that Freud's path-breaking research led to the foundation of psychoanalysis as a science of 'self-reflection'.[21]

Psychoanalysis is relevant to us as the only tangible example of a science incorporating methodical self-reflection ... It provides theoretical perspectives and technical rules for the interpretation of symbolic structures.

HABERMAS, 1987: 214

In Pêcheux's terms psychoanalysis represents an attempt to decode of the symbolic order vis-à-vis unconscious structures of subjection. Such analysis can potentially reveal the repressive mechanisms of symbolic domination in so far as such beliefs are typically misrecognized in *conventional* forms of social interaction.

---

20   Although the State prescribes the official language/s within its territory this fact does not prevent dominant and dominated ideologies existing within the 'same' linguistic structures. This is due to certain pragmatic norms permitting different enunciative effects within seemingly identical forms of language (cf. Haroche *et al.,* 1971; Austin, 1962).

21   Pêcheux uses the work of both Freud and Lacan to demonstrate that the linguistic basis of ideology is typically unconscious, however, any 'self-reflection' provided by psychoanalytic inquiry must be delimited by the *ideological structure of meaning* that is concealed in 'automatic discourse' (Pêcheux, 1995).

We can therefore advance the hypothesis that this repression (which affects both the discursive process itself and the interdiscourse with which it is articulated by relations of contradiction, subservience and encroachment) is unconscious in character, in the sense that ideology is constitutionally unconscious of its own existence ....

PÊCHEUX, 1995: 139

State legitimacy may, constitute an unconscious ideology which tacitly justifies the existence of certain repressive conditions for the 'social-integrative preservation' of existing social relations.[22] The discourse of 'freedom' (non-coercive coercion) and the subject as cause of itself would then serve as part of the 'background consensus' by which various aspects of state power are legitimated. According to Pêcheux:

Being the most fully developed form of ideology, bourgeois ideology tells us a great deal about earlier historical forms, as well as about the workings of the ideological instance in general ... Insofar as it is a 'representation of an imaginary relationship', the autonomy of the subject is in fact closely bound up with the appearance and extension of bourgeois juridico-political ideology.

ibid.: 126

Moreover, a given discursive formation exhibits specific conditions of enunciation that correspond to the social system in which it is used, therefore, lexical structures correspond to particular modes of production. "We are advancing the hypothesis that a given state of conditions of production corresponds to a definite structure of the process of production of discourse within the language" (ibid.: 82). The 'free subject' is the ideological correlate of a free society.

One main postulate, in Pêcheux's programme, is the following ... the obviousness of being a subject, a free subject, is essentially illusory. It is constructed inside the discursive-ideological process ... this materialist perspective claims that there is no such thing as a free, prior subject, and that subjectivity is a preconstructed effect.

GILLOT, 2014: 103

---

22   According to Althusser the State is fundamentally repressive in so far it organizes the structure-in-dominance vis-à-vis the relations of production. "The hard core of the state is its *repressive apparatus*. It is endowed with a force and a power of resistance that are by definition meant to be 'fail proof'" (Althusser, 2014: 152).

Habermas suggests that the unconscious functions via the occlusion of its effects 'inside' various forms of behavior (e.g., gesture and speech). Thus, the method of psychoanalysis primarily functions to reveal how certain psychic agencies convey the symbolic basis of self-subjection.

> Psychoanalytic interpretation is concerned with those connections of symbols in which a subject deceives itself about itself ... Freud coins the phrase 'internal foreign territory' to capture the character of the alienation of something that is still the subject's very own.
>
> HABERMAS, 1987: 218

The symbolic order transmitted in discursive formations is integrated by the programmatic restrictions of occluded subjection where agency is attributed to intentionality, however, this process of subordination is – in principle – determined by imaginary mechanisms of ideological mis/recognition associated with customary speech patterns (e.g., ideologies of self-evident meaning). According to Habermas:

> The institutions of social intercourse sanction only certain motives for action. Other need dispositions, likewise attached to interpretations in ordinary language, are denied the route to manifest action, whether by the direct power of an interaction partner or the sanction of recognized social norms. These conflicts, at first external, are perpetuated intrapsychically; insofar as they are not manifest consciously, this perpetuation takes place as a permanent conflict between a defensive agency representing social repression and unrealizable motives for action.
>
> ibid.: 223

In Pêcheux's terms A (semantic) and B (syntactic) ideologies produce particular forms of symbolic stratification that define interdiscursive speech acts via ideological state apparatuses. Such interdiscursive repression is manifest in various forms of psychic 'censorship'. According to Habermas interpretations of reality outside of social norms are suppressed by unconscious parsing (i.e., self-censorship) and any content not supported by institutionally guaranteed discourse is repressed by defence mechanisms which manage the conflict of intrapsychic agencies.[23] Symptomatically instances of unconscious repression

---

23   Freud notes: "Repression may, without doubt, be correctly described as the intermediate stage between a defensive reflex and a condemning judgement" (Freud, 1960: 175).

may appear as parapraxes whereby the latent structure of censorship is temporarily bypassed and what is 'private' becomes 'public'.[24] Habermas suggests that public discourse represents what is socially acceptable and appears to exclude (repress) anything from the 'privatized language of unconscious motives'. Self-alienation occurs, according to Habermas, when the the subject seems to disagree with a speech act that 'ought' to have been repressed given the existing forms of discourse, in consequence, 'the ego deceives itself about its identity in the symbolic structures that it consciously generates' (ibid.: 227). The self-censorship of subjective experience prevents manifest discord in relation to official ideologies: thus, any latent motives not prescribed by the symbolic order are displaced and repressed by censorial effects of 'consciousness'. According to Habermas:

> both psychological and official censorship suppress linguistic material and the meanings articulated in it. Both forms of censorship make use of the same defence mechanisms: the procedures prohibiting and rewriting a text correspond to the psychic mechanisms of omission (repression) and displacement.
>
> ibid.: 225

Pêcheux's research advances Freud's repressive hypothesis to explain how ideology functions as a self-generating form of subjection vis-à-vis Lacan's symbolic order.[25] According to Gillot:

> The crucial implication here is that the subjectivation process responds to the very logic of ideology, in so far as such a logic is linked to the *logic of Unconscious itself* (the effectiveness of an absent cause).
>
> GILLOT, 2014: 105

The subject's ego, Habermas suggests, 'deceives itself' by articulating speech which has occluded origins, i.e., the absent cause of linguistic subjection (i.e., self-evident meaning). Discourse analysis – as conceived by Pêcheux – attempts to explain such 'self-deception' with recourse to unconscious structures

---

24   Freud's research in *The Psychopathology of Everyday Life* (1981) addresses the symptomology of unconscious mistakes, parapraxes and other 'bungled actions' revealed in psychoanalytic investigation.

25   Lacan adapts Saussure's research to explain how Freud's theory of the unconscious is the missing link (absent cause) between the signifier and the signifed in the subject-form of discourse (Lacan, 2006: 412–441).

of symbolic domination: the subject unconsciously subjects 'itself' to the Munchausen effect via certain forms socially prescribed discourse (i.e., ideological state apparatuses).

> Pêcheux's linguistic and philosophical understanding of the subterranean effectiveness of ideology leans of a precise and neuralgic use of psychoanalytical categories, such as... the 'strangeness in the familiar', according to Pêcheux's particular understanding of the Freudian *Unheimlichkeit* [uncanny].
>
> GILLOT, 2014: 106

Dominant interpretations of existing social relations are defined, according to Pêcheux, by ISAs (ideological state apparatuses), however, these structures of authority are not typically perceived as the source of a subject's discourse.[26] Such discursive mis/recognition is identified by Habermas in certain cases of 'public communication'.

> The institution of power relations necessarily restricts public communication. If this restriction is not to affect the appearance of intersubjectivity, then the limits to communication must be established in the interior of subjects themselves ... The starting point of psychoanalytic theory is the experience of resistance, that is the blocking force that stands in the way of the free and public communication of repressed contents.
>
> HABERMAS, 1987: 228–229

Habermas further considers the problem of 'meaning' generation in "Toward a Critique of the Theory of Meaning" where he proposes that 'meaningful' interaction implies satisfactory 'understanding'. "*A theory of meaning should answer the question: what is it to understand the sense of a – well-formed – symbolic expression?*" (Habermas, 1992: 57; emphasis added). Although Habermas appraises a number of competing theories of semantic phenomena, e.g.,

---

26   Pêcheux describes two kinds of forgetting that form the basis of ideological subjection. Forgetting 1 designates the institutional structure that pre-defines speech activity and forgetting 2 designates the supposedly immediate meaning of subjective experience. "In other words, we are positing the view that the relationship between forgetting 1 and forgetting 2 relates to the relationship between, one the one hand, the non-subjective conditions of existence of the subjective illusion and, on the other, the subjective forms of its realization" (Pêcheux, 1995: 139).

'intended meaning', 'literal meaning' and 'meaning as use', he does not appear to directly pursue the hypothesis that meaning is an ideology. Where Pêcheux seeks to explain 'meaning effects' within certain discursive conditions Habermas generally appears to support the specious belief that meaning exists in words. However, Habermas does identify – following Wittgenstein – that semantic interpretations are preconstructed by particular social conditions.

> Learning to master a language or learning how expressions in a language should be understood requires socialization into a form of life. The latter *antecedently* regulates the use of words and sentences within a network of possible purposes and possible actions.
>
> HABERMAS, 1992: 63

The Saussurian break defines a theoretical point of no return for linguistics as a science and Pêcheux seeks to apply this working principle to the study of discourse. He identifies 'meaning' as a prescientific (ideological) residuum that mis/represents forms of subjective experience via his *materialist* theory of discourse. Thus, Pêcheux begins the project of demonstrating how meaning is produced in discursive formations whereas Habermas typically continues to further the *philosophy* of meaning. I am not suggesting that Habermas was unaware that meaning may function in the service of ideologies, rather, this theoretical oversight appears to reflect a repressed element in his theories of symbolic interaction.[27] In "Themes in Postmetaphysical Thinking" Habermas details a double structure in which subjects 'freely' choose their linguistic means and are, simultaneously, situated by the same activity: he suggests such relations are 'equiprimordial' (i.e., co-constitutive).

> Subjects capable of speaking and acting who, against the background of a common lifeworld, come to an understanding with each other about something in the world, relate to the medium of their language *both autonomously and dependently* ... Both moments are equiprimordial.
>
> HABERMAS, 1992: 43; emphasis added

Autonomous language *use* appears to parallel Pêcheux's 'Munchausen effect' (ME) where the subject is attributed the cause of its own discourse, however, this is, in fact, illusory as the subject is dependent on the intelligibility

---

27   Habermas' research on 'understanding' is haunted by the problem of *subjective* consensus. In this sense 'meaning' *enigmatically* establishes agreement. Pêcheux attempts to overcome such theoretical failings by outlining a non-subjective theory of meaning effects.

of pre-existing discursive structures to achieve 'mutual understanding'.[28] Habermas seems to accept that the subject cannot be located outside the discursive formations which permit communication, yet his solution to the 'equiprimordial' double structure of language is understanding by consensus, which seems to repeat Jean-Jacques Rousseau's imaginary 'social contract'.

> On the one hand ... subjects always find themselves already in a linguistically structured and disclosed world; they live off of grammatically projected interconnections of meaning. To this extent, language sets itself off from the speaking subjects as something antecedent and objective ... On the other hand, the linguistically disclosed and structured lifeworld finds its footing only in the practices of reaching understanding within a linguistic community. In this way, the linguistic formation of consensus, by means of which interactions link up space and time remains dependent upon the autonomous 'yes' and 'no' positions that communication participants take toward criticizable validity claims.
>
> ibid.: 43

Broadly considered, Habermas' research remains on the terrain of philosophical solutions to linguistic problems and, consequently, despite his awareness of Saussure's break, regresses towards fictions of a consensus model to explain symbolic interaction.[29] Pêcheux, by contrast, attempts to align his theory of discourse with methods of scientific practice. According to Herbert/Pêcheux a scientific field is established in two stages 1) theoretical-conceptual transformation (i.e. from ideology to science) 2) conceptual-experimental verification (methodical reproduction of the scientific object). Habermas clearly finds that existing norms of language evince a double structure between individual autonomy and social dependence, but, he does not appear to pursue objective verification principles as a means to address such ideological issues. Programmatically, Habermas appears to endorse 'communicative hermeneutics' to further 'understanding' and 'consensus' via dialogue (e.g., ideal speech

---

28   In the first instance the State apparatus functions to guarantee legitimate consensus, yet, such agreement may function as an ideology if it is based on 'natural' language. This is due to the fact that everyday discourse typically conveys pre-established meanings which have been occluded by habit (cf. Pêcheux, 1995; Sapir, 1921).

29   Habermas works in the the tradition of critical theory and his research attempts to define how perceptible reality is related to symbolically prestructured forms of interaction – theoretically – he appears to conflate consensus and objectivity.

situations). Yet, this theory of consensus does not adequately engage with pre-existing forms of discursive dominance in so far as the pragmatic conditions of consensual speech activity (e.g., acceptability) are regulated by structures of repression (e.g., ideological state apparatuses). Hence, a 'well-formed symbolic expression' – in Habermas' ideology of meaning – must comply with an existing normative framework that is administered by institutional forms of authority.[30]

---

30   According to Althusser the ideology of the state apparatus leads subjects to 'work by themselves' such that the structure-in-dominance is reproduced without *significant* interference. Pêcheux thus advances Althusser's general theory of ideology to demonstrate that the primary vehicle of ideological subjection is language (i.e., the means of subjection is found in certain forms of symbolic interaction).

CHAPTER 15

Émile Benveniste (1902–1976)

Pêcheux appears to suggest that Benveniste's theory of enunciation tacitly supports the Munchausen effect [ME] in so far as the sovereign individual proclaims its linguistic deeds from the unrestricted (free) space of *self-generating* subjectivity (Pêcheux, 1995: 137).[1] But such a reading would not account for the broad continuity of Benveniste and Pêcheux's research in relation to the function of discourse for the *reproduction* of social reality.[2] According to Benveniste:

> Language *re-produces* reality. This is to be understood in the literal sense: reality is produced anew by means of language. The speaker recreates the event and his experience of the event by his discourse. The hearer grasps the the discourse first, and through this discourse, the event which is being reproduced. Thus the situation inherent in the practice of language, namely that of exchange and dialogue, confers a double function on the act of discourse; for the speaker it represents reality, for the hearer it recreates that reality.
>
> BENVENISTE, 1971: 22

In Pêcheux's materialist theory of discourse the linguistic base 'realizes the real' vis-à-vis particular discursive formations. This process – which is typically unconscious – systematically situates subjects within the linguistic structures defined by ideological state apparatuses. In homologous terms Benveniste outlines a theory of symbolic interaction which describes the realization of social reality *linguistically*.

> Why are the individual and society, together and of the same necessity, *grounded* in language? Because language represents the highest form of a faculty inherent in the human condition, the faculty of *symbolizing*. Let us understand by this, very broadly, the faculty of *representing* the real by

---

1 Pêcheux also cites Bally and Jakobson as sources for the illusions associated with the subject-form of discourse.

2 The reproduction of the relations of production, according to Pêcheux, is a consequence of certain linguistic norms which are supported by preconstructed forms of discourse (e.g., the subject as cause of itself).

a 'sign' and of understanding the 'sign' as representing the real – the faculty, then, of establishing a relation of 'signification' between one thing
and another.

ibid.: 23

This symbolic representation of reality is determined – in Pêcheux's research –
by the linguistic base that prescribes certain interdiscursive and intradiscursive forms of speech (Pêcheux, 1982).[3] Moreover, the unconscious dynamics of
the symbolic order are not neglected by Benveniste: he, like Pêcheux, refers to
the research of Freud to explain the formation of subjective speech acts.

All through Freudian analysis it can be seen that the subject makes use of
the act of speech and discourse in order to 'represent himself'... Language
[*langage*] is thus used here as the act of speech [*parole*], converted into
that expression of instantaneous and elusive subjectivity which forms
the condition of dialogue.

BENVENISTE, 1971: 67

For Pêcheux the mis/recognition of linguistic immediacy determines the spontaneous existence of the always-already-there as a pre-constructed linguistic product. Because discursive formations are assumed to be obvious their
operation may pass unnoticed in the reproduction of daily life.[4] According to
Williams the research of Benveniste addresses how a given enunciation *situates* the speaking subject (1999: 175). Ideological conditions of enunciation are
represented by the collocation of subject and situation given that the structure of language determines *parole* [speech] systematically (Pêcheux, 1982).
In this respect Benveniste highlights how forms of speech and societal norms
are mutually dependent on the symbolic systems used to determine social
structures.

---

3   Following the work of Leroi-Gourhan interdiscourse and intradiscourse function via the
    interiorized exteriority of symbolic systems. Phonic and graphic symbols thus represent
    external reality internally in so far as ideo-cultural practices support the transmission of lin-
    guistic technicity.
4   For example, in natural language meaning appears self-evident because the 'associations'
    that connect semantic and syntactic structures are taken for granted, i.e., words *naturally*
    'have' meaning.

In placing man in his relationship with nature or in his relationship with man, by the mediation of language, we establish society ... For language always realizes itself in *a language* in a definite and specific linguistic structure which is inseparable from a definite and specific society.

> BENVENISTE, 1971: 26

One of Pêcheux's main theses is that through language the structure of society may be transmitted unconsciously because individuals fail to identify (i.e., 'forget about') the preconstructed conditions of communicative activity.[5] Individual agency, then, represents an illusory effect via certain unconscious mechanisms which determine the *appearance* of linguistic intentionality in subjective form. Furthermore, Williams maintains that Benveniste's research was instrumental for the development of 'post-structuralism' and its ensuing deconstruction of the subject as cause of itself (i.e., Pêcheux's 'Munchausen effect).

Benveniste's contribution to post-structuralism has not been widely recognized ... Benveniste's work, together with that of Lacan ... lay behind the decentring of the subject, deriving as it did from the French linguist's analysis of the subject in language in terms of the subject of enonciation.

> WILLIAMS, 1999: 175

Yet, Williams also supports Pêcheux's thesis regarding the ideological basis of Benveniste's work, in fact, Williams suggests Pêcheux found Benveniste to be a proponent of pre-Saussurian metaphysics.

Pêcheux saw Benveniste, above all, as a linguist of subjectivity in whose work he identified the possibility of a return to the question of psychological subjectivity, which structuralism and the work of Saussure had banished from linguistic theory.

> ibid.: 177

There is, then, an apparent *contradiction* between the views of Pêcheux and Benveniste regarding psychological subjectivity and its potentially ideological ramifications.[6] I find that Benveniste does, in some cases, support 'creative'

---

5 Forgetting no. 1 describes the fact that individual agency is prescribed by existing sociolinguistic structures and forgetting no. 2 designates the phantasmatic effect of self-evident meaning that is spontaneously occluded in forms of ordinary language (Pêcheux, 1995).

6 Contrary acts of diction (i.e., contradictions) imply *subjective* forms of understanding given that what is being contradicted may be disputed.

language use (i.e., linguistic spontaneity), although, he also suggests that certain elements of discourse are the product of unconscious structures.[7] Benveniste states:

> All psychoanalysis is grounded on a theory of symbolism. Now, language is nothing but symbolism ... The profound analyses Freud gave to the symbolism of the unconscious also illuminate the different ways that language is realized ... We thus come back to 'discourse'. By following this comparison, one would be put on the way to productive comparisons between the symbolism of the unconscious and certain typical procedures of the subjectivity manifested in discourse.
>
> BENVENISTE, 1971: 73–74

For Benveniste symbolic structures are, in certain respects, *unconsciously realized* in speech acts. Metonymy, metaphor, euphemism, allusion, antiphrasis, preterition, litotes, synecdoche, and – more generally – 'syntactic conventions', are enumerated by Benveniste to indicate how subjects 'use' certain linguistic devices without being explicitly aware that they are doing so.[8] According to Benveniste: "the reality of language, as a general rule, remains unconscious; except when language is especially studied for itself, we have no more than a very faint and fleeting awareness of the operations which we accomplish in order to talk" (ibid.: 55). Pêcheux's 'subject-form of discourse' is an unconscious – phantasmatic – linguistic effect (the subject as cause of itself) whereby subjectivity is attributed to an ideological structure of intentionality (Pêcheux, 1982). Hence, structures of verbal interaction may be associated with particular forms of subjection:

> The fundamental point of Benveniste's work is that it is only through language that humankind is constituted as a subject ... This is because it is through language that humankind constitutes itself as subject, since it is

---

7 For Pêcheux 'creative' speech activity supports the illusion of linguistic spontaneity, i.e., speech acts which are outside social determination. The Saussurian break, then, registers how speech activity may appear spontaneous via the ideology of self-evident meaning found in ordinary language.

8 Benveniste's observations regarding unconscious linguistic structures are in broad agreement with a number of Pêcheux/Herbert's findings in 'For a General Theory of Ideologies' in so far as syntactic and semantic linguistic structures define the 'realization' of the social reality via tacit forms of discourse (cf. Herbert, 1968; Benveniste, 1971).

only language that establishes the concept of ego in reality ... Importantly, it is also the source of social identity.

WILLIAMS, 1999: 183

The individual subject is constituted via the symbolic order socially: the 'I' of intradiscourse is a grammatical complement to the 'you' of interdiscourse. This double structure defines the paradoxical system of 'self-evident' subjectivity.

> The condition for the constitution of the subject-form is precisely the absorption-forgetting of the interdiscourse in the intradiscourse ... This inversion of causality lies at the heart of the subject-form: the forgetting of an exteriority (the preconstructed, the interdiscourse based upon an intertwining – 'intrication' – between discursivity and ideology)... produces this 'interiority without exteriority', which accounts for the *fantasmatic* structure of subjective identity.
>
> GILLOT, 2014: 98

While Pêcheux suggests that 'meaning' is a pre-scientific category for linguistics (i.e., a theoretical ideology) Benveniste appears to champion its ideological effects. According to Pêcheux a given meaning relies on 'subjectivity' to be effective, i.e., meaning effects require the subject-form of discourse to *recognize* that some part of speech or writing is 'meaningful' (Pêcheux, 1982). This correlation between the subject and 'its' meaning is described by Benveniste in the following terms:

> In language, organized into signs, the meaning of a unit is the fact that it has meaning, that it is meaningful ... When we say that a certain element of a language, long or short, has a meaning, we mean by this a certain property which this element possesses *qua* signifier: that of forming a unit which is distinctive, contrastive, delimited by other units, and identifiable for native speakers for whom this language is language. This 'meaning' is implicit, inherent in the linguistic system and its parts.
>
> BENVENISTE, 1971: 108

If preconstructed semantic 'facts' are implicitly accepted by users of a given language such suppositions appear to indicate that the genesis of meaning is not understood as a consequence of interdiscursive and intradiscursive linguistic systems, i.e., in Pêcheux's terms, the double structure of semantic and syntactic ideology defines a 'complex whole in dominance' supported by the ideological superstructure. Benveniste notes that language has 'two planes' which determine its structure, one material, the other mental:

> language is a special symbolic system organized on two planes. On the one hand it is a physical fact ... On the other hand, it is an immaterial structure, a communication of things signified, which replaces events or experiences by their 'evocation'. Such is language – a two-sided entity.
>
> ibid.: 25

This duality of language has been well documented since its initial description in Saussure's *Course in General Linguistics* (see Lacan, 2006; Haroche *et al.*, 1971; Derrida, 1997; Barthes, 1967). Benveniste describes the Saussurian rupture in the following terms:[9]

> Everything in language is to be defined in double terms; everything bears the imprint and seal of an opposing duality: the articulatory/acoustical duality; the duality of sound and sense; the duality of the individual and society; the duality of *langue* and *parole*; the duality of the material and the immaterial ... the duality of the synchronic and the diachronic, etc.
>
> BENVENISTE, 1971: 36

For Pêcheux the Saussurian revolution establishes that language can be studied scientifically without appealing to the fictions of indwelling agency (e.g., myths of subjectivity) that operate 'behind the scenes' of linguistic structures, i.e., Saussure's rupture begins the study of language as a process without a subject. In consequence, Saussure's research outlines the basic framework for a non-subjective theory of language.

> I should like to stress the fact that every epistemological break provides the opportunity for a 'shake-up', a specific redistribution of the relationship between materialism and idealism, to the extent that, as I have said,

---

9 Although Benveniste asserts that meaning is a fact, he does not establish *how* such semantic facts are, really, determined. Thus, the genesis of semantic facticity is not addressed by Benveniste in non-ideological, i.e., scientific terms. Rather, Benveniste simply *insists* that elements of language 'possess' meaning. Following the work of Skinner and Hirst words possess meaning in the same way that individuals are 'possessed' by demons, i.e., as pre-scientific beliefs (cf. Skinner, 1972; Hirst, 1983).

every break exhibits and challenges, in its own field, the effects of the subject-form.

PÊCHEUX, 1982: 139

Within the field of linguistics Saussure's epistemological 'shake-up' represents the denegation of self-evident 'meaning effects' vis-à-vis the institutional materiality of graphic (writing) and phonic structures (speech).[10] According to Benveniste language is a device that facilitates the transmission of culture through various forms of symbolic interaction:

> By means of his language, man assimilates, perpetuates or transforms his culture. Now, each culture, as does each language, makes use of a particular set of symbols in which each society is identified ... It is definitely the symbol which knots that living cord between man, language, and culture.
>
> BENVENISTE, 1971: 27

Saussure's epistemological breakthrough in the domain of linguistics commences the scientific analysis of a field historically determined by pre-scientific culture, e.g., philology, grammar, and the philosophy of language. If, following Benveniste, cultures can be differentiated via symbolic systems, then, it may be possible to distinguish scientific culture from ideological culture by demonstrating how they differ *linguistically*. To some extent this strategy appears to conform to the broad aims of Pêcheux's research programme. According to Helsloot and Hak:

> Pêcheux outlines the preliminaries of a 'general theory of ideologies', which would make possible a scientific study of how ideologies function. Such a theory is necessary for both an understanding of how ideologies can function as obstacles for the establishment of a science and of how they are superseded through an epistemological break.
>
> HELSLOOT and HAK, 1995: 9

---

10   Saussure's epistemological break separates sound (phonation) from meaning (understanding) via the concept of 'association'. Consequently, sound and meaning are only associated in certain forms of social practice. According to Derrida the history of metaphysics is replete with examples of logocentrism and phonocentrism which reveal the theological verity of writing and speech. Therefore, Saussure's work constitutes an important moment in the development of linguistic *science* given that his research does not support the ideology of innate ideas (cf. Saussure, 1959; Derrida, 1997).

Hence, the role of ideological state apparatuses in the reproduction of pre-scientific culture should not be overlooked when considering how social domination is symbolically determined.[11] According to Poulantzas:

> The dominant ideology ... is embodied in the state apparatuses ... This is true *par excellence* of those which have been termed *ideological state apparatuses*, whether they retain a 'private' juridical character (e.g., the Church or religious apparatus, the educational apparatus, the official information network of radio and television, the cultural apparatus). Of course, the dominant ideology also enters into the organization of other apparatuses (army, police, judicial system, prisons, state administration) whose principal responsibility is the exercise of legitimate physical force.
>
> POULANTZAS, 1978: 28–29

For Pêcheux, however, there is not one – undifferentiated – 'dominant ideology', rather, distinct ideological effects are realized in particular syntactic and semantic beliefs which find articulation vis-à-vis technical and political practices:

> Pêcheux makes a distinction between two forms of ideologies: 'empirical' ideologies (which have technical origins) and 'speculative' ideologies (which have political origins)... The ideological process must be understood as combination of the semantic effect and the syntactic effect ... The first effect produces the reality of the signified, whereas the second assigns it its proper place between all other things that can be present in discourse *in the given ideological conjuncture*.
>
> HELSLOOT and HAK, 1995: 9–10

The authority of the State defines the accepted forms of syntax (symbolic order) within a specific territory and, furthermore, the state apparatus can also physically enforce the legitimacy of its definitions, if necessary, via the system

---

11   For example, using *fiction* the state apparatus actively promotes and instils various kinds of 'make believe' and other fables via the 'education' system. According to Terry Eagleton the literary mode of production (LMP) creates the literature that is consumed, distributed, and exchanged throughout society. "Every text obliquely posits a putative reader, defining its producibility in terms of a certain capacity for consumption" (Eagleton, 1976: 48). Thus, the State appears to require a kind of literary inculcation which supports the ideology of self-evident meaning. One obvious example of state inscription is represented by its official language/s.

of law.[12] The ideological apparatus and the repressive apparatus function coefficiently to uphold semantic domination (i.e., self-evident meaning). Following the work of Benveniste children learn to think and speak in terms of a language that predates their birth. Hence, children are trained to adopt a preconstructed language:

> Language and society cannot be conceived without each other. Both are *given*. But both are *learned* by the human being, who does not possess innate knowledge of them. The child is born and develops in the society of men. It is adult human beings, his parents, who inculcate in him the use of words. The acquisition of language is an experience in the child that goes along with the formation of symbols and construction of objects ... Thus there awakens in him the awareness of the social milieu in which he is immersed and which little by little will shape his mind by the intermediary of language.
>
> BENVENISTE, 1971: 26

The practice of socialization via language, then, *prescribes* certain 'forms of consciousness' which are supported by existing systems of knowledge.[13] Moreover, according to Benveniste, this symbolic order is the *sine qua non* for any conceptual activity whatsoever:

> such a system of symbols ... reveals to us one of the essential facts – perhaps the most profound – about the human condition; that there is no natural, immediate, and direct relationship between man and the world or between man and man. An intermediary is necessary; this symbolizing apparatus which has made thought and language possible.
>
> BENVENISTE, 1971: 26

State apparatuses prescribe certain modes of discursive interaction, however, subjects may not cognize the preconstructed effects of inculcation-prescience

---

12   Althusser notes the superstructure (law-state-ideology) *guarantees* that the relations of production are defined in accordance with the expectations of the structure-in-dominance. "Law is a formal, systematized, non-contradictory, (tendentially) comprehensive system *that cannot exist all by itself.* On the one hand, it rests on part of the state repressive apparatus for support. On the other hand, it rests on legal ideology a little supplement of moral ideology for support" (Althusser, 2014: 68).

13   According to Trân Duc Thao consciousness is *"the idealized form of the motion of inner language"* (Thao, 1984: 29). The material history of human cognition is outlined by Thao in his remarkable *Investigations into the Origin of Language and Consciousness.*

which are the prior condition for social cohesion-dominance.[14] Poulantzas maintains that the institutional materiality of the state is realized in ideologies which secure the legitimacy of its epistemic dominance:

> In their capitalist forms of army, law-courts, administration and police (not to mention ideological apparatuses) these state apparatuses involve the practical supremacy of a knowledge and discourse – whether directly invested in the dominant ideology or erected on the basis of dominant ideological formations from which the popular masses are excluded.
>
> POULANTZAS, 1978: 56

Such forms of state sanctioned symbolic control – following Pêcheux's general theory of ideologies – reveal syntagmatic systems of linguistic authority in so far as state power legitimates certain signifying structures to the exclusion of the symbolically subjected. The Saussurian break appears to establish how symbolic control is determined:

> Language ... is always built up on two planes, those of the 'significant' and the 'signified'... it is the point of interaction between the mental and the cultural life in man, and at the same time the instrument of that interaction.
>
> BENVENISTE, 1971: 14

State discourse represents an interiorized exteriority of social life in so far as ideological effects are disseminated throughout the relations of production of a particular society (e.g., 'capitalist' society). According to Poulantzas:

> It is precisely because politico-ideological relations are already present in the actual constitution of the relations of production that they play such an essential role in their reproduction; that is also why the production and exploitation involves reproduction of the relations of politico-ideological domination and subordination. This elementary datum is at the root of the State's presence in the constitution and reproduction of the relations of production, as the factor which concentrates, condenses,

---

14   For Pêcheux ordinary language occludes the ideological basis of speech activity in its effects given that meaning appears self-evident in everyday forms of interaction (Pêcheux, 1995).

materializes and incarnates politico-ideological relations in a form specific to the given mode of production.

POULANTZAS, 1978: 26–27

In *Automatic Discourse Analysis* Pêcheux attempts to clarify how discursive formations function in relation to existing institutions and he finds that certain meaning effects are inseparable from the linguistic norms instantiated by the ideological superstructure (Pêcheux, 1995: 124–132). For Benveniste language is an instrument of culture functioning via symbolic systems, however, certain forms of discourse are prescribed by ideological systems. This discursive embedding is apparent in the syntax which supports locutionary acts involving 'subjectivity' and 'personality'.

> What then is the reality to which *I* or *you* refers? It is solely a 'reality of discourse', and this is a very strange thing. *I* cannot be defined except in terms of 'locution'... *I* signifies the 'person who is uttering the present instance of the discourse containing *I* ... It is thus necessary to stress this point: *I* can only be identified by the instance of discourse that contains it and by that alone. It has no value except in the instance in which it is produced ... the form of the *I* has no linguistic existence except in the act of speaking in which it is uttered.
>
> BENVENISTE, 1971: 218

In Pêcheux's theory of discourse the 'very strange thing', that Benveniste describes, is called the Munchausen effect where the subject is represented as the cause of itself while – simultaneously – being the discursive effect of pre-existing syntactic conditions.

> This contradiction between *'causa sui'* and 'result' is also fundamental in the constitution of the subject as other than itself, that is, as a speaking subject necessarily grasped into the symbolic network of *shifting effects* and into the *signifier process*.
>
> GILLOT, 2014: 98

The 'meaning' of I *shifts* depending on certain contextual conditions: I – as a referent – is related to how the subject 'uses' this pronoun in a given situation.[15]

---

15   According to Jakobson personal pronouns are 'shifters'. Shifters assign information between interlocutors (e.g., addressee/addresser) depending on their role within the 'message' (Jakobson, 1971).

> It is by identifying himself as a unique person pronouncing *I* that each
> speaker sets himself up in turn as the 'subject'. The use thus has as a con-
> dition the situation of discourse and no other ... This sign is thus linked to
> the *exercise* of language and announces the speaker as speaker.
>
> BENVENISTE, 1971: 220

Although the subject of discourse is realized by the use of 'I' this syntactic
device alone does not explain the material structure of the social system which
permits the legitimate locution of the first-person.[16] Therefore, a locutionary
act cannot be separated from its social situation if the pragmatic structures of
superordinate and subordinate discourse are explained in terms of you and I
(i.e., shifters). A dual structure then functions between you and I that is situationally defined by the conditions of addressivity within what Benveniste calls
the 'reality of discourse'.

> The definition can now be stated precisely as: *I* is 'the individual who
> utters the present instance of discourse containing the linguistic instance
> *I*'. Consequently, by introducing the situation of 'address', we obtain a
> symmetrical definition for you as the 'individual spoken to in the present
> instance of discourse containing the linguistic instance *you*'.
>
> ibid.: 218

Such linguistic symmetries, do not, however, reveal the dissymmetries of certain social situations that are revealed in terms of Pêcheux's Munchausen
effect (i.e., the subject as cause of itself). Benveniste remarks how you and I are
verbal categories in so far as these pronouns represent the 'present instance'
of a speech situation. In this sense you and I may convey ideological subject
positions via the norms of grammar.

> These definitions refer to *I* and *you* as a category of language and are
> related to their position in language ... Yet it is a fact both original and
> fundamental that these 'pronominal' forms do not refer to 'reality' or to
> 'objective' positions in space and time but to the utterance ... that con-
> tains them, and thus they reflect their proper use. The importance of
> their function will be measured by the nature of the problem they serve
> to solve, which is none other than that of intersubjective communication.
>
> BENVENISTE, ibid.: 218–219

---

16   Following the research of Althusser and Pêcheux the superstructure (law-state-ideology)
     is the absent cause which legitimates the authority of subjective statements.

The present instance of intersubjective communication a result of prede-
fined (i.e., historical) symbolic systems which are 'immediately' understood
via conditions of addressivity (e.g., accepted speech situations). These syntactic systems are performatively instantiated by specific enunciative acts which
denote forms of address, such as you and I.

> When the individual appropriates it, language is turned into instances
> of discourse, characterized by this particular linguistic construction he
> makes use of when he announces himself as the speaker.
>
>> ibid.: 220

Furthermore, ideological state apparatuses prescribe the forms of intersubjective communication which are accepted in a given territory.[17] The subject-form
of discourse and the Munchausen effect (i.e., the subject as cause of itself)
are derived – linguistically – from the institutional materiality of the state.
According to Poulantzas:

> It is in this precise sense that we cannot imagine any social phenomenon
> (any knowledge, power, language or writing) as posed in a state prior to
> the State: for all social reality must stand in relation to the State ... once
> the latter is posited, every social reality must be conceived as maintaining
> constitutive relations with it.
>
>> POULANTZAS, 1978: 39–40

Intersubjective communication is *authorized* by state power in so far as the
'meaning' and 'origin' of a given speech act is defined by the educational apparatus.[18] The discourse of the state:

---

17   According to Eagleton the appearance of national unity is the product of politico-
      linguistic practices that are preserved and defined by the hegemonic power of the State
      (Eagleton, 1976).

18   The ideological state apparatus supplies the self-evident meaning which all subjects are
      expected to accept. If an individual fails to comply with this existing ideology such insub-
      ordination will activate the repressive apparatus. The 'bad subject' will then be corrected
      according to the level of infraction. This 'putting right' may ensue as informal coercion
      (rhetoric/cajolement) or formal censure (criminal proceedings, sentencing, incarcer-
      ation). Thus, subjects must *freely accept their subjection* to avoid the implications of
      counter-identification (cf. Pêcheux, 1982; Althusser, 2014).

must always be *heard* and *understood* ... This presupposes that, in the various codes of thinking, the State itself is *overcoded* ... Through a process of measured distillation, this overcoding is inculcated in the totality of subjects. Thus, the capitalist State instals a uniform *national language* and eliminates all other languages. This national language is necessary not only for the creation of a national economy and market, but still more for the exercise of the State's political role. It is therefore the mission of the *national State* to organize the processes of thought by forging the materiality of the people-nation.

    ibid.: 58

Hence, the institutional materiality of the state governs the accepted forms of discourse within a given territory (i.e., a nation-state) to ensure that such 'processes of thought' – as Poulantzas calls them – conform with the existing social order.

This spreads through the entire material ritual of the State down to such a precise feature as *writing*. Of course, there has always been a close relationship between the State and writing ... But writing plays a quite specific role in the case of capitalism, representing, still more than the spoken word, the articulation and distribution of knowledge and power within the State. In a certain sense, nothing exists for the capitalist State unless it is written down – whether as a mere written mark, a note, a report, or a complete archive.

    ibid.: 59

Poulantzas explains how writing and speech literally *represent* state power:

Unlike the precapitalist States or the Church, this State does not retain a monopoly of writing: it spreads it (in schools) in response to the concrete necessity of training labour-power. But it thereby *reduplicates* writing, the more so as the spoken word of the State itself be heard and understood ... It is this State which has systematized, if not invented, grammar and orthography by establishing them as networks of power.

    ibid.: 59–60

The State defines *speech activity* in so far as its official language is inscribed via the institutional materiality of ideological apparatuses. According to

Benveniste – subjectivity – 'in' language constitutes the basis of *personal* experience, i.e., pronouns and other orthographic structures permit the subject to represent 'itself':

> It is in and through language that man constitutes himself as a subject, because language alone establishes the concept of 'ego' in reality, in its reality which is that of the being. The 'subjectivity' we are discussing here is the capacity of the speaker to posit himself as 'subject'... That is where we see the foundation of 'subjectivity', which is determined by the linguistic status of 'person'.
>
> BENVENISTE, 1971: 224

The function of the I embeds the subject in its discourse self-referentially, however, as Poulantzas explains, the social system which make this possible is *preconstructed* by the institutional materiality of the state.[19] While Benveniste, in some cases, suggests that the subject is *causa sui* the fact remains – as demonstrated by the institutional materiality of his writings – that subjectivity is a product of particular linguistic practices.

> Then, what does *I* refer to? To something very peculiar which is exclusively linguistic: *I* refers to the act of individual discourse in which it is pronounced, and by this it designates the speaker ... The reality to which it refers is the reality of the discourse. It is in the instance of the discourse in which I designates the speaker that the speaker proclaims himself as the 'subject'. And so it is literally true that the basis of subjectivity is in the exercise of language.
>
> ibid.: 226

Following the work of Poulantzas a subject's discourse – and the writing system that supports it – is established by the state apparatus and, therefore, such inscription constitutes the realization of legal person-ality. Furthermore, this interiorized orthographic structure appears to be the 'accepted' form of superordinate and subordinate experiences of subjectivity that are conveyed via the official language (e.g., the legal system).[20]

---

19 The ideological state apparatus determines the linguistic structure-in-dominance that sanctions the 'realization of the real' in forms of ordinary language.

20 According to Ragnar Rommetveit the graphic and phonic structures of discourse are not intrinsically meaningful. These structures exhibit 'semantic content' after particular

It is precisely through a system of general, abstract and formal rules that law *regulates* the exercise of power by the state apparatuses, as well as access to these apparatuses themselves.

POULANTZAS, 1978: 91

Pêcheux maintains that although speech may appear individuated in terms of 'subjective' origination the real basis of discourse is, in effect, occluded by 'forgettings' of symbolic sovereignty (e.g., the rule of law). Automatic discourse (i.e., self-evident meaning) is thus a preconstructed effect of state ideology in so far as speech acts are the un/conscious realization of its institutional materiality. The normative conditions of state power, therefore, prescribe the dominant vision of social reality, yet, its subjects must appear to *voluntarily* accept their own subjection. The voluntary acceptance of prestructured forms of communication supports the interior-exterior of state authority vis-à-vis symbolic determination of subjectivity (e.g., internalized orthography).

The 'subjectivity' we are discussing here is the capacity of the speaker to posit himself as 'subject'. ... How we hold that that 'subjectivity'... is only the emergence of a fundamental property of language. That is where we see the foundation 'subjectivity', which is determined by the linguistic status of 'person'.

BENVENISTE, 1971: 224

Evidently there is an important institutional connection between the linguistic status of a 'person' and state apparatuses in so far as this relationship defines the normative and judicial framework of a given social order. Yet, Benveniste's theory of linguistic performativity seems to trivialize such pragmatic issues, i.e., the assumed intentionality of a speech act takes precedence over the speech situation. "*I* use *I* only when I am speaking to someone who will be a you in my address ... Language is possible only because each speaker sets himself up as a *subject* by referring to himself as *I* in his discourse" (ibid.: 224–225). The constitutive process whereby the 'speaker sets himself up' does not receive detailed examination by Benveniste, instead, he suggests, elliptically, how advent of subjectivity 'creates' *personal* meaning.[21]

---

psycholinguistic connections are established 'internally' by hierarchically organized protocols of meaning activation (Rommetveit, 1971).

21   Benveniste appears to explain linguistic subjectivity in ideological terms, i.e., he does not present an account of how the material base of society prescribes certain forms of

The establishment of 'subjectivity' in language creates the category of person – both in language and also, we believe, outside of it as well. Moreover, it has quite varied effects in the very structure of languages, whether it be in the arrangement of the forms or in semantic relationships.

ibid.: 227

For Pêcheux subjectivity (i.e., the subject-form of discourse) is a phantasmatic linguistic concept used for ideological descriptions of 'personal' experience in which the speaker 'sets himself up' with a point of view via 'spontaneous' speech activity.

To take the subject-form as point of departure is to consider that there is on one side 'the point of view of the sciences' on the real, and on the other, 'the point of view of ideology'... *In fact, every 'point of view' is the point of view of a subject*; a science cannot therefore be a point of view on the real, a vision or a construction which represents the real ... a science is the real in the modality of its necessity-thought.

PÊCHEUX, 1982: 128; emphasis added

The subjective 'point of view' is, according to Pêcheux, a fiction which typically used in journalism, literature, and creative writing.[22] According to Benveniste: "If one really thinks about it, one will see that there is no other objective testimony to the identity of the subject except that which he himself gives about himself" (Benveniste, 1971: 226). Here Benveniste maintains that subjectivity is, in fact, self-defined which, in Pêcheux's terms, denotes an ideological point of view. I find that although Benveniste clearly appreciates the theoretical significance of Saussure's research for the field of linguistics he does not register that the Saussurian rupture between *langue* and *parole*

---

language to reproduce the structure-in-dominance. Thus, the subordinate and superordinate systems of enunciation which prescribe certain subject positions may seem *prima facie* 'natural'. In effect the 'meaning' of ordinary language is supported by the structure-in-dominance to reproduce the relations of production via certain speech acts.

22　Following the work of Eagleton, the primary source of ideological discourse is 'literature' and the principal institution that supplies it is the educational apparatus. "From the infant school to the University faculty, literature is a vital instrument for the insertion of individuals into the perceptual and symbolic forms of the dominant ideological formation, able to accomplish this function with a 'naturalness', spontaneity and experiential immediacy possible to no other ideological practice" (Eagleton, 1976: 56).

dispels the subject as cause of itself as a pre-scientific myth. Benveniste does not attempt to address how the subject is preconstructed by ideological conditions syntagmatically.[23] Nonetheless Benveniste's references to Saussure and the field of psychoanalysis do – to a limited extent – support Pêcheux's hypotheses regarding the unconscious inscription of discursive structures as assumed forms of subjectivity.

---

23 Syntagmatic preconstruction defines subject positions based on superordinate and subordinate speech acts, however, the structure-in-dominance may not appear as the immediate source of this discourse due to systems of ideological mis/recognition. In this respect the State functions as the absent cause of 'subjective' speech in so far as individuals 'forget' that their discourse is always-already-prescribed by its institutional materiality.

CHAPTER 16

Michel Foucault (1926–1984)

To develop his theory of discourse analysis Pêcheux made liberal use of Michel Foucault's research. In the bibliographies of *Language, Semantics, and Ideology* and *Automatic Discourse Analysis* there are references to Foucault's 'Orders of discourse', *The Archaeology of Knowledge*, and *Discipline and Punish* (Pêcheux, 1982, 1995). According to Pêcheux's colleague Paul Henry:

> There are – at the theoretical if not the practical level – many similarities between Foucault's work on discourse analysis and that of Pêcheux. The concept of a 'discursive formation' can, for instance, be found in Foucault, even though he uses the term in a slightly different sense.
>
> HENRY, 1995: 33

Pêcheux advances a *non-subjective theory of subjectivity* that is clearly aligned with Foucault's concept of 'discursive formations' (cf. Pêcheux, 1982; Foucault, 1972). Foucault does not provide a positive definition for the 'subject of discourse', instead, he identifies subject *positions* based on certain forms of discursive interaction.[1] This interdiscursive approach also appears in the research of Lacan and Derrida where the subject is an effect of discourse rather than its cause (Henry, 1995: 34). The speaking subject is, therefore, *situated* vis-à-vis particular discursive formations that structure the experience of what is called 'subjectivity'.[2] In Pêcheux's view Foucault does not, however, study discourse in relation to class structures. Despite the fact that Pêcheux finds *The*

---

1   The subject is determined by the function/s it performs 'in' discourse. The notion of agency indicates how a subject is the *agent for a given discourse* or set of discursive practices. According to Foucault: "Religious discourse, juridical and therapeutic as well as, in some ways, political discourse are all barely dissociable from the functioning of a ritual that determines the individual properties and agreed roles of the speakers" (Foucault, 1972: 225). Consequently, superordinate and subordinate subject positions may be derived from particular discursive regularities that seem self-evident in 'autonomous' forms of subjection (cf. Rommetveit, 1971; Pêcheux, 1982).

2   Althusser lists some points for a preliminary theory of subjectivity in 'Three Notes on the Theory of Discourses'. One of his notes detailing 'The character of the unconscious' suggests that the *subjectivity-effect* is determined linguistically. "The theory of the production of the subjectivity-effect falls within the province of the theory of the signifier" (Althusser, 2003: 48).

Archaeology of Knowledge 'of extraordinary interest for the theory of discourse' he contends that Foucault 'regresses into the sociology of institutions and roles, because he fails to recognize the existence of the (ideological) class struggle' (Pêcheux, 1982: 181). On the other hand, Poulantzas finds that Foucault's work is particularly useful for the study of state apparatuses and the politics of the 'individual person' in regard to the 'microphysics of power' and 'state writing' (Poulantzas, 1978, 2008).[3] According to Foucault a 'discursive formation' is a group of statements that is not defined exclusively by grammatical, proposi- tional, or psychological relations, by contrast, it represents a set of enunciative conditions (i.e., institutional sites, subject positions, and truth procedures) that define certain speech acts.

> Now, what has been described as discursive formations are, strictly speaking, groups of statements ... To describe statements, to describe the enunciative function of which they are the bearers, to analyse the con- ditions in which this function operates, to cover the different domains that this function presupposes and the way in which those domains are articulated, is to undertake to uncover what might called the discursive formation ... the discursive formation is the general enunciative system that governs a group of verbal performances ... What has been called 'dis- cursive formation' divides up the general plane of things said at the spe- cific level of statements.
>
> FOUCAULT, 1972: 115–116

Paul Henry suggests Pêcheux's research programme presents discourse as an interposed structure permitting the theoretical juxtaposition of language – as a system of representation – and ideology – as a system of mis/recognition.[4]

> Pêcheux works in the space between the 'subject of language' and the 'subject of ideology'. This has a bearing on all his work ... he attempts to clarify the links between the 'obviousness of meaning' and the

---

3   Discursive formations are part of the institutional materiality of the State. Thus, the author- ity of state power is realized in various forms of discourse (e.g., law, social policy, educa- tion &c.). According to Poulantzas: "Through its discursiveness and characteristic texture, law-regulation obscures the politico-economic realities, tolerating structural lacunae and transposing these realities to the political arena by means of a peculiar mechanism of concealment-inversion" (Poulantzas, 1978: 83).

4   Althusser outlines a general theory of discourse which, in principle, may be read as an analog to Pêcheux's theoretical problematic described in *Language, Semantics, and Ideology* (cf. Pêcheux, 1982; Althusser, 2003).

'obviousness of the subject' and locates discourse in a region intermediate between language and ideology.

HENRY, 1995: 39

Pêcheux, then, connects the functioning of particular discursive formations to ideological state apparatuses in so far as the linguistic base of society generally prescribes the enunciative superstructure. Forms of discourse are prescribed or prohibited by state systems vis-à-vis socio-political 'consensus' (e.g., legal norms). Poulantzas suggests that the ideological basis of state legitimacy is guaranteed by specific conditions of institutional materiality, including epistemic structures (i.e., structures of knowledge).[5]

> It goes without saying that repression and ideological inculcation are present in the materiality of the State's current functions ... Not only does the State proclaim the truth of its power at a certain 'real' level; it also adopts the necessary means to elaborate and formulate political tactics. It produces knowledge and techniques of knowledge which go far beyond ideology, while naturally remaining imbricated in it.
>
> POULANTZAS, 1978: 30–32

Poulantzas finds that legitimate knowledge – as authorized by the State – is, in fact, the means of its own continuity as an ideological system (e.g., 'accepted' speech acts). A discursive formation (e.g., law, psychiatry, national language, 'literature', social science, &c.), according to Foucault, is not necessarily a science – in many instances – it will have the institutional status of a 'discipline'.

> A discipline is not the sum total of all the truths that may be uttered concerning something; it is not even the total of all that may be accepted, by virtue of some principle of coherence and systematisation, concerning some given fact or proposition ... *Disciplines constitute a system of control in the production of discourse, fixing its limits through the action of an identity taking the form of permanent reactivation of the rules.*
>
> FOUCAULT, 1972: 223–224; emphasis added

---

5 Applying Foucault's research from the *Archaelogy of Knowledge* to the State theory outlined by Poulantzas suggests that the ideological state apparatus has the capacity to generate specific 'knowledge effects' that function to *inscribe* or write certain subject positions into existence. The orthographic basis of state power is exhibited in the discursive formations which consolidate its *literal* authority (cf. Foucault, 1972; Poulantzas, 1978).

The subjection and *imagined* subjectivity of sovereign individuals, is, then – via the application Foucault's theory – a result of discursive formations functioning as ideological 'disciplines'.[6] The legitimacy of such subjection will find expression in various rule-based procedures associated with the acquisition, preservation, and dissemination of certain speech acts (i.e., enunciative conditions of discourse) vis-à-vis institutional authorities. The process by which these rules are discovered Foucault calls 'archaeology': the study of discursive *archives*. 'Archaeology defines the rules of formation of a group of statements' (ibid.: 167). Every discipline has its own archive: the historical record of the statements made which define its object domain (e.g., law, psychiatry, grammar, philosophy, sociology &c.). Archives designate the 'already-said' of a given discursive formation. 'Archaeology describes discourses as practices specified in the element of the archive' (ibid.: 131). The ideology of 'subjectivity' – as the spontaneous source of self-identity – is, according to Foucault, determined by the miscognition of speech activity (e.g., ordinary language). Foucault finds that questions regarding consciousness typically support the illusions of self-generating subjectivity. Thus, he proposes to investigate the relationship of discursive practice to archaeology rather than the relationship of 'consciousness' to knowledge (ibid.:183). Pêcheux's Munchausen effect is then a form of discursive practice vis-à-vis 'self-knowledge' in so far as the subject is situated by forms of discourse which it spontaneously recognizes as self-evident. According to Gillot:

> Pêcheux's approach to *discourse analysis* ... is partly indebted to Michel Foucault's own theorization of discourse analysis. It seems that Pêcheux borrowed from Foucault the concept of discursive formation, first introduced in *L'Archéologie du savoir* (*The Archaeology of Knowledge*) ... Nevertheless, Pêcheux himself, while acknowledging his debt to Foucault, also stresses the singularization of his own theorization of discourse, in the frame of Marxism and and of a materialist theory of social-ideological formations.
>
> GILLOT, 2014: 110

---

6 The speculative ideologies of the social sciences and humanities function to instil and sustain conventional forms of subjective (imagined) 'knowledge' which are not verified using the methods found in the exact sciences. These imaginary epistemic structures facilitate the legitimacy of the ideological superstructure in various forms of discourse (e.g, literature, philosophy, law, psychology &c.).

Both Pêcheux and Foucault dismiss the subject as cause of itself as a pseudo-problem for discourse theory (i.e., a philosophy of consciousness) because any given enunciation will be correlated to a number of different archives which represent the historical *a priori* of a given statement. Hence, statements can be related to those disciplines which govern the rules of formation for a particular discourse and subject position. Furthermore, Foucault maintains that the archaeology of knowledge – to some extent – involves certain principles from psychoanalysis, epistemology and historical materialism (the history of social formations):

> in seeking to define, outside all reference to a psychological or constituent subjectivity, the different positions of the subject that may be involved in subjectivity, archaeology touches on a question that is being posed today by psychoanalysis ... in trying to reveal the rules of formation of concepts ... it touches on the problem of epistemological structures ... in studying too the conditions of appropriation of discourses, it touches on the analysis of social formations. *For archaeology, these are so many correlative spaces.*
>
> FOUCAULT, 1972: 207; emphasis added

Foucault suggests that psychoanalytic, epistemological and social structures are potential co-ordinates for certain forms of discursive practice. "Statements should not longer be situated in relation to a sovereign subjectivity but recognize in the different forms of speaking subjectivity effects proper to the enunciative field" (ibid.: 122). According to Pêcheux/Herbert 'meaning effects' guarantee the self-evidence of the 'always-already-there' as a preconstructed social reality and Foucault's research appears to support this theory in so far as discursive formations can be traced to institutional sites via archaeological investigation (e.g., with reference to the archival material of 'disciplines'). Discussing one application of Foucault's work for his materialist theory of discourse Pêcheux writes:

> A discursive formation is not a closed structural space in that it is constantly being invaded by elements from elsewhere (i.e., from other discursive formations). They are reproduced within it and provide it with its basic discursive truths (in the shape of 'preconstructs' or 'transverse discourses').
>
> PÊCHEUX, 1995: 237

Gillot notes Pêcheux's 'reworking' of Foucault's research suggests how the subject is a result of discursive preconstruction.[7] "It permits us to conceive the subject not as a principle, but as an 'effect': the effect of a certain discursive-ideological device" (Gillot, 2014: 101). Poulantzas – who applied Foucault's research to the question of state power – notes that ideological inculcation cannot be reduced to the realm of ideas alone, rather, it is manifested in particular conditions of embodiment.[8]

> Ideology does not consist merely in a system of ideas or representations: it also involves a series of *material practices* ... The state cannot enshrine and reproduce political domination exclusively through repression, force or 'naked' violence, but directly calls upon ideology to legitimize violence and contribute to a consensus of those classes and fractions which are dominated from the point of view of political power.
>
> POULANTZAS, 1978: 28

Poulantzas appears – in principle – to follow Foucault's research regarding the material composition of the 'modern soul' in so far as 'subjective' ideologies are determined vis-à-vis state power (cf. Poulantzas 1978; Foucault, 1984). According to Foucault:

> This real, noncorporal soul, is not a substance; it is the element in which are articulated the effects of a certain type of power and the reference of a certain type of knowledge, the machinery by which the power relations give rise to a possible corpus of knowledge, and knowledge extends and reinforces the effects of power ... The soul is the effect and instrument of a political anatomy; the soul is the prison of the body.
>
> FOUCAULT, 1984: 177

---

7 The subject as cause of itself seems to coincide with the position of speaking subjects interposed by the structure-in-dominance, yet, as Pêcheux's research in *Automatic Discourse Analysis* indicates the Munchausen effect occludes the origin of subjective speech activity by dissimulating the ideological basis of immediate meaning (Pêcheux, 1995).

8 For Foucault enunciative modalities (descriptions, biographies, interpretations, reports &c.) are typically determined by certain 'authorities of delimitation' which administer the norms of existing discursive formations. Poulantzas appears to advance this theory of Foucault's to explain how State ideology authorizes general forms of subjection via the institutional materiality of 'state writing'. Institutional structures and somatic singularities (i.e., individual persons) are 'connected' to generate 'subjective' meaning effects in forms of everyday practice (such as writing and speech) which embody established ideologies.

The subject (or 'soul') is the result of certain material activities which define its composition as a form of discourse (i.e., subjectivity is the result of discursive practice).[9]

> On this reality reference, various concepts have been constructed and domains of analysis carved out; psyche, subjectivity, personality, consciousness, etc.; on it have been built scientific techniques and discourses, and the moral claims of humanism ... The man described for us ... is already in himself the effect of a subjection much more profound than himself.
>
> ibid.

Foucault does not attempt to disclose the personal interiority of a subject's ahistorical 'consciousness': he seeks to define the *objective conditions of discursive practice* that have produced a a particular statement (i.e., its *disciplinary* conditions of existence). How does a speech act relate to historically determined archives of knowledge? With which disciplines can the speaking subject be associated? Why was one statement made and not another?

> Thus conceived, discourse is not the majestically unfolding manifestation of a thinking, knowing, speaking subject, but, on the contrary, a totality, in which the dispersion of the subject and his discontinuity with himself may be determined. It is a space of exteriority in which a network of distinct sites is deployed ... it must now be recognized that it is neither by recourse to a transcendental subject nor by recourse to a psychological subjectivity that the regulation of its enunciations should be defined.
>
> FOUCAULT, 1972: 55

The 'spontaneous' subjectivity expressed in a given speech act is then always related – via certain socio-historical conditions – to the exterior space of discursive formations in so far as such statements are defined by institutional disciplines. This institutional materiality is, therefore, legitimated by the authority of disciplinary systems. Thus, the State – following Foucault's

---

9 Althusser's materialist theory of ideology suggests that 'subjectivity' is a form of mis/recognition induced by certain superstructural exigencies (Althusser, 2014). In this Althusserian view subjective beliefs serve to secure the imaginary basis for the subjection prescribed by the economic base.

research – exercises the capacity to control the 'consciousness' of the population within its territory via forms of discourse.[10]

> Interest at the level of the consciousness of each individual who goes to
> make up the population, and interest considered as the interest of the
> population regardless of what the particular interests and aspirations
> may be of the individuals who compose it, this is the ... target and funda-
> mental instrument of the government of population.
>
> FOUCAULT, 1991: 100

The *authority* of the State is legitimated by discursive formations in terms of
the triumvirate 'sovereignty-discipline-government' (ibid.: 102). According
to Foucault 'governmentality' determines the institutional authority used to
secure a *legitimate* State. In one example Foucault defines governmentality as:

> ensemble formed by the institutions, procedures, analyses and reflec-
> tions, the calculations and tactics that allow the exercise of this very
> specific albeit very complex form of power, which has as its target the
> population, as its principal form of knowledge political economy, and as
> its essential technical means apparatuses of security.
>
> ibid.

Foucault does not attempt to define discourse in terms of 'innate ideas', subjective interiority, or other incorporeal agencies, instead, he examines the fundamental exteriority of discursive practice in relation to specific institutional
systems (e.g., pedagogy, penal codes, clinical norms &c.).

> Thus, what I am writing is not a history of the mind ... I do not question
> discourses about their silently intended meanings, but about the fact and
> the conditions of their manifest appearance ... about the field where they
> coexist, reside and disappear. It is a question of an analysis of the dis-
> courses in the dimension of their exteriority.
>
> ibid.: 60

---

10   Although a national language may appear as a 'natural' language the language of the
      nation-state is, in fact, an *official* language. Hence, the State may officially determine spe-
      cific 'forms of consciousness' (legal, historical, political, &c.) to regulate the institutional
      materiality of the structure-in-dominance (cf. Saussure, 1959; Poulantzas, 1978).

The institutional materiality of the State regulates discourse by virtue of its assumed legitimacy (e.g., social order is guaranteed by the official language).[11] The State, then, may determine speech acts with reference to the institutional norms prescribed by the discursive practice of 'subjective' disciplines (e.g., law, psychiatry, social science &c.) (cf. Althusser, 2014; Herbert, 1966). Such authority ensures that statements may be repeated – and as required – regenerated – to regulate 'interior' experience via forms of instituted discourse.

> The repeatable materiality that characterizes the enunciative function reveals the statement as a specific and paradoxical object ... the statement as it emerges in its materiality, appears with a status, enters various networks and various fields of use, is subjected to transferences or modifications, is integrated into operations and strategies in which its identity is maintained or effaced.
>
> FOUCAULT, 1972: 105

Disciplines regulate the statements that circulate within the enunciative fields of discursive formations.[12] Such normative procedures structurally demarcate the subjects who are ostensibly 'communicating' within certain discursive formations.[13] These discoursing subjects are thus – typically unbeknownst to them – interposed linguistically by the institutional materiality of the State. This institutional 'context' suggests that disciplinary systems determine

---

11   In Henry's terms it seems that the State defines its own 'context' *in* discourse (Henry, 1971). In this sense superordinate and subordinate subject positions are contextually inferred by certain structures of authority (i.e., State loci). The ideological basis of particular institutional norms thus supports the self-evident meaning of the structure-in-dominance as a form of contextualized subjection which is generally accepted via the institutional materiality of the State.

12   According to Martin Kusch statements are grouped by Foucault in terms of succession, coexistence and procedures of rewriting. As a network of statements every discursive formation is then structured with reference to a heterogeneous multiplicity of operations, e.g., conditions of enunciation, conceptual criteria, strategic requirements, and institutional norms (Kusch, 1991).

13   The interlocutors of a given speech act (e.g., addresser/addressee) 'communicate' according to preconstructed forms of discourse. Such meaning effects are determined by specific kinds of social interaction that reproduce the relations of production within the structure-in-dominance. Superordinate and subordinate subject positions are, then, regulated by relatively autonomous structures of authority that are defined in advance by the ideological state apparatus (cf. Pêcheux, 1982; Henry, 1971).

accepted forms of agency to ensure that the modern soul (i.e., the subject) acts in accordance with the linguistic norms guaranteed by the State.

> The norm consequently lays claim to power. The norm is not simply and not even a principle of intelligibility; it is an element on the basis of which a certain exercise of power is founded and legitimized ... the norm brings with it a principle of both qualification and correction. The norm's function is not to exclude and reject. Rather, it is always linked to a positive technique of intervention and transformation, to a sort of normative project.
>
> FOUCAULT, 2003: 50

According to Herbert empirical ideologies are supported by certain discursive practices which realize the relations of production within a given social formation (Herbert, 1968). Throughout this *relatively* autonomous system certain statements are approved by institutional authorities to reproduce 'accepted' forms of subjection (e.g., self-evident meaning). The archives (epistemic disciplines) associated with a given 'enunciative field' would constitute the recorded history of a discursive formation (e.g., theoretical concepts, legislative norms, received truths &c.)

> At the very outset, from the very root, the statement is divided up into an enunciative field in which it has a place and a status, which arranges for its possible relations with the past, and which opens up for it a possible future. Every statement is specified in this way ... a statement always belongs to a series or a whole, always plays a role among other statements, deriving support from them and distinguishing itself from them: it is always part of a network of statements, in which it has a role, however, minimal it may be, to play.
>
> FOUCAULT, 1972: 99

The repeatable materiality of statements is subject to institutional verification and this occurs via the 'legitimacy' of state power (e.g., the legal apparatus, public records, curricula &c.). Furthermore, discursive formations provide a certain amount of security over a given territory in so far as ideological state apparatuses define the semantic and syntactic representations within it. Thus, the State establishes certain linguistic forms of security (e.g., an official language, law &c.) (cf. Foucault, 2007; Pêcheux, 1982). According to Foucault the function of security is to "plan a milieu in terms of events or series of events or possible elements, or series that will have to be regulated within a multivalent and transformable framework" (Foucault, 2007: 20). Pêcheux's Munchausen effect (i.e., the 'free' subject) can be translated into Foucault's theory of security in terms of relatively autonomous self-subjection. Discursive formations both limit and enable certain forms of social interaction, however, the State, in the last instance, retains control of the always-already-there (i.e., the pre-constructed systems of institutional authority). The subject as cause of itself is a discursive correlate of 'legitimate' freedom in so far 'liberty' is defined by state apparatuses, i.e., within a particular territory *subjective* freedom is prescribed by disciplinary mechanisms. Foucault calls this "the ideology of freedom" (ibid: 48). "So this problem of freedom ... really was one of the conditions of development of modern or, if you like, capitalist forms of the economy. This is undeniable" (Foucault, 2007: 48). For Foucault liberal ideology engenders the *belief* that society functions as if it was simply the outcome of 'free activity' when, in fact, it is the direct result of disciplines and security. Liberal society reflects a social order which is the product of specific mechanisms of *organized* freedom (including 'free' speech).

> The game of liberalism – not interfering, allowing free movement, letting things to follow their course; *laisser faire, passer et aller* – basically and fundamentally means acting so that reality develops, goes its way, and follows its own course according to the laws, principles, and mechanisms of reality itself.
>
> ibid.: 48

Pêcheux's Munchausen effect, then, appears to be a 'natural' consequence of a liberal society. The subject as cause of itself is thus an ideo-technical achievement for the secure administration of a free society (cf. Pêcheux, 1982; Foucault, 2007). According to Foucault:

> *More precisely and particularly, freedom is nothing else but the correlative of the deployment of apparatuses of security* ... It is not an ideology; it is not exactly, fundamentally, or primarily an ideology. First of all and above all it is a technology of power, or at any rate can be read in this sense.
>
> FOUCAULT, 2007: 49[14]

---

14   Göran Therborn maintains that ideological domination is used to maintain various forms of political power whereby mechanisms of subjection (i.e., technologies of power) are used to secure certain forms of political 'rapport' (e.g., consensus, legitimacy, 'free choice' &c.) (Therborn, 1999).

Despite the fact that discursive formations are instantiated by state power the subject of discourse is assumed to act with regard to its own intentionality. "A real subjection is born mechanically from a fictitious relation" (Foucault, 1995: 202). The Munchausen effect situates a given subject within a discursive panopticon where its own 'self-observation' is facilitated by the power of security apparatuses functioning as disciplines.[15] Thus the 'free choice' a subject makes with regard to its speech acts is, in effect, a product of ideological state apparatuses that surveil and regulate certain forms of discourse. Furthermore, Pêcheux's research suggests that the apparent spontaneity of a subject's discourse really derives from a given 'discursive corpus', i.e., the body of speech traceable to certain 'production conditions'.

> 'Discursive corpus' is to be understood as meaning a set of texts (or discursive sequences) of variable length deriving from conditions of production which may be regarded as being stable, or as a set of textual images bound up with the 'virtual' text (with, that is, the discursive process which dominates and generates the various discursive sequences belonging to the corpus).
>
> PÊCHEUX, 1995: 133

Discursive formations – particularly in so far as these are regulated by writing systems – represent specific conditions of production for given statements. Furthermore, these speech acts can then be correlated with institutional sites vis-à-vis a discursive corpus. Foucault notes *literal* discipline inscribes certain forms of social control (e.g., orthographic subjection):

> A 'power of writing' was constituted as an essential part in the mechanisms of discipline ... Hence the formation of a whole series of codes of disciplinary individuality ... These codes were still very crude ... but they marked a first stage in the 'formalization' of the individual within power relations. The other innovations of disciplinary writing concerned the correlation of these elements, the accumulation of documents, their seriation, the organization of comparative fields making it possible to classify, to form categories, to determine averages, to fix norms.
>
> FOUCAULT, 1995: 189–190

---

15   The Munchausen effect is a theoretical corollary of a free society, however, the ideological justification for this 'internal agent' is to subject individuals to 'their own' subjectivity. In Althusser's terms individuals appear to 'freely choose' their subjection based on the illusions of subjectivity found in bourgeois society (Althusser, 2014).

Writing, then, appears to function as an epistemic panopticon that defines the interiorized-exteriority of state inscription where the subject is eventually designated as the cause of itself – and its own subjection – by a rigorous practice of disciplined normalization.[16] Generalized writing – as a disciplinary system – enables two important modalities for the state control of subjectivity: individual description and comparative analysis across groups of inscribed individuals. According to Foucault:

> the whole apparatus of writing ... opened up two correlative possibilities, first, the constitution of the individual as a describable, analyzable object ... in order to maintain him in his individual features ... his own aptitudes or abilities, under the gaze of permanent corpus of knowledge; and, second, the constitution of a comparative system that made possible the measurement of overall phenomena, the description of groups, the characterization of collective facts, the calculation of the gaps between individuals, their distribution in a given 'population'.
>
> ibid.: 190

The transformation of 'human nature' into a written code was represented by forms of bio-graphic description, in consequence, the modern soul was defined vis-à-vis systems of disciplinary power. "The turning of real lives into writing is no longer a procedure of heroization; it functions as a procedure of objectification and subjection" (ibid.: 192). According to Pêcheux the corpus of given discourse will exhibit particular correlations with its conditions of production in terms of the linguistic surface, the discursive object, and the discursive process.

> Linguistic surface is to be understood as meaning an oral or written sequence of variable dimensions, usually greater than a sentence ... Discursive object is to be understood as meaning the result of the transformation of the linguistic surface of discourse into a theoretical object ...

---

16 Following the work of Kusch (1991) normative disciplines may be studied genealogically (i.e., as social histories) in terms of power mechanisms, social networks, interests, systems of exclusions and prohibitions, and forms of coercion. Hence, a geneaology of writing – as a technical practice – would demonstrate how networks of authority define subject positions vis-à-vis certain socio-historical systems of orthographic power. Furthermore, it may then be possible to determine how writing functions as political instrument used to establish 'legitimate' rule in the specific forms of administration (e.g., judicial, bureucractic, pedagogic &c.) that support ruling ideologies (cf. Therborn, 1978, Kusch, 1991).

Discursive process is to be understood as meaning the result of the controlled interrelating of discursive objects corresponding to linguistic surfaces that represent stable and homogeneous conditions of production.

PÊCHEUX, 1995: 142

The linguistic base supplies the syntactic 'raw material' that is subsequently
transcribed and normalized in discursive processes, however, as Pêcheux notes,
the relation of the subject to this corpus may be the consequence of imaginary
effects.[17] Within a 'concrete situation' – Pecheux suggests – a given statement
is derived from preconstructed discursive corpora (e.g., ideological state apparatuses). Moreover, such 'meaning' may represent an imaginary relationship
between the linguistic surface and the discursive object (e.g., ordinary language). "The concrete analysis of a concrete situation implies, in our view, that
discursive materiality in an ideological formation must be regarded as an articulation of processes" (ibid.: 145). Such 'meaningful' processes appear to refer
those regulated forms of discourse which determine the stability of ideological conditions of production (e.g., disciplinary apparatuses). Hence, 'concrete
situations' (e.g., speech acts, relations of production, pedagogical practices
&c.) are based on certain conditions of institutional materiality structured by
social norms.

In many respects, Foucault's work can be seen as focusing upon norma-
tivity. His preoccupation was with how the actions of norms in the life
of human beings determine the kind of society in which they themselves
appear as subjects ... The norm is not external to its field of application,
and the focus must be on its application and the way in which it thereby
produces and reproduces itself. The question shifts to what legitimates it.

WILLIAMS, 1999: 285

Across social structures disciplinary norms are realized in the discursive systems that regulate what is called 'subjectivity'.[18]

---

17   In *Automatic Discourse Analysis* and *Language, Semantics, and Ideology* Pêcheux suggests
      that the subject is typically unaware of its subjection to certain forms of discourse – it
      simply accepts the veracity of self-evident meaning – despite the fact that the genesis of
      discourse (e.g., natural language) is occluded by existing systems of authority.

18   In principle an 'archaeology of subjectivity' would describe the institutional basis of the
      subject-form vis-à-vis certain discursive corpora. The archive (discursive corpora) of a
      given discipline may then be studied in terms of how it 'represents' subjective phenom-
      ena in order to differentiate scientific practice from the scientific ideologies found in the

The productivity of the norm for Foucault is involved in the same process of knowledge and power by reference to its productivity in exposing
the action of a norm ... Being a subject is being subjected, not merely in
the sense of submitting to some external order that supposes a relation
of pure domination, but in the sense of the insertion of individuals in
networks which are homogeneous and continuous. This involves a normative disposition which reproduces them and transforms them into
subjects.

> ibid.: 287

Evidently social norms are instituted via disciplinary apparatuses which regulate discursive formations according to particular forms of enunciation. In
the case of Pêcheux's Munchausen effect the subject 'forgets' that its discourse
is the result of certain normative conditions which define the assumptions
of self-evident meaning. Moreover, in both Pêcheux and Foucault's research,
the established norms of disciplines (e.g., social science and governmentality)
present a view of 'reality' that is prestructured, i.e., the norms of discourse represent what are assumed to be social facts.[19]

Meaning came to be conceived in terms of the relationship between signs
and references within a theory of enunciation ... It involved Pêcheux's
theory of the subjective illusion of *parole*. It was the key which opened
the way to linking the linguistic work of enonciative linguistics with
Foucault's work on the normative.

> ibid.: 309

Society then appears to function as an invisible linguistic panopticon in so far
as enunciations conform to the expectations of socially sanctioned forms of
discourse, yet the origins of this normative system are effaced in the subjective

---

humanities and social sciences which typically accept and support the imaginary experience of subjectivity.

19   Ludwik Fleck presents a theory of 'thought collectives' which attempts to describe how
individual cognition is determined by social structures. "Cognition is therefore not an
individual process of any theoretical 'particular consciousness'. Rather it is the result of
a social activity, since the existing stock of knowledge exceeds the range available to any
one individual ... Although the thought collective consists of individuals, it is not simply
the aggregate of them. The individual within the collective is never, or hardly ever, conscious of the prevailing thought style, *which almost always exerts an absolutely compulsive
force upon his thinking and with which it is not possible to be at variance*" (Fleck, 1979: 38–41;
emphasis added).

self-evidence of a process that functions 'automatically' in certain kinds of linguistic behavior. Thus, a subject's interdiscourse is the product interdiscursive observation via certain forms of discipline. While the enunciative field of the State seems non-coercive this impression can only be achieved by strictly disciplined security apparatuses which successfully produce a 'free' society within precisely prescribed limits. State apparatuses, therefore, produce freedom by constructing it normatively using certain forms of discourse: this belief system consequently produces the 'subjective illusion' that Pêcheux outlines *in Language, Semantics, and Ideology* and *Automatic Discourse Analysis*. The State guarantees an ideology of freedom which aligns the linguistic base with the security necessary to support the Munchausen effect as a necessary illusion of subjection.

Conclusion

Writing this text has permitted me to consider some of the most significant theorists of language vis-à-vis Pêcheux's account of discourse analysis and, as a result, I have found that the *philosophy* of language will not further the Saussurian break in any *real* way. Philosophical interpretations of linguistic systems are a form of ideological practice. That being so, I think the techniques of reading, writing, and speaking – as instances of social practice associated with certain discursive formations – should be re-viewed from a strictly *physical* perspective and any theoretical appeal to subjective phenomena should be completely dispensed with. I shall, therefore attempt, in my next book, to produce a theory of social science using strictly physical principles. As the problem of ideology is remarkably pervasive in the existing social sciences and humanities this predilection for metaphysics appears to be the reason why the objective basis of these disciplines has not been formally established: for in their present state, they are closer to systems of religion than systems of science. In *Reading Capital* Louis Althusser alludes to such problems as the 'religious myth of reading', although, in some respects, he sought to be a pious believer rather than an agent of its repudiation. The research of Lucien Lévy-Bruhl (1857–1939) appears highly instructive in this regard – not for any alleged or evident ethnocentrism – but for the purpose of determining how ideology can function via 'collective representations' within the domain of social science itself. I note that scientific ideologies assume particular forms of collective experience and Lévy-Bruhl presents a detailed study of how such beliefs are supposed to function in *How Natives Think (Les Fonctions Mentales Dans Les Sociétés Inférieures)*.

> Thus it is that a language, although, properly speaking, it exists only in the minds of the individuals who speak it, is none the less an incontestable social reality, founded upon an ensemble of collective representations, for it imposes its claim on each of these individuals; it is in existence before his day, and it survives him.
>
> LÉVY-BRUHL, 1979: 13

I do not unequivocally support Lévy-Bruhl's speculations regarding 'primitive mentality', yet, his research can be adapted to examine how collective representations – specific to different forms of cultural practice – are embedded within language. For example, when one examines the material basis of vernacular forms of language such an enquiry will lead – in due course – to the social institutions which reproduce the collective representations of a given society (which in Pêcheux's terms are ideological state apparatuses). A critical re-consideration of Lévy-Bruhl's theory, then, appears to suggest that the collective representations of 'developed' societies may be founded on forms of mystical participation that are enshrined by the functioning of such apparatuses. In English-speaking countries, the collective representations that are socially 'accepted' derive from the English alphabet and the history of its instituted use. The collective representations of the social order are guaranteed by the legitimacy of state authority (i.e., an official language). I must emphasize that such legitimacy is only *customary* and is not established – as far as I can see – by any scientific principles. Given that the social sciences, are in many cases, interpretive *literary* disciplines, it is not implausible to posit that these scientific ideologies reproduce the collective representations of an advanced society as contemporary examples of what Levy-Bruhl calls – prelogical – mysticism.

> The attitude of the primitive's mind is very different. The natural world he lives in presents itself in quite another aspect to him. All its objects and all its entities are involved in a system of mystic participations and exclusions; it is these which constitute its cohesion and its order.
>
> LÉVY-BRUHL, 1923 35

Pêcheux's theory of discourse analysis attempts to convey that everyday language is, in fact, an ideology through which subjects communicate via self-evident – imaginary – semantic structures, i.e., 'meaning' amounts to mystical participation in which collective representations are normalized by ideological state apparatuses. The objective rupture between the physical properties of language and the 'mental' properties of semantic subjection – in Pêcheux's development of Saussure's research – designates the inauguration of real social science.

None other than Sir Karl Popper (1902–1994) also strives to characterize how 'ordinary' knowledge is distinguished from scientific knowledge in *The Logic of Scientific Discovery*. While his discussion of scientific discovery is informed by a number of philosophical questions he proposes to demonstrate how scientific practice is empirically determined. "I suggest that it is the task of the logic of scientific discovery, or the the logic of knowledge, to give a logical analysis of this procedure; that is, to analyse the method of the empirical sciences" (Popper, 1968: 27). Pêcheux refers to Popper as an 'ideologist' in *Language, Semantics, and Ideology*, however, they generally agree on two key principles of method. First, unconditional *belief* is irrelevant for epistemology, and second, scientific knowledge is verified by experimental procedures (cf. Pêcheux, 1982; Popper, 1968). Popper's research in The *Logic of Scientific Discourse* presents some important concepts to further Pêcheux's materialist theory of discourse. Foremost among these are falsification, testability, and corroboration.[1]

> According to my proposal, what characterizes the empirical method is its manner of exposing to falsification, in every conceivable way, the system to be tested. Its aim is not to save the lives of untenable systems but, on the contrary, to select the one which is by comparison the fittest, by exposing them all to the fiercest struggle for survival.
>
> POPPER, 1968: 42

In other words, there is nothing gratuitous about the empirical method: all the theoretical statements of a science must be corroborated by the most rigorous testing. In practice, this amounts to formulating hypotheses which may be falsified by experimental means. In Pêcheux's research self-evident 'meaning' generally functions via untested beliefs and other imaginary forms of cognition. Popper's research outlines a number of methodological procedures which may be used to avoid the mysticism associated with such kinds of primitive thought. In this respect, Pêcheux's materialist theory of discourse stands to be improved by demonstrating how meaning is generated in collective representations and *falsifying* the imagined basis of such ideologies empirically.

---

1   See, in particular, Chapter IV. Falsifiability, Chapter VI. Degrees of Testability, and Chapter x. Corroboration, or How a Theory Stands up to Tests from *The Logic of Scientific Discovery* (Popper, 1968).

References

Althusser, Louis. (2003). *The Humanist Controversy and Other Writings (1966-67)*. New York: Verso.

Althusser, Louis. (2006). *Philosophy of the Encounter*. London: Verso.

Althusser, Louis. (1990). *Philosophy and the Spontaneous Philosophy of the Scientists*. New York: Verso.

Althusser, Louis. (2014). *On the Reproduction of Capitalism*. New York: Verso.

Althusser, Louis. (1996). *Writings on Psychoanalysis*. New York: Columbia University Press.

Althusser, Louis. (1970). *Reading Capital*. London: NLB.

Althusser, Louis. (2005). *For Marx*. London: Verso.

Althusser, Louis. (1976). *Essays in Self-Criticism*. London: NLB.

Aristotle. (1926). *The "Art" of Rhetoric*. London: William Heinemann.

Arnauld, Antoine., Nicole, Pierre. (1850). *Logic; Or, the Art of Thinking: Being the Port Royal Logic*. London: Sutherland and Knox.

Austin, J. L. (1962). *How To Do Things With Words*. Massachusetts: Harvard University Press.

Austin, J. L. (1979). "How to Talk" in *Philosophical Papers*. Oxford University Press [Published to Oxford Scholarship Online: November 2003].

Austin, J. L. (1979a). "The Meaning of a Word" in *Philosophical Papers*. Oxford University Press [Published to Oxford Scholarship Online: November 2003].

Austin, J. L. (1979b). "A Plea for Excuses" in *Philosophical Papers*. Oxford University Press [Published to Oxford Scholarship Online: November 2003].

Bachelard, Gaston. (2002). *The Formation of the Scientific Mind*. Manchester: Clinamen Press.

Bachelard, Gaston. (2012). "Correlationalism and the Problematic". *Radical Philosophy*, 173 May/June.

Bahktin, Mikhail. (1994). *The Bakhtin Reader: Selected Writings of Bakhtin, Medvedev, Voloshinov* [Pam Morris, ed.]. London: Arnold.

Barsky, Robert F. (2011). *Zellig Harris: From American Linguistics to Socialist Zionism*. Massachusetts: MIT Press.

Barthes, Roland. (1972). *Mythologies*. New York: The Noonday Press.

Barthes, Roland. (1967). *Elements of Semiology*. New York: Hill and Wang.

Barthes, Roland. (1988). *The Semiotic Challenge*. Oxford: Basil Blackwell.

Benveniste, Émile. (1971). *Problems in General Linguistics*. Florida: University of Miami Press.

Bloom, Allan. (1991). *The Republic of Plato*. New York: Basic Books.

Brown, Cecil, H. (1974). *Wittgensteinian Linguistics*. The Hague: Mouton.

Canguilhem, Georges. (1994). *A Vital Rationalist*. New York: Zone Books.

Carswell, E. A. & Rommetveit, Ragnar. (1971). *Social Contexts of Messages*. Academic Press: London.

Chomsky, Noam. (1966). *Cartesian Linguistics*. New York: Harper & Row.

Chomsky, Noam., Herman, Edward S. (1988). *Manufacturing Consent: The Political Economy of the Mass Media*. New York: Pantheon Books.

Chomsky, Noam. (1965). *Aspects of the Theory of Syntax*. Massachusetts: The M.I.T. Press.

Chomsky, Noam. (2005). *Language and Mind*. Cambridge: Cambridge University Press.

Chomsky, Noam. (1957). *Syntactic Structures*. Paris: Mouton Publishers.

Chomsky, Noam. (1999). "An On-Line Interview with Noam Chomsky: On the nature of pragmatics and related issues" [interviewed by Briggite Stemmer]. *Brain and Language*, Volume 68, Number 3.

Clérambault, Gatian de. (2002). "Part II: Translation of the work Gatian de Clérambault's on Automatisms" in *Mental Automatisms*. Hermes Whispers Press.

Derrida, Jacques. (1988). *Limited Inc*. Evanston: Northwestern University Press.

Derrida, Jacques. (1982). *Margins of Philosophy*. Sussex: The Harvester Press.

Derrida, Jacques. (1997). *Of Grammatology*. Baltimore: The John Hopkins University Press.

Derrida, Jacques. (1981). *Positions*. London: The Athlone Press.

Derrida, Jacques. (1978). *Writing and Difference*. London: Routledge.

Derrida, Jacques. (2011). *Voice and Phenomenon: Introduction to the Problem of the Sign in Husserl's Phenomenology*. Illinois: Northwestern University Press.

Downing, Eric. (1984). An Essay on Aristotle's "Muthos". *Classical Antiquity*. Vol. 3, No. 2.

Eagleton, Terry. (1976). *Criticism and Ideology: A Study in Marxist Literary Theory*. London: Verso.

Elhammoumi, Mohamed. (2012). "Michel Pêcheux" in *Encyclopedia of the History of Psychological Theories*. Springer Science+Business Media.

Eastwood, John. (2002). *Oxford Guide to English Grammar*. Oxford: Oxford University Press.

Fairclough, Norman. (1989). *Language and Power*. New York: Longman.

Fichant, Michel (1969). L'Idée D'une Historie Des Sciences [The Idea of the History of the Sciences]. *Sur L'Historie Des Sciences*. Paris: Maspero.

Fleck, Ludwik. (1979). *Genesis and Development of a Scientific Fact*. Chicago: University of Chicago Press.

Foucault, Michel. (1972). *The Archaeology of Knowledge (and the Discourse on Language)*. New York: Pantheon Books.

Foucault, Michel. (2003). *Abnormal: Lectures at the Collège de France 1974-1975*. London: Verso.

Foucault, Michel. (1995). *Discipline and Punish: The Birth of the Prison*. New York: Vintage Books.

Foucault, Michel. (2007). *Security, Territory, Population: Lectures at the Collège de France 1977-1978*. Basingstoke: Palgrave Macmillan.

Foucault, Michel. (1991). *The Foucault Effect: Studies in Governmentality*. Chicago: University of Chicago Press.

Foucault, Michel. (1984). *The Foucault Reader*. New York: Pantheon Books.

Foucault, Michel. (2008). *The Birth of Biopolitics*. New York: Palgrave Macmillan.

Freese, John Henry. (1926). "Introduction". *The "Art" of Rhetoric*. London: William Heinemann.

Freud, Sigmund. (1953). "Fragment of an Analysis of a Case of Hysteria" in *The Standard Edition of the Complete Psychological Works of Sigmund Freud* (Volume VII). London: The Hogarth Press.

Freud, Sigmund. (1961). "Introduction" in *The Standard Edition of the Complete Works of Sigmund Freud* (Volume XV). London: The Hogarth Press.

Freud, Sigmund. (1960). "The Relation of Jokes to Dreams and to the Unconscious" in *The Standard Edition of the Complete Psychological Works of Sigmund Freud* (Volume VIII). London: The Hogarth Press.

Freud, Sigmund. (1981). *The Psychopathology of Everyday Life*. London: The Hogarth Press.

Gadet, Françoise. (1989). *Saussure and Contemporary Culture*. London: Century Hutchinson.

Gadet, F., Leon, J., Maldidier, D., and Plon, M. (1995). "Pêcheux's Linguistic References" in *Automatic Discourse Analysis*. Amsterdam: Rodopi.

Gillot, Pascale. (2014). "The Munchausen Effect: Subjectivity and Ideology", in *Multistable Figures: On the Critical Potential of Ir/Reversible Aspect-Seeing*, ed. Christoph F. E. Holzhey, Cultural Inquiry, 8, pp. 89-111.

Greimas, Algirdas. (1990). *The Social Sciences: A Semiotic View*. Minnesota: University of Minnesota Press.

Greimas, Algirdas Julien. (1989). "On Meaning". *New Literary History*. Vol. 20, No. 3.

Habermas, Jürgen. (1979). *Communication and the Evolution of Society*. London: Heinemann.

Habermas, Jürgen. (1987). *Knowledge and Human Interests*. Cambridge: Polity Press.

Habermas, Jürgen. (1992). *Postmetaphysical Thinking: Philosophical Essays*. Cambridge: Polity Press.

Haroche, Cl., Henry, P., Pêcheux, M. (1971). "La sémantique et la coupure saussurienne: *langue*, langage, discours" [Semantics and the Saussurian Break: Language, Speech, Discourse], *Langages*, No. 24.

Harris, Roy. (1990). *Language, Saussure and Wittgenstein*. London: Routledge.

Harris, Zellig, S. (1954). "Distributional Structure", *Word*, 10, pp. 146-162.

Harris, Zellig, S. (1988). "Science Sublanguages and the Prospects for a Global Language of Science", *The ANNALS of the American Academy of Political and Social Science*.

Harris, Zellig, S. (2002). "The Background of Transformational and Metalanguage Analysis" in *The Legacy of Zellig Harris: Language and Information into the 21st Century, Vol. 1: Philosophy of Science, Syntax, and Semantics*. Amsterdam: John Benjamins Publishing.

Harris, Zellig, S. (1964). "Transformations in Linguistic Structure", *Proceedings of the American Philosophical Society*, Vol. 108.

Harris, Zellig, S. (2002). "The structure of science information", *Journal of Biomedical Informatics*, volume 35, issue 4.

Harris, Zellig, S. (1985). "On Grammars of Science" in *Linguistics and Philosophy: Essays in Honor of Rulon S. Wells*. Amsterdam: J. Benjamins.

Harris, Zellig. S. (1957). Co-Occurrence and Transformation in Linguistic Structure. *Language* (Linguistic Society of America), vol.33, no.3.

Harris, Zellig. (1952). "Discourse Analysis" in *Language* (Linguistic Society of America). Vol. 28. No.1.

Harris, Zellig. (n.d.). *The Direction of Social Change* (Tentative Title). Unpublished Manuscript [<http://www.zelligharris.org>].

Harris, Zellig, S. (1951). *Structural Linguistics*. Chicago: The University of Chicago Press.

Henry, Paul. (1995). "Theoretical issues in Pêcheux's Automatic Discourse Analysis (1969)" in *Automatic Discourse Analysis*. Amsterdam: Rodopi.

Henry, Paul. (1971). "On Processing of Message Referents in Contexts" in *Social Contexts of Messages*. New York: Academic Press.

Helsloot, Neils & Hak, Tony. (1995). "Pêcheux's contribution to discourse analysis" in *Automatic Discourse Analysis*. Amsterdam: Rodopi.

Herbert, Thomas. (1966). "Réflexions sur la situation théorique des sciences et, specialement, de la psychologie sociale [Reflections on the Theoretical Situation of Social Science, and Especially, of Social Psychology]", *Cahiers pour l'Analyse* (Volume 2).

Herbert, Thomas. (1968). "Pour une théorie générale des idéologies [For a General Theory of Ideologies]", *Cahiers pour l'Analyse* (Volume 9).

Hirst, Paul. (1983). "Ideology, Culture, and Personality". *Canadian Journal of Political and Social Theory/Revue canadienne de théorie politique et sociale*, Vol. 7, Nos. 1-2.

Hriso, Paul. (2002). *Mental Automatisms: Translations and Commentaries on the works of Gatian De Clérambault*. Hermes Whispers Press.

Jakobson, Roman. (1980). *The Framework of Language*. Michigan Studies in the Humanities.

Jakobson, Roman & Halle, Morris. (1956). *Fundamentals of Language*. 's-Gravenhage: Mouton & Co.

Jakobson, Roman. (1978). *Six Lectures on Sound and Meaning*. Massachusetts: The MIT Press.

Jakobson, Roman. (1971). *Selected Writings II – Word and Language*. The Hague: Mouton.

Kusch, Martin. (1991). *Foucault's Strata and Fields: An Investigation into Archaeological and Genealogical Science Studies*. London: Kluwer Academic Publishers.

Lacan, Jacques. (2006). *Écrits*. New York: W. W. Norton & Company.

Lacan, Jacques. (2008). *My Teaching*. London: Verso.

Lacan, Jacques (1988). *The Seminar of Jacques Lacan. Book I: Freud's Papers on Technique 1953-1954* [Miller, Jacques-Alain ed.]. New York. W. W. Norton & Company.

Lacan, Jacques. (1988a). *The Seminar of Jacques Lacan. Book II: The Ego in Freud's Theory and in the Technique of Psychoanalysis 1954-1955*. New York: W.W. Norton & Company.

Langacker, Ronald W. (1972). *Language and Its Structure: Some Fundamental Linguistic Concepts*. New York: Harcourt Brace Jovanovich, Inc.

Larkin, Sister Miriam Therese. (1971). *Language in the Philosophy of Aristotle*. The Hague: Paris.

Lemco, Ian. (2006). "Wittgenstein's Aeronautical Investigation". *Notes Rec. R. Soc*, 61, 39–51.

Leroi-Gourhan, André. (1993). *Gesture and Speech*. Massachusetts: The MIT Press.

Lévi-Strauss, Claude. (1963). *Structural Anthropology*. New York: Basic Books.

Lévi-Strauss, Claude. (1978) "Preface" in *Six Lectures on Sound and Meaning*. Massachusetts: The MIT Press.

Lévy-Bruhl, Lucien. (1979). *How Natives Think*. New York: Arno Press.

Lévy-Bruhl, Lucien. (1923). *Primitive Mentality*. New York: The Macmillan Company.

Lucy, John A. (2001). "Sapir-Whorf Hypothesis" in *International Encyclopedia of the Social & Behavioral Sciences*, 2nd edition, Volume 20.

Macherey, Pierre. (1978). *A Theory of Literary Production*. London: Routledge & Kegan Paul.

Marx, Karl. & Engels, Friedrich. (1976). *Collected Works of Karl Marx and Friedrich Engels, 1845-47, Vol. 5: Theses on Feuerbach, The German Ideology and Related Manuscripts*. New York: International Publishers Co.

Montgomery, Martin & Allan, Stuart. (1992). "Ideology, Discourse, and Cultural Studies: The Contribution of Michel Pêcheux", *Canadian Journal of Communication*, Volume 17, No. 2.

Morris, Pam. (1994) "Introduction" in *The Bakhtin Reader: Selected Writings of Bakhtin, Medvedev, Voloshinov*. London: Arnold.

Online Etymology Dictionary. (2021) "lecture, n." https://www.etymonline.com.

OED Online. (2020) "sentence, n." Oxford University Press.

OED Online. (2020) "lecture, n." Oxford University Press.

OED Online. (2020) "myth, n." Oxford University Press.

Pashukanis, Evgeny B. (2003) *The General Theory of Law and Marxism*. London: Transaction Publishers.

Pêcheux, Michel. (1971). "A Method of Discourse Analysis Applied to the Recall of Utterances" in Carswell E.A. (ed.) *Social Contexts of Messages*. London: Academic Press.

Pêcheux, Michel. (1983). La langue introuvable. *Canadian Journal of Political and Social Theory*, 7 (1–2), 24-28.

Pêcheux, Michel. (2014) "Dare to Think and Dare to Rebel! Ideology, Marxism, Resistance, Class Struggle". *Décalages*, Vol. 1.

Pêcheux, Michel. & Balibar, Etienne. (1971). "Definitions". *Theoretical Practice*, 3/4.

Pêcheux, Michel. (1982). *Language, Semantics, and Ideology*. New York: St. Martin's Press.

Pêcheux, Michel. (1988). "Discourse: Structure or Event?", trans. Warren Montag in Nelson and Grossberg (eds.) *Marxism and the Interpretation of Culture*. Chicago: University of Illinois Press.

Pêcheux, Michel. (1971). "A Method of Discourse Analysis Applied to Recall of Utterances" in *Social Contexts of Messages*. New York: Academic Press.

Pêcheux, Michel. (1995). *Automatic Discourse Analysis*. Amsterdam: Rodopi.

Plon, Michel. (1974). "On the meaning of the notion of conflict and its study in social psychology". *European Journal of Social Psychology*. 4 (4).

Plon, Michel. (1974a). "On a question of orthodoxy". *European Journal of Social Psychology*. 4 (4).

Popper, Karl. (1968). *The Logic of Scientific Discovery*. Harper & Row: London.

Poulantzas, Nicos. (1978). *State, Power, Socialism*. Verso: London.

Poulantzas, Nicos. (2008). *The Poulantzas Reader: Marxism, Law and the State*. London: Verso.

Poulantzas, Nicos. (1975). *Classes in Contemporary Capitalism*. London: NLB.

Rommetveit, Ragnar., Cook, Malcolm., Havelka, Nenad., Henry, Paul., Herkner, Werner., Pêcheux, Michel. and Peeters, Guido. (1971). "Processing of Utterances in Context" in *Social Contexts of Messages*. New York: Academic Press.

Rommetveit, Ragnar. (1971). "Words, Contexts, and Verbal Message Transmission" in *Social Contexts of Messages*. New York: Academic Press.

Resch, Robert Paul. (1992). *Althusser and the Renewal of Marxist Social Theory*. Berkeley: University of California Press.

Rodríguez, Juan Carlos. (2002). *Theory and History of Ideological Production*. Newark: University of Delaware Press.

Sapir, Edward. (1921). *Language: An Introduction to the Study of Speech*. New York: Harcourt, Brace & Co.

Saussure, Ferdinand (1959). *Course in General Linguistics*. New York: Philosophical Library.

Searle, John, R. (1969). *Speech acts: An Essay in the Philosophy of Language*. Cambridge: Cambridge University Press.

Searle, John, R. (1995). *The Construction of Social Reality*. New York: The Free Press.

Searle, John, R. (2007). "What is Language: Some Preliminary Remarks" in Tsohatzidis, Savas L. (ed.) *John Searle's Philosophy of Language: Force, Meaning, and Mind.* Cambridge: Cambridge University Press.

Skinner, B.F. (1957). *Verbal Behavior.* London: Methuen & Co Ltd.

Skinner, B.F. (1972). *Beyond Freedom and Dignity.* New York: Alfred A. Knopf.

Skinner, B.F. (1990). "Can Psychology be a Science of Mind?". *American Psychologist,* Vol. 45. No. 11.

Skinner, B.F. (1987). "Whatever Happened to Psychology as the Science of Behavior?". *American Psychologist,* Vol. 42. No. 8.

Skinner, B.F. (1963). "Operant Behavior". *American Psychologist,* 18 (8).

Smith, Bryant. (1928). "Legal Personality". *Yale Law Journal.* Vol. XXXVI, No. 3.

Taylor, T. Wardlaw. (1898). "Law and Responsibility". *The Philosophical Review,* vol. 7, No. 3.

Thao, Trân Duc. (1984). *Investigations into the Origin of Language and Consciousness.* Boston: D. Reidel Publishing Company.

Therborn, Göran. (1999). *The Ideology of Power and the Power of Ideology.* London: Verso.

Therborn, Göran. (1978). *What Does the Ruling Class Do When it Rules?* London: NLB.

Wallis, Darian A. (1998) "Language, attitude, and ideology: An experimental social-psychological study". *Journal of Pragmatics,* 30.

Wallis, Darian A. (2007) "Michel Pêcheux's theory of language and ideology and method of automatic discourse analysis: A critical introduction". *Text & Talk,* vol. 27, no. 2.

Watson, John B. (1994). "Psychology as the Behaviorist Views It". *Psychological Review,* Vol. 101. No.2.

Williams, Glyndwr. (1999). *French Discourse Analysis.* London: Routledge.

Wittgenstein, Ludwig. (1974) *Tractatus Logico-Philosophicus.* London: Routledge.

Wittgenstein, Ludwig. (1969). *The Blue and Brown Books.* Oxford: Basil Blackwell.

Wittgenstein, Ludwig. (1963). *Philosophical Investigations.* Oxford: Basil Blackwell.

Wittgenstein, Ludwig. (1978). *Culture and Value.* Oxford: Basil Blackwell.

Index